More praise for **Brand New World**

"Max takes us into the boardrooms (and favorite bars) of far-flung ad agencies and gives insight into the people and trends that will dominate the coming decades. It's the next best thing to getting on a plane yourself."

Sean MacPhedran,
Director, Creative Strategy of Fuel Industries

"You need to read this book to understand where marketing and consumers in the global economy are going and how to successfully be a part of it."

Karl Moore,
Ph.D., Associate Professor,
Desautels Faculty of Management, McGill University

"Lenderman's behind-the-scenes tour of hyper-markets is an important read for any marketer looking to stay ahead of the new world order."

Andrew Simon,
SVP, Creative Director of DDB

"An eye-opening book [that] paints the picture of a field evolving with dizzying speed towards a brash new reality where the old rules barely apply."

Christophe Bergeron,
Editorial Director, *Hour* (Montreal)

"Everyone knows the BRIC countries will change everything, but Lenderman actually gives you a roadmap, vividly bringing to life the universal human insights driving change in these countries."

Mary Maddever,
VP, Editorial Director, Brunico Communications,
Executive Editor, *Strategy* magazine, *Stimulant*, and *Media in Canada*

BRAND NEW WORLD

A Sneak Peek

Just how impressive is the emerging marketplace of hyper-developing countries? Here are some stats to ponder. If you're not a "numbers person," feel free to skip ahead to the Table of Contents.

In 2007, for the first time in history, China, India, and Russia combined accounted for more than half of the world's economic growth.[1]

India's GDP is growing at 9 percent annually. The stock market grew 278 percent between 2002 and 2006. Goldman Saks believes India will be the world's third-largest economy by 2050, overshadowing Japan by 2030.[2]

By 2009, it is estimated that seven of the world's 10 largest malls will be located in China.[3]

In 2007, China accounted for 800,000 of the world's millionaires, including 250 people worth more than $1 billion. India has more than 100,000 millionaires and is adding to that number faster than any other country.[4]

There are 9,000 listed companies in India, making it the world's largest market of small and mid-cap public companies.[5]

China's capital city, Beijing, alone has 17 million people. The United States has nine cities with a population of one million people or more; China has more than 90.[6]

The combined population of India and China is about 2.6 billion people, or 37 percent of humanity.[7]

Over 10 million small stores in India account for 95 percent of sales; only 4 percent of India's retail outlets can be classified as supermarkets, department stores, or malls. China has 23 million retail outlets, of which 78 percent are considered to be mom-and-pop operations.[8]

According to the 2007 Grant Thornton *International Business Report*, Indian business leaders—along with their colleagues in Argentina—work the longest, at 57 hours per week, and were the third-most-stressed workers in the world, behind those in China and Taiwan.[9]

In Brazil, the number of credit cards per person was 2.25 in 2006. In China, that number was 0.93 per capita; in Russia, it was .56 per capita; and in India, it was 0.08 cards per person.[10]

In the three years between 2003 and 2006, the number of Visa credit cards issued in China increased from 1.7 million to 11.7 million.[11]

Nielsen Media Research has projected that Russia may become the largest consumer market in Europe—and the fourth largest in the world—by 2025.[12]

India's savings rate is above 30 percent, with the investment rate around 33 percent. China's investment rate of over 40 percent is a world record.[13]

The Organisation for Economic Co-operation and Development (OECD) indicated that India generated more than 11 million new jobs every year between 2000 and 2005, a rate higher than that of Brazil, Russia, and China. The four countries together created over 22 million jobs each year, which is more than 5 times the net employment gains recorded in OECD countries over the same period.[14]

India has 380 universities and 11,200 higher education institutions that produce around 6,000 PhDs, 200,000 engineers, and 300,000 science graduates and post-graduates each year.[15]

The BRIC nations—Brazil, Russia, India, and China—will account for more than 775 million new PCs by 2015, according to a report by Forrester Research. The vast majority of growth in the PC and related industries will come from emerging markets.[16]

Compared with American youth, China's under-25 set has higher rates of at-home broadband Internet access, ownership of computer phones, and digital video cameras.[17]

China is the biggest blogging market in the world. It is also the biggest instant message market in the world.[18]

The entertainment and media market spending in BRIC countries, particularly China and India, will continue to grow annually at double-digit rates from 2007 to 2011. It will account for 24 percent of global entertainment and media growth during that five-year period.[19]

BRIC countries have overtaken the United States in dominating the global energy industry in 2007. In 1991, by market capitalization, 55 percent of the 20 largest companies in the energy industry were American and 45 percent were European. In 2007, 35 percent of the 20 largest energy companies were from BRIC countries, about 35 percent being European and 30 percent American.[20]

In the United States, the main use of the Internet is for information gathering and exchanging; in China, it's for entertainment.[21]

Over the past three years, ad spending in the BRIC markets has grown four times faster than the world average.[22]

A single Chinese telephone company, China Mobile, had over 301 million cell phone customers at the beginning of 2007. As of July 2006, the total population of the United States was estimated at 298 million.[23]

QQ, a Chinese social network site run by Tencent Inc., has 300 million active accounts. It also boasts revenues of $523 million, about four times more than Facebook, the most popular social network site in North America. QQ's operating profit is over $224 million. Facebook logged a $50-million loss in 2007.[24]

Between 2.5 and 3 billion people—nearly half of the world's population—use a stove every day in conjunction with solid fuel such as wood, coal, or dung.[25]

The United Nations' Human Settlements Program projects that one-quarter of the global population will live in so-called slums by the year 2020.[26]

BRAND NEW WORLD

BRAND
NEW WORLD

How Paupers, Pirates, and Oligarchs
Are Reshaping Business

MAX LENDERMAN

 Collins

HarperCollins Publishers Ltd
2 Bloor Street East, 20th Floor
Toronto, Ontario, Canada
M4W 1A8

www.harpercollins.ca

Library and Archives Canada Cataloguing in Publication
Lenderman, Max
Brand new world : how paupers, pirates,
and oligarchs are reshaping business / Max Lenderman.

ISBN 978-1-55468-397-0

1. Branding (Marketing). I. Title.
HF1416.L45 2010   658.8'27   C2010-900811-1

9 8 7 6 5 4 3 2 1
Printed and bound in the United States

To my girls: Summer, Marley, and Lara

CONTENTS

CHAPTER FOUR: No Logo Metropolis
How Much Advertising Is Too Much?

CHAPTER FIVE: The World Is Poor
And the Meek Shall Inherit the Mall

A Note from an Ad Man

In 2001, Goldman Sachs global economist Jim O'Neill coined the term "BRIC"—an acronym that refers to Brazil, Russia, India, and China—and predicted that by 2050 the combined economies of these four countries would eclipse the economic markets of the United States, Europe, and Japan. At the beginning of 2009—during the early throes of the current global economic downturn—he bullishly and confidently announced that "the BRIC consumer is going to rescue the world." How? Mostly by shopping. According to O'Neill, "since October 2007, the Chinese shopper alone has been contributing more to global GDP growth than the American consumer."[1]

More astonishingly, the BRIC economies are doing better than O'Neill's seminal forecast eight years ago. Back then, the London-based economist predicted that the BRIC countries would account for 10 percent of global economic output by 2010; today, they have already eclipsed 15 percent. The BRICs, it seems, are on track for economic dominance.

Of course, the economic annus horribilis that is enveloping the world markets is certain to adversely affect the red-hot BRIC economies—China's economy grew at close to 10 percent for three decades and may now slow to 7.3 percent in 2009, while India's growth rate may drop as low as 6.5 percent in 2009, from 9 percent in 2008. Brazil and Russia—dependent on natural resources and commodities—will see more of a significant growth slowdown.[2] Nonetheless, the 2.8 billion people living and shopping in these countries may well be the world's economic saviors: a horde of superhero super-consumers who are entering a brand new world. These are the shoppers of the future.

Because of this, there is an enormous amount to learn from the way marketing and consuming is conducted in these hyper-developing nations. And we in the West need to take these lessons to heart and apply them here in our own businesses. The exciting and dynamic marketing tactics that are emerging and maturing in the hyper-developing world must be both a window and a mirror for thoughtful business leaders, marketing mavens, and global-conscious influentials who are craving new business stories and marketing adventures. Globalization is not just a catchphrase. It's a how-to for all global marketing of the future. There are profound lessons to be learned from marketing beyond our own borders; indeed, it's entirely possible that everything interesting in marketing and advertising is actually happening in the so-called Third World.

To lend credence to such an assertion, this book presents case studies and campaigns that are redefining the way brands engage their consumers, both in the hyper-markets and here in the West. Perhaps more important, this book presents some really big ideas that ground the reader in the massive cultural shifts and trends that are blossoming in hyper-developing nations, and suggests how these shifts and trends will invariably alter our perception of the marketing, advertising, and media landscapes here at home.

The insights presented in this book have been created from notions, observations, interviews, conferences, and personal experiences in the hyper-markets of Brazil, Russia, India, and China. They are meant to stimulate the creative juices of anyone wishing to understand the incredibly dynamic changes that are fundamentally transforming these massive countries. They can also be used as primers for executives wishing to do business in other hyper-developing nations across the globe. Or they can be read as a sort of quasi-travelogue of a guy who's interested in how people live, love, consume, and inspire.

Most important, this book shows that we are globally connected beyond business needs and synergies. Many books and articles have been written on how to penetrate the BRIC markets, each one espousing and extolling the nuances of local business conditions and the cultural eccentricities of the local consumer. Needless to say, any such pertinent knowledge should be instrumental to doing business in these hyper-markets. In essence, this book examines massive and complex paradigm shifts in these countries through a simple lens: consumer behavior and the marketing that is being invented to influence it.

To be sure, the case studies and examples presented in this book (which use US dollars unless otherwise indicated) are prevalently viewed from an advertising and marketing perspective. But they are used to present a work that, I hope, is bigger than just that. In traveling through the BRIC countries, meeting colleagues and strangers alike, I have uncovered a global hyper-market that should be approached with a humanistic bent. In doing so, I may have stumbled on the simple thesis of this book: human insights trump cultural ones.

More than ever before in the history of this world, it is obvious that we all—*we all*—share the same human aspirations and trepidations. As an ad man, simple-minded as I am, the emerging marketplace has to be approached existentially. It is the only way in which I could begin to fathom the vast complexities of each of the BRIC countries.

Overall, the tone and sentiment of these chapters is of awe, amazement, and inspiration. The almost unimaginable economic growth being witnessed in these markets is one story. Another is how everyday people are adapting to it, how they are living their commercially engaged lives, what they are into, and why they are into it. Billions of people are entering a brand-centric marketplace for the very first time. The stories of how brands, companies, and consumers are doing it will, I hope, provide a glimpse into the future of marketing throughout the world.

This means that to stay relevant within our own society and marketplace, marketers must become bolder and more inclusive. Our insights must be more empathetic; our tactics should be more innovative. Brands will need to unequivocally become virtuous forces in the marketplace. Those that can't offer up a clear and meaningful benefit to the marketplace will be rejected. Marketing in the future will be personal. I don't mean targeted. I don't mean customized. I mean *personal*. Marketing will be something that is shared between people rather than directed at them. And it will be a force for the global good, an industry that no longer annoys, but inspires.

CHAPTER ONE

Think Like an Oligarch

(Anything Goes)

I have seen my father cry only once. We were on an Aeroflot flight from St. Petersburg (then called Leningrad), and as the stairs pulled away I saw his tears. It was 1979 and my family was emigrating from the Soviet Union. Although I was a bit too young to know exactly the disheartening situation facing my family, I could clearly intuit that this wasn't a vacation we were embarking on. We were never returning to our homeland.

I'm writing this sentence on another Aeroflot flight. This time, I am flying into Moscow to meet with top Russian agency heads and tapped-in ex-pats. As it happens, the international news is on fire with dispatches of unrest in the city. Opposition forces—led by world chess champion Gary Kasparov—began a peaceful march in downtown Moscow, which ended with a brutal police crackdown in Pushkin Square, right underneath the statue of Russia's greatest poet. Truncheons swung on the heads of young and old alike.

The next day, marchers were out in the streets of St. Petersburg and more police clashes ensued. Opposition leaders are denouncing the "heavy hand" of President Vladimir Putin, the ex-KGB colonel who has consolidated his power in the vein of the past Communist apparatchiks. The crackdown is exposing the true nature of the authoritative regime.*

The unrest began with a newspaper interview. A Russian oligarch named Boris Berezovsky, speaking to the UK's *Guardian* newspaper, openly called for revolution. And although it is pretty easy to incite violence from the posh offices of a genteel gentleman's club in a fashionable neighborhood of London, the repercussions were immediate on the streets of Moscow and St. Petersburg: placards unfurled, marchers gathered in Pushkin Square, and the riot police started running amok.

In no uncertain terms, Berezovsky called for a coup d'état. "I am calling for revolution and revolution is always violent," he said in a telephone interview from London. This O.O.—Original Oligarch—also indicated that he was in contact with members of the Russian political elite who oppose Putin and was helping finance efforts to oust the president.

Although he is one of the businessmen who became wealthy in the 1990s through their influence over then president Boris Yeltsin, Berezovsky supported Putin's election in 2000. He later fell out with the Russian president and fled Russia for the UK in 2001 to avoid charges that included fraud. (Parenthetically, Berezovsky is accused of stealing $50 million from Aeroflot, among a plethora of other schemes and offenses. *Forbes* magazine estimates that his personal fortune is worth $1.1 billion.)

Berezovsky escaped extradition in 2003 when the UK

---

* Since Vladimir Putin is now Russia's prime minister, some elements of this context have changed. His grip on Russian society has not.

granted him political asylum. To repay his former patron, he has since accused Putin of ordering the 2006 murder of former Russian intelligence agent Alexander Litvinenko in London, and declared in the interview that he wanted to restore democracy to Russia by removing what he described as a "terrorist regime."* It's not hard to imagine why some may want to oppose Putin. Since coming into power in 2000, he has stifled all opposition in Parliament, nationalized the media, and killed off direct elections for regional governors. Conversely, the iron-fisted former KGB colonel is probably Russia's most popular politician. He has been fortunate to see an economic windfall that has practically doubled average wages for most workers in the country.

This boon is evident everywhere, especially in Moscow. In 2007, it was rated the world's most expensive city.[1] London was a distant second. Living in Moscow is almost 35 percent more expensive than living in New York City. A two-bedroom, one-bathroom apartment in Moscow now rents for $4,000 a month; a CD costs $24.83, and an international newspaper sets you back $6.30. At the Moscow Ritz-Carlton, rooms start at $1,000 per night.**

For real estate deals, the city is the third-largest market after London and Paris.[2] According to a PricewaterhouseCoopers report, Moscow ranks first among 27 European cities in terms of investment risk, but places second in terms of future returns on invested capital. The capital was also recommended as the best choice among all surveyed cities for purchasing commercial property. In 2006, deals involving office space in Russia made

---

* Litvinenko was a vocal critic of the Putin regime who died on 23 November in a London hospital from poisoning by the radioactive isotope polonium-210. Nice. His deathbed confession accused Putin of murder. Real nice.

** In 2005, it was reported that home builders in a northwest suburb of Moscow—the same one in which Putin had a home—were offering to throw in a helicopter with every purchase of a new home.

up almost one-quarter of all transactions in eastern and central Europe. Reports show that the value of commercial property deals in Russia in 2007 reached $5 billion, compared with $3 billion in 2006 and $1 billion in 2005.[3]

Russia has quietly become the world's biggest energy producer, supplying western Europe with more than one-third of its natural gas and pumping out more oil than Saudi Arabia. The energy bonanza has given Russia the third-largest reserve of foreign currency in the world, dwarfing that of any other European country.[4] This massive swell of capital and deal-making has made billionaires out of many Russians who had previously toiled as low- to mid-level bureaucrats, or who have the luxury of knowing someone high up on the government food chain. These are the so-called oligarchs, a group of men who have made fortunes from the privatization foibles and shenanigans that engulfed the country in the nineties.

To characterize this period as a gold rush is an understatement. The country's industries, natural resources, real estate, and capital were gobbled up by those who had means, gumption, and—often—murderous henchmen who would systematically assassinate those who stood in the way of making a buck.

Today, these oligarchs are the celebrities of Russia. A recent poll of youngsters indicated that their heroes weren't sports or cinema stars. They were the guys in Brioni suits, with palaces in Dubai, and a retinue of bodyguards who travel in Mercedes or BMW cavalcades through the streets of Moscow.

First You Get the Money, Then You Get the Power, Then You Get . . .

The oligarchs are at the helm of the economic boom, and the ones who profit most from it. The wealth they are accruing is staggering, and fluid. As recently as April 2007, *Forbes* magazine had identified Roman Abramovich—the much-maligned owner of London's Chelsea Football Club—at the top of the pack, with a personal fortune valued at $21 billion in 2007. In early 2008, Oleg Deripaska, the head of holding company Basic Element, overtook Abramovich with a personal wealth estimated at $28.6 billion.

The top 100 oligarchs closest to him increased their personal wealth by an average of 36 percent from 2006 to 2007.* In London alone—a favorite home-away-from-home for the newly rich—there are at least 10 Russian billionaires and more than 1,000 Russian millionaires living the good life.[5] In March 2008, *Forbes* announced that for the first time ever Moscow had overtaken New York as the home of the world's most billionaires. The former bastion of Communism had 74 billionaires, three more than were found in the mecca of capitalism.[6]

The fat cats aren't the only ones getting fatter. The average Russian has also benefited greatly by Putin's directive for stability and rule of law—even if that law is tailored for his cronies and hangers-on. Disposable dollars are now freely being spent on such things as home appliances, real estate, and luxury goods. But for a true, self-respecting Russian—and especially a Muscovite—the money is spent on two things: clothes and a car.

It is absolutely mind-boggling to see Moscow's Tverskaya Street teeming with Bentleys, Maseratis, Ferraris, BMWs, and the ubiquitous Benzes. Considering that only two decades ago the average Russian couldn't even afford a car—never mind a luxury vehicle—this transformation is astounding. The only cars available in the past were the locally produced Ladas or Zhigulis—box-like, bare-bones cars that make Yugos seem

---

* The 100 richest citizens of Russia are estimated to be worth 25 percent of the nation's GDP, while 20 percent of the country lives below the poverty line (*The Observer*, 17 February 2008).

like Cadillacs. These days, if you don't have a foreign car, you haven't made it.

And if you don't have a shiny belt buckle from Dolce & Gabbana or Versace, you are a shabby dresser. For some reason, the Russians have appropriated the belt buckle as the status symbol du jour, the way hip-hop has appropriated the bling-bling necklace or iced-out watch. Around this belt buckle, the typical Russian metrosexual can assemble an entire foreign wardrobe ensemble.

The streets of Moscow are veritable catwalks for both men and women. Hugo Boss stores are on almost every corner down-town, and every purse is either Gucci or Louis Vuitton. Longines and Rolex grace the wrists of most mid-level managers, and it is not uncommon to see Muscovite teens turn their noses up to brands such as Polo, Levis, and Tommy Hilfiger. These brands are considered to be sub-par.*

The similarities to the hip-hop culture are somewhat uncanny because for all the bling and bluster that nouveau riche Russians display, they still go home to tiny flats that they prob-ably share with their mothers. Perhaps the analogy is closer to Los Angelenos: the apartment may be $1,000 per month, but the car payments are three times that.

Salaries are skyrocketing, but not as fast for civil servants and for those average folks who have not capitalized on the cash wind-fall from the oil, gas, timber, mineral, consumer packaged goods (known as CPG), real estate, and banking sectors. These people have to rely on a different method to make ends meet: bribes.

The pay-off has become an art in Russia, as well as in many

---

* It has been noted of late that the Moscow look is becoming more understated, with fashion-forward Muscovites eschewing the Gucci ensemble for a more "casual luxury" look. The label driving this fashion trend is run by Abramovich's girlfriend, Dasha Zhukova, whose father is a Russian real estate oligarch in his own right.

other developing nations. It is common knowledge in Moscow that cops officially make around $300 to $400 per month, but consistently take home more than $3,000. That is because their day-to-day activities are centered on keeping the peace . . . for a price.

Although bribery has propped up the system for decades, it really began to flourish after the Communist state system fell apart. And when the police are on the take, so is everyone else. Those Russians who can navigate the treacherous waters of bribe giving and taking come out ahead. Those of a more scrupulous nature are left far, far behind.

My first day in Moscow proved just how inept I am at this dance between the giver and the taker. I had decided to take in a soccer match between CSKA Moscow and Spartak Nalchik. The hotel had arranged the tickets, and I set off with a few beers in my coat pockets for a good old-fashioned game of footie. Unfortunately, I entered the wrong door at the stadium. And since I encountered the OMON—the special paramilitary police known for its enthusiasm for enforcing a "quick peace"— every fifteen feet, getting to the right section proved extremely difficult. After a few attempts, I found the endeavor impossible. I decided to seek help, and the policeman at the entrance to Section 5 seemed like a nice chap. I told him my predicament and showed him my ticket.

He shrugged and said just one thing: "You have to pay." (I became quite used to that phrase in the days to come in Moscow.) I mistook him to mean that I needed to buy another ticket, and naively asked him where I should buy it.

He looked at me as if I was from another planet. "Right here," he said.

It dawned on me that he was referring to himself. I asked how much. He proffered 300 rubles, or about $12. The figure seemed reasonable, until the math proved that my little "gift" to him to let me pass into the stadium—which in theory my ticket already allowed me to do, although from a different door—was more than 5 percent of his entire monthly salary.

It's par for the course: the Russian prosecutor general has estimated that government officials in the country take in about $240 billion each year in bribes—roughly equal to the national budget.[7]

I began to fumble with the ruble notes that I fished out of my pocket, counting out the multicolored and somewhat indistinguishable bills. He slapped my hand down and scowled at me. "What are you doing?" he growled. (I almost noticed him moving his hand closer to his holstered pistol.) "This is not how we do it here."

I apologized profusely and scrambled to get him as many rubles as I possibly could in the split second before his comrades and superiors could swoop in on the action.

If bribery is an art form, I proved to be a true hack. Nevertheless, in his benevolence the officer did let me in. Even wished me luck on my stay in Moscow. CSKA won 2–0. (Both goals were scored by Brazilian players.)

From One Tragedy to the Next

Graft is at the heart of the philosophy of Russian business. This isn't to say that one must partake in it to succeed. Rather, the notion of graft complements the imperative for connections or an inside man to make deals happen. And for all intents and purposes, that inside man will most likely have an office inside the Kremlin or in one of its hundreds of satellite buildings in the rest of the country. Transparency International recently placed Russia at the bottom of the list of countries that are the least transparent places in which to do business, placing it on par with Rwanda. To do business here, you need to know someone in the government to make things happen.

To any ordinary Russian, this situation is terribly common-place and historically unchanged. The best way to get a car in the Soviet days was to belong to the Communist Party. A *dacha* (summer home) was possible only through a bribe or favor. All trips abroad needed to be approved by the bureaucrats. Life didn't progress unless someone said it could and produced a stamped and signed document in triplicate to prove it.

This fetish for bureaucracy is still a staple of Russian business. Nothing can be accomplished without a letter or document from a top-tier authority. Everything is stamped and signed. In my hotel, for instance, each page of the room service menu was stamped and hand signed by some paper pusher in the Ministry of Health or Tourism. Every single page.

But a cursory perusal of Russia's history—or rather, the personal history of its people—can explain this bureaucratic overkill. Russia is by far the world's largest country, spanning an area more than 11 million square miles (17 million km²). It has nearly twice the total area of the second-largest country, Canada. It covers both Europe and Asia and has the world's ninth-largest population. With such a huge territory to cover, and the vast number of people dispersed in it, control has always been a dominant preoccupation for Russia's rulers.

Even since the time of the first nomads on the steppes of Eurasia—Slavs, Turks, Tatars, Mongols, Norse, and even Vedics—the notion of ruling over wide swathes of land on which fierce and war-like tribes uneasily coexisted has always been practically quixotic. Not until the tenth century do we witness a central authority arising in Russia, as the state of Kievan Rus' became the largest in Europe and one of the most prosperous, due to diversified trade with both Europe and Asia.

In 1547, Ivan the Terrible was officially crowned the first czar of Russia. That says a lot, don't you think? Your first ruler is dubbed "the Terrible"? That certainly doesn't bode well for the Russian peasant. After a civil war in the early 1600s called the Time of Troubles, the atrocities of Ivan the Terrible were easily forgotten as the reign of the Romanov dynasty took hold. From 1613 to the Russian Revolution in 1917, the Romanov line ruled Russia with an iron fist. At the close of the 1917 Revolution, a Marxist political faction called the Bolsheviks seized power in St. Petersburg and Moscow under the leadership of Vladimir Lenin. The Bolsheviks soon changed their name to the Communist Party.

A bloody civil war ensued, pitting the Bolsheviks' Red Army against a loose confederation of anti-socialist monarchist and bourgeois forces known as the White Army. The Red Army triumphed, and the Soviet Union was formed in 1922.

Many in the West either forget or overlook that millions of Russians died in two practically overlapping wars: World War I and the Russian Civil War. By 1922, Russia had been at war for eight years, during which time some 20 million of its people had lost their lives (to go with 3 million surrendered to Poland in the Treaty of Brest-Litovsk). The Russian Civil War alone had taken an estimated 15 million lives. Compare this abominable figure to the 970,000 men and women who fell in the US Civil War. The naked magnitude of the loss of life through armed conflict just within the borders of Imperial Russia is historically unprecedented.

Famine and drought claimed millions more. In 1920 alone, over 3 million died of typhus. Massacres and pogroms were all too commonplace. The combined effect of these years plays havoc on the Russian psyche today, and has influenced the course of history irrevocably. The total disregard for life and the sheer numbers that Russians were able to put up—either in war or in peace—is staggering.

And again, in the guise of control (this time under the "egalitarian" banner of Communism) central authoritarian powers subjugated the Russian people. The megalomaniac Soviet dictator Joseph Stalin both embodies the kinds of rulers the Russian people have endured and equally illustrates just how docile and pliable the same people are in the face of a dominating force ruling from the top. By the time this shrewd Caucus-born dictator keeled over in 1953, his forced industrialization plans had killed off millions of peasants in widespread famines. His "devotion" to keeping his cadres in power led to the Great Purges (everything in Russia is done on a grand scale), which saw the murder or exile of even more millions of fellow comrades.

On the heels of famine and systematic executions came another little hardship for the Russian people: World War II. In by far the costliest front of the war (the Eastern Front contained more combat than all the other European fronts combined), Soviet forces lost close to 9 million soldiers . . . and 18 million civilians!

This sacrifice has never been forgotten in Russia, and losing so many of its citizens has affected the country ever since. Post-Stalin Soviet Russia can therefore be described as years of shell shock and industrial malaise. Although the Soviet Union still pounded loudly on UN desks, shot a man into space first, and attacked Afghanistan, the Soviet system was fundamentally washed out: economically, morally, spiritually, viscerally. By the time the last Soviet leader, Mikhail Gorbachev, was chased out of office in 1991, the Soviet Union did not exist any more. Russia took up the mantle of reinventing itself.

Pause a moment, please. It is remarkably easy to forget that the Russia I am writing about now is only 18 years old. Compare the nineties and first decade of the twenty-first century with what the country endured in the greater part of the twentieth. It is almost inconceivable to think of the differences.

The past 100 years of the country have been marked by brutal and bullying systems of government and a slavish acquiescence to them by the majority of the populace. The years have seen revolution and two world wars. They have seen massive industrial build-up and, concurrently, forced collectivization of all private property. The twentieth century took Russia from a feudal, agrarian monarchy to a country that has the largest nuclear arsenal in the world and could rightly claim to be the ultimate beacon of Communism to social revolutions around the world. (Where would China be now without the historic events perpetrated in Russia?)

But these past 18 years—these mere 18 years—have not passed without another roller coaster ride for the Russians. As the Soviet system fell, a period of free-for-all capitalism was quickly followed by a massive economic crash. Slowly, under the firm and controlling hand of Prime Minister Vladimir Putin and his cronies, the country and the economy has rebounded magnificently.

So it's fairly easy to forgive the typical Russian for spending a little something on himself or herself. Materialism is good pampering for a battered body and soul. This is what friends tell those who have gone through a long period of grief or hardship: "Take care of yourself, do something nice for yourself. Get out there and try to have a little fun." In a way, that's exactly what Russia is doing. Russians can breathe again. People can let their hair down. They can turn their music up. And brands are more than happy to oblige.

To many aging Russians, the crumbling of state control and the reckless rush to obscene wealth has been a corrosive and displacing occurrence in the country's history. To the younger generation that grew up in post-Gorbachev Russia, the go-go corrupt system that allowed the oligarchs to become the new rock stars has fundamentally affected their value system.

Most middle-aged Russians—the ones who are truly driving the new Russian economy—are straddling the nostalgia of a glorified Soviet Union and the contemporary reality of a competitive marketplace. It is this generation that can deliver the direction for the country in the immediate future: a slide back to the unpleasant past or a head-first leap into an uncertain future.

This market-driving Russian generation is aptly embodied in Alex Korobov, the president of TBWA\Russia. I meet him in a cute, Parisian-inspired bistro next door to his fashionable office address, which rests in an alley-like street literally shrouded by the shadow of the Kremlin's western wall. (In fact, the office is so close to the heart of government that the Russian secret service had to come over and officially conclude that the two floors that hold the bustling TBWA operation were not viable places for a sniper to get a clear shot into Putin's personal chambers.)

Korobov is suave, intellectual, and driven. He orders a cappuccino and sits at the table next to me and Mickie Thorpe, an American ex-pat and the senior account director at TBWA\Russia. Like almost every Russian I encounter, he is quick to light up a cigarette and inhale it like a man released from a long stay in one place.

Alex is a product of a privileged Soviet—that is to say, apparatchik—upbringing. His parents were of the Soviet elite. As a born Muscovite, he went to the best schools and institutes on his way to becoming a foreign service employee, a diplomat in the Ministry of Foreign Affairs. Fluent in Korean and Japanese, he is now the head of a 300-person ad shop in a homeland that 18 years ago didn't have any ads.

When talking with Alex, I get the impression that his new profession as ad man is another form of diplomacy, and perhaps much more important in its impact on everyday Russian life. It has something to do with the aimless freedom that is a signature of present-day Russian society. Because in as far as diplomacy seeks to attain a modicum of normality between nations, it is conceivable that advertising could contribute to a social normality in Russia. It could provide the commercial framework for freedom and establish aspirational goals to curb the aimlessness. In other words, commercial messaging could help to normalize Russian society.

Alas, the commercial messaging that is seemingly pervasive in Russia today is inundated with Russian celebrities. It is unclear how this clutter of fake personalities and talking heads will help to normalize Russian society. If anything, it just may contribute to its rabid preoccupation with money, goods, access, and privilege—not a far cry from our very own Hollywood-soaked media.

Russians are obsessed with their A-listers. They are obsessed with D-listers, too. First on the list of celebrities are the oligarchs. Without a doubt, the most respected and sought-after personalities are the billionaires. And just to be clear: Donald Trump is a mere millionaire. For the Russians, seven figures are for the hoi polloi.

Second on the list are the sports heroes and the TV personalities. Musicians and film actors are close behind. There is also the "famous because they are famous" segment of celebrities. Among all these types, you cannot escape their mugging faces on screen, poster, billboard, or page.

Alex thinks the celebrity-focused obsession that Russians are increasingly falling prey to is a by-product of history. It's not today's headline-whoring celebrities who instigate this fake hysteria. It's the fact that less than 20 years ago, no headline whoring existed in the Russian media landscape.

"We had a clear system of coordinates in Soviet times. You worked in a system, so to speak. You were guided from childhood to adulthood with a very clear path for school, career, family, a [Communist] party organization. Everything was very organized," he recalls. "We had celebrities in Soviet times: cosmonauts, sports heroes . . . heroes of the state. Suddenly that is gone. And there is a vacuum that needs to be filled with something."

Unfortunately, this vacuum is being filled with scoundrels, idiots, hacks, sluts, and meatheads. (Okay, there are a lot of Russian tennis stars above this blanket statement. But the generalization still holds.) The parade of Russian celebrities—grand marshaled by the oligarchs who occupy the business, political, and gossip pages—is akin to a train wreck, and the Russian people are unable to look away.

Paris Hilton Is Small Fry

Whereas Korobov is philosophical in his explanation of the insufferable phoniness of Russian celebrity-hood, Alex Shifrin is more . . . um . . . blunt. A columnist for the infamous Moscow *eXile*, an English-language alternative newspaper published in the capital until 2008, he describes Russian celebrity culture as "nothing more than a glammed-up PR engine for a really expensive prostitution ring." Writing in his Reklama Review column, Shifrin reflects on an ad he recently saw, and in doing so, exposes the deep-rooted cynicism that accompanies the Russian obsession:

> The celebrity idea carries a very different understanding in Russia. In America, celebrity spotting is something to behold. In a country of over 300 million, the celebs are distributed all over the place: LA, New York, Seattle, wherever. Spotting someone of note is a hunt, the payoff rewarding. In Russia, a country with a population of 150 million and falling, almost every celebrity is found within Moscow's Boulevard Ring. At any given moment, they are probably all in one of ten clubs or restaurants . . . Furthermore, if you have ever attended or organized any sort of corporate function, you know that every mug that you find on [TV] can be rented for between $5,000 and $25,000.[8]

Shifrin leaves his best for the celebrity oligarchs who dominate the modern Russian psyche. In contemplating the use of their image and endorsement of consumer goods and brands, he poses one simple question: "Would Coca-Cola Inc. ask Pablo Escobar to endorse Coke?"

Alex Korobov is more cerebral in his assessment of the shallow scene in Russian pop culture, but in the small, smoky café you can't but feel a bit of his rueful disappointment in the Russian audience he is trying to reach. "There is a clear lack of understanding of what the values are. Where do we go now? Who are our idols, our ideal people? There is a need for heroes and figures that you can identify with," he laments. "Our celebrities are fake. They are nobodies."

But the top ones, perhaps, are not nobodies at all. The oligarchs certainly are not nobodies. And some celebrities, with the help of the Kremlin, could be the next generation of business and political leaders in the country. Russian celebrities may embody the nadir of Russian mores and marketing, but the people dig them.

One night, I was invited for a humble meal at a relative's house. Normally, a formal Russian dinner is composed of eight courses or more, with a cornucopia of delicacies washed down fervently with ice-cold shots of vodka. And although Aunt Gala didn't have more than a half hour to put something together, I was greeted with a kitchen table full of typical Russian fare: salad oliviet, boiled and baked potato, red caviar, stuffed cabbage, borscht soup, pickled herring, sauerkraut, canned tomatoes and peppers, fried perch, rye bread, butter, and, of course, an ice-cold bottle of vodka.

As we sat down to eat and talk, Gala was reminded by her sister to turn on the TV. Much like *American Idol* or *Dancing with the Stars*, a reality show had captured the attention of the Russian masses and become a pop culture phenomenon. The show, loosely translated as "Under the Big Top," had a relatively simple premise: Russian celebrities compete against each other in front of a panel of judges to find the best circus performer among them. Yes, that's right. A circus performer.

Certainly, the circus tradition has deep roots in European, and especially eastern European, societies. So rather than compete in the boardroom, like on *The Apprentice*, these celebrities were put to the test under the big top. There was nothing particularly peculiar about the concept until I looked more closely at what these celebrities were made to do.

One had to walk a tightrope without a safety net. Another threw knives (after a week's training) at a petrified fellow celebrity. A TV news anchor was forced to get into a tiger cage to cajole four ferocious felines to jump through a ring of fire.

What kind of celebrity would agree to these kinds of stunts, I wondered. It's great TV! No doubt. But what respectable Hollywood agent would ever allow their clients to get into a tiger cage or get a hatchet thrown at their head? (All of you agents in Los Angeles, please stop snickering.)

On my third shot of vodka, I asked Gala who these celebrities were. She really didn't know. A few faces she recognized, but the rest were a bit unfamiliar to her.

So that's how they get convinced to do these things. They're not really celebrities. They are just people who work on TV or appear on stage. Sure, the same can be said for their US counterparts on a celebrity show like *Dancing with the Stars*. But the difference is that the US celebrities have actually done something to get there. (Please stop snickering, Mario Lopez.)

And they didn't have a political patron in a high-powered position in some Russian ministry, oil conglomerate, or real estate firm. For Russian celebrities, a ride to the top is a manufactured process, usually with the blessing and backing of the power elite in government or industry. One such glaring example is the meteoric ascent of a certain girl named Ksenia Sobchak, who is now the Paris Hilton of Russian pop culture.

Her rise and stay at the top of Russian buzz form a perfect indicator of how things are done here. Her father, Anatoly Sobchak, was the mayor of St. Petersburg and Putin's boss years ago, before Putin was chosen as Boris Yeltsin's successor. (It is common knowledge that when Sobchak lost the mayoral election in 1996, the victor offered all his protégés a place in the new administration. All accepted except for Putin, who declared that "it was better to be hung for loyalty than for betrayal.")

Putin owes his office to Ksenia's dad and has done all he can to help his patron's offspring. In fact, almost everyone in Russia is convinced that he is her personal Svengali, and that without his patronage she would not be a celebrity. The Paris Hilton comparisons are obvious.

Ksenia, as she is universally known, is a career celebrity. As the host of *Dom 2*—a reality show akin to *Big Brother*—she vamps on TV in a sultry (almost slutty) way, encouraging the contestants to make out, hook up, or go even further. The action is so racy that a group of conservative deputies in the Russian Parliament accused her of running a brothel on the set.

She has started her own clothing line, starred in a movie called *Thieves and Prostitutes* (the irony does not escape anyone in Russia), and published a bestselling book titled *Marriage of a Higher Sort*. In it, Ksenia dispenses invaluable advice on how to use sex to woo men, manipulate suitors for expensive jewelry, and shave in all the right places—all in the hope of snaring a rising oligarch. (The subtitle is *How to Marry a Millionaire*.) The book's back cover says it all: "There are enough oligarchs in Russia to go round! If you're dreaming of great love, an oligarch is the last person you need. You need an oligarch if you're dreaming of money, big money."

The astronomical sales of the tome have proven once and for all that for teen girls and young women in Russia, the allure of marrying an oligarch is many times more powerful than acquiring fame or intellectual status. Many of her indelible lessons are being taken to heart by millions of teenagers, and some brands are taking notice. For instance, a prime weapon of seduction for a Ksenia acolyte is the stiletto shoe. You won't see a single leggy billionaire huntress standing on anything less than five inches of heel. This is a Ksenia must: a "show 'em what you got" mini and "fuck me" shoes.

This lesson has been appropriated by so many girls in Russia that *Glamour* magazine annually organizes and sponsors the High Heel Race in the capital. Hundreds of girls line up for a mad 100-meter dash in five-inch heels, hoping to win $4,000 in cash and a bit of bragging rights. In the latest race, a girl named Masha ran the track in 12 seconds. The world record for the 100-meter sprint, held by Florence Griffith-Joyner, is 10.49 seconds.

And since politics and the tentacles of the political state permeate almost every facet of Russian life—much like it did in the Soviet times—Ksenia is now set on becoming a politician. She has started her own "youth movement" called All Free. On the surface, it can be construed as a progressive, youth-oriented political party, but almost all political commentators are convinced that All Free is a Putin-ordered affair created and co-opted by the Kremlin.

Another youth political movement called Nashi—or "Ours" in Russian—is a quasi-right-wing nationalist organization that models itself as a hybrid of the Boy Scouts, evangelical movements, and student political groups of the sixties. It's both an idealistic and a dangerously narrow-minded movement, and one which has taken the country by storm. Nashi members have picketed the US embassy in outrage at excessive "meddling" in Russian culture. At massive camp-out rallies in the Russian countryside, Nashi leaders urge couples to go into the woods to have sex so that the Russian race will not die out. Nashi is a Putin-sponsored party. Attendance at the rallies is monitored by compulsory electronic badges worn by all attendees. Anyone who misses three rallies is expelled.

All Free, like Nashi, is part of the so-called managed democracy or sovereign democracy that Putin has instilled in Russia. In an interview with the UK's *Guardian* newspaper, Ksenia toed the party line perfectly, stating that "freedom should always be restricted, or otherwise you have anarchy. If we stay within the law, young people can decide what's right for themselves."[9] Apparently, her brand of "fighting for your rights" doesn't include protesting in Pushkin Square.

Nor is her personal brand worth that much. You see, dear reader, Ms Sobchak comes cheap. According to the Russian edition of *Forbes* magazine, Ksenia is the seventh-best-paid celebrity in Russia: she made $1.5 million in 2007. (Tennis player Maria Sharapova came in first, with an annual income of $23 million.) Of course, the editor of the magazine readily admitted that a list of the incomes of Russian celebrities is extremely hard to compile, because Russian stars are usually paid in cash.[10] But still, getting a brand into the hands of Russia's It Girl is relatively inexpensive when compared with her bimbo counterpart in Malibu.

In fact, Kira Plastinina—another oligarch's daughter—recently paid Ms Paris Hilton a cool $2 million just to attend her Moscow catwalk show. You see, her daddy gave Kira $100 million to start her own fashion label. And, surprise, the business is a big hit. Hooray!

At a time when many young Russian girls are aspiring to be debutantes, oligarchs' wives or mistresses, international fashion models, or designers, the 16-year-old Kira runs a multi-million-dollar fashion empire as a leading voice of the "spoilt bratski" generation—the mega-wealthy kids of just-got-rich oligarchs.

Kira Plastinina sells about 40,000 pieces of clothing each month at 15 Moscow stores and 12 outlets in other cities. Although she is the daughter of Russia's milk and juice magnate, her fashion line is targeted at the burgeoning middle class of Russia. Her average piece retails at about $100. Kira is also the official designer on the massively popular Russian TV show *Star Factory*, an *American Idol* rip-off. I wonder how she got that gig.

Regardless of Kira Plastinina's success, Ksenia Sobchak is still Russia's darling. She is seen in one of the 10 most fashionable restaurants within the Moscow Boulevard Ring every night. She is on TV. She is on the nightly news. She has her own political party. Eat your heart out, Lindsay Lohan.

And to prove the point further that Ksenia is something totally different from the rest of the Russian common folk, she is chauffeured around town in a Mercedes with a Russian flag on the license plate. That means it's a state car, one of a small number given out to state officials, and cannot be stopped by the police. Apparently, the Moscow cops can't make a living off Ksenia Sobchak.

But some very ingenious (and brave) entrepreneurs are making a living off Vladimir Putin, the man who put Ksenia on the map. The Russian politician is also a star, a true celebrity, a Cecil B. DeMille type. In fact, for those who choose to overlook his dictatorial tendencies, or because of them, he is nearing a cult of personality status. He is Ronald Reagan and Chuck Norris rolled into one.

Just a year before he was to leave office, Vladimir Putin was at the top of his popularity both as politician and celebrity. A poll released in April 2007 by the respected Yuri Levada Analytical Center found that 79 percent of Russians were happy with Putin's performance—79 percent!

They were so happy, according to another poll, that two-thirds wanted Putin to remain in office for a third term, instead of quitting after the March 2008 presidential election, as the constitution required. Putin repeatedly went on record to deny that he was seeking a third term, but the mass adulation added to the rumors that he would finagle a way to stay in power.[11] And so he did. Vladimir Putin is currently Russia's prime minister, and still calling the shots.

With an 80 percent approval rating and a virtual lock on state-controlled media, it is not outrageous to suggest that Vladimir Putin is the biggest and best celebrity Russians have. And in much the same way that celebrities are leveraged by marketers to be sponsors and spokespeople, Putin's celebrity status has been appropriated by some risk-taking brands in a truly Russian manner.

For instance, Putin's name and visage have graced the label of a highly successful vodka line called Putinka. The Kristall Distillery, which began producing Putinka in the third year of Putin's presidency, has grown the pun label into the third-largest vodka brand by sales in Russia. In less than five years, a vodka named after an authoritarian ruler is a run-away success in a country whose population drinks more vodka than any other in the world.

And although a Russian law exists forbidding companies to use a person's name for marketing purposes without their permission, a preserved foods company called the Russian Canning Company, located in the southern province of Astrakhan, has named its products "PUIN." It prints the name with a sword through it that takes the place of the T. Incidentally, the sword closely resembles the historical symbol for the KGB. So by placing a sword in the shape of a letter—and providing an unmistakable nod to the president's KGB pedigree—the company got their celebrity spokesman without all those pesky fees and contractual negotiations.

Sales have been brisk since the brand launch in December 2006, allowing the Russian Canning Company to break into national supermarket chains, all because of the name and the clever way of presenting it to the consumer.

If your spokesperson enjoys 80 percent popularity, why not name your products after him or her?[*] It makes perfect sense. But can you imagine if Coca-Cola's Glaceau Water brand decided not to pay Jennifer Aniston her $10 million plus company shares for being a spokeswoman for Vitamin Water and just called the product Aniston instead . . . without her consent?

In Russian business, it is not inconceivable to sell a lot of vodka named after the Russian president without his consent.

Because it can't be shut down if it isn't tried. And if you have enough clout with the new power structure, it won't be shut down at all. So why not try it? This type of free thinking is both genius and insidious. This is the thinking of a Russian oligarch. And aptly, marketers outside Russia should learn from it. Not one of them made their fortune by thinking small.

The Ads That Changed a Country

The rise of the oligarchs could never have occurred were it not for a TV ad—two TV ads, to be precise. They were written and shot by Igor Lutz, who is now president and executive creative director of BBDO Moscow. Titled *Wedding* and *Graduation*, the two spots introduced the concept of "loans for shares" to the Russian people.

As the Yeltsin government—the first post-Soviet leadership—began to privatize state-owned enterprises, the regime

---

[*] When Putin announced that he was nominating Dmitry Medvedev to succeed him as president, alcohol manufacturers all over Russia began scrambling to register new trademarks using the name Medvedev. According to the *Moscow Times*, Inso Energia registered "Medvedka" and "Tsar-Medved," while the rights to "Medvedevka" belong to a Russian company called LaTerma (Svetlana Osadchuk, "Advertising Campaign Cashes in on Medvedev," *Moscow Times*, 4 August 2008, www.themoscow-times.com).

became worried that too much wealth was being hoarded by too few (and often unscrupulous) individuals. The government introduced the notion of loans for shares in an effort to spread share ownership of former Soviet businesses, as well as to shore up political support for Yeltsin among the increasingly grumbling and dissatisfied masses.

The government instituted a system of free vouchers to jump-start privatization. It also allowed people to use their own money to purchase shares of stock in privatized businesses. Yet for most people who had grown up with a state-controlled economy that professed a strict ban on capitalism, the idea of privatization wasn't easily digestible or readily accepted.

The Yeltsin government asked a tiny advertising agency to come up with a communication platform to convince them otherwise. These were tumultuous times for ordinary Russians. Their world was being torn asunder, the value system under which they lived was being rejected, and their leaders looked somewhat helpless in trying to control the ensuing chaos and confusion of political breakdown. Igor Lutz was living all this personally, and to counteract the frightening prospect of an unknown future, he decided to base his ads on the comforting notion of parochial tradition and solemn transition. Hence the idea for *Wedding* and *Graduation*, both symbols of enduring Russian traditions couched in the context of change and progress.

The 60-second spots are beautiful to watch. They are rich in cinematic artistry, each presenting the emblems of Russian tradition. A somber wedding in a Russian Orthodox church—in itself a groundbreaking portrayal for people emerging from a secular, anti-religious Communist past—allows the narrator to talk about responsibility to your spouse in terms of responsibility to your country, and coupled with the religiousness of the wedding ceremony, gives the topic a sense of divine approbation.

Clearly, at a time when most Russians were spooked out of their minds by the prospect of giving up their sparse cash for an unknown and unproven capitalist scheme, the symbols of Church and divinity worked to calm their fears and gave a benediction to the venture.

The symbolism of *Graduation* was not lost on the public either. The country was growing up, moving into a new phase, ready to take on the world. As most Russians hold secondary and post-secondary degrees, the familiarity of the graduation ceremony gave them pride in their country and faith in its success. It gave capitalism the veneer of a challenge, one to be taken on with the same enthusiasm as their coursework and first job out of university.

These two spots arguably made privatization happen in Russia. (BBDO Moscow was even charged with designing the actual vouchers!) Without TV, the Russia we see emerging as an economic heavyweight—pulling no punches in a hyper-capitalistic market-place—would never have happened.

Wedding and *Graduation* made capitalists out of the stooped babushkas in pastoral villages along the Volga and the weathered herders in the endless expanses of Siberia. The spots also helped garner a nod of approval from the skeptical West, which was looking for a sign that all those millions of people previously yoked under a Soviet regime really only wanted a bit of the American dream. What better way to show it than with a TV ad?

Even though initially each Russian citizen was issued a voucher of equal face value, within months of the program most vouchers converged in the hands of intermediaries who were snatching them up for cash right away. Ordinary people needed money. The state system was falling apart. Speculators were more than happy to take the shares off their hands. The shares were quickly, and often ruthlessly, accumulated by the upstart oligarchs.

Although the vouchers were meant to finance the average Russian's easy passage into capitalism, they quickly became the main currency by which budding entrepreneurs could generate an obscene amount of wealth and power. In hindsight, many Russians think the voucher scheme was a complete failure for ordinary Russians. But everyone can agree that it was a massive windfall for the oligarchs. And this was how the new Russian economy—fraught with shady politicians, shadier cronies, and budding oligarchs— came to be.

It is therefore conceivable that Igor Lutz's two TV spots at BBDO Moscow may have sparked an entire modern marketplace and initiated the birth pangs of a premature economy that today is fueling a modern gold rush. So how could I not ring their bell?

The offices of BBDO Moscow are in a nondescript building in a shabby-chic part of town, only a few blocks from Tverskaya Street—the grand boulevard of the Russian capital. A small plaque denotes the agency overtly, but a trained eye can always spot an outdoor scrum of "creative types" huddled over glowing cigarettes. Every agency has that cabal, and BBDO Moscow is no exception. The small lobby holds only a few seats, but contains a gaggle of bubbly receptionists, who constantly buzz the heavy, security-conscious doors for agency staff going in and out. It's a vibrant place, a place where you can feel that people believe in their work.

This is the vibrancy that BBDO Moscow's managing director, Igor Kirikchi, wants to keep in his shop. He heads the largest and most-respected agency in Russia, one that appeared in the country only in 1989 and operated with five employees out of two rooms at the Hotel Ukraine. Back then, the agency was called BBDO Marketing because at the time, as Igor says matter-of-factly, "no one needed advertising in Russia."

Igor is an incredibly bright and intellectual guy somewhere in his early thirties, someone who speaks of advertising with a passion and pathos not easily found in the West. He is a polyglot and can carry a conversation into fascinating tangents and conclusions in flawless English. As for appearance, the pale skin, some gray streaked through dark hair, and a noncaffeinated restlessness suggest that here's a guy who can stoically shrug off many late nights at the office. And yet he has that unmistakable Russian soft spot for family and friends, a wholly admirable code that requires the interruption of an interview for a call from his wife. He also has a fondness for heaping praise on his agency's accomplishments in the Russian advertising industry. It is much deserved.

It is somewhat zany to consider that TV advertising was nonexistent in Russia prior to the early 1990s. "Advertising didn't exist in the Soviet Union," says Kirikchi. "First of all, there was a total deficit of goods. When there is a deficit of goods, if any product is any good, it will be bought right away. Moreover, many goods were sold under the counter. For instance, if Czech shoes—maybe the best shoes you could buy in the Soviet Union at the time—came into the shop, an ordinary person off the street would never even see them because the salesperson would be hiding them and selling them for a better price to their relatives, friends of relatives, et cetera. Why would you need advertising when goods are sold in this way?"

The business of advertising and its effectiveness on the Russian people had another hurdle to clear. In Soviet times, the only advertising on TV was used to push the industrial complex's overstock. What the Soviets couldn't sell in Hungary or Poland, they pushed onto their own people.

Before the Communists fell from power, everyone in Russia knew that practically all the products being advertised on TV or out-of-home were the stuff that nobody else wanted.* So even today, advertising that looks too much as if it comes from the West

---

* "Out-of-home" generally means billboards, posters, ads on public transportation, and other ad signage.

is mistrusted because the Russian people naturally assume that the products are overstock that can't be sold over there, so now it's being pushed over here. Interestingly, this makes the typical Russian consumer much more suspicious of advertising than his or her American counterpart.

So the real demand for advertising started in 1991, after the demolition of the Soviet state. As the first private TV channels appeared in the marketplace, they began to sell advertising. They needed the money. At the same time, the first non-state-owned production companies opened their doors. Almost overnight, a market for advertising was created.

Overall, the ad market in Russia is on a tear. It is by far the fastest-growing market in Europe and is contributing to roughly half of all European growth in advertising. According to London-based media buyer Group M, Russia will become the fifth-largest ad economy in Europe and among the top 10 in the world by 2009. In fact, the Russian ad market has seen double-digit growth for eight years straight.[12] Official statistics point in the same direction. Advertising spending in the first half of 2007 in Russia surged to a record $4.1 billion as companies fought for market share in an expanding economy. Spending jumped 24 percent to 105 billion rubles, or $4.1 billion, from 84.5 billion rubles a year earlier, according to the Association of Communication Agencies in Russia. The top advertisers in the period, TNS Gallup AdFact revealed, were Procter & Gamble, the American company whose products include Pantene shampoo; Unilever, the European maker of Axe deodorant and Knorr soup; and Mars, the chocolate maker. TV ads account for half of all spending.[13]

The ad economy is obviously being driven by the country's rapid economic expansion, propped up by oil and commodity prices. The booming economy has instigated consumer demand,

and not just from those living in St. Petersburg and Moscow. "Consumers have spending power," says Adam Smith, futures director at Group M. "Five years ago, if you talked about Russia you were talking about Moscow and St. Petersburg. Now it means any city over 100,000."[14] TV ad demand is huge, but other media formats are gaining strength and popularity, especially outside the two main urban hubs. Radio is shifting from Moscow to the regions as 50 percent of all radio investment is now outside Moscow and St. Petersburg, compared with 30 percent just a few years ago.

Radio is also the leading format for branded programming and sponsorship, a key indicator of just how unevolved the media landscape is in Russia. In fact, when looked at through a historical prism, this particular piece of information harkens back to the early days of US media when radio carried almost all of the branded messaging burden, until TV took over with the likes of sponsored entertainment.

Interestingly, out-of-home advertising is also benefiting from too much TV demand. So is the online segment, albeit slowly. Russia's Internet growth "does not rely on e-commerce and direct response; advertisers mainly use the Internet for branding," says the Group M report.[15] This reality is confirmed by Kirikchi: "Unfortunately, Russia is still a country of dial-up. And in a country of dial-up, opportunities for making interesting advertising materials is very limited. I hope that in two or three years, there will be a broadband revolution. Then the Internet can become a medium to watch television. Only then can we talk about the Internet as being an important part in Russian advertising."

This is a powerful statement, for it presupposes that the Internet in Russia may not foster open conversation. It may not be used in the same way as it is over here. It may be a medium only, and not a conduit for dialogue, not an enhancer of consumer experience, not a gateway to myriad communities and groups.

And yet it is a sober examination of what is contextual and compelling to a Russian: something on TV. This makes "something not on TV" an interesting proposition for marketers seeking to break through in the Russian marketplace.

Allow me a digression: it may prove to be the key to marketing—or doing business—in Russia.

Na Zdroviya! (To Your Health!)

When we talk about Russia, we must talk about vodka. So when we talk brands, why not talk vodka brands? Or rather, let's talk about vodka branding. But first, a little bit of background on the ubiquitous elixir.

Its name comes from the diminutive word for water, *voda*. That's right. Vodka to Russians is water's cute little cousin, and so it flows as freely. And if you want to do business in Russia—any type of business—you must get intimately acquainted with vodka.

The classic Russian and Polish vodka is 40 percent alcohol content by volume (or 80 proof). This can be attributed to the Russian standards for vodka production introduced in 1894 by Czar Alexander III from research undertaken by the Russian chemist Dmitri Mendeleev. According to the Vodka Museum in Moscow, Mendeleev found the perfect percentage to be 38. However, since spirits in his day were taxed on their strength, the percentage was rounded up to 40 to simplify the tax computation. The taxes on vodka became a key element of government finances in czarist Russia, providing at times up to 40 percent of state revenue. By 1911, vodka constituted 89 percent of all alcohol consumed in Russia.

That number hasn't really wavered since. In the Soviet era, vodka seemed like the only thing that kept the system going: the workers would get drunk to forget their measly existence, and the bosses would get drunk to forget their corruption. (The more unscrupulous ones would celebrate it, I suppose.)

Generally, before taking a shot of vodka, one exclaims, "Na zdroviya!"—To your health!—and then proceeds to chase it with a *zakuska*—a bite-sized snack that brings out the flavor of the drink or dulls its burn. Each shot is typically followed by some caviar (for the well connected), or simply rye bread and a pickle. Consequently, one could assume that Russians are the healthiest people on the planet (which they are certainly not).

Russia is the world's biggest market for hard liquor, and vodka takes up almost all of it.* According to a market research agency called Biznes Analitika, 2.4 billion liters of vodka were sold in Russia in 2006. This figure represents official sales—to the tune of $15.7 billion. Another 1.2 billion liters were sold on the black market.[16]

The Russian thirst for vodka is insatiable, and yet successive administrations have tried to crack down on it, curb it, misdirect it—anything, really—to force Russians to drink less. The Putin administration has increasingly put restrictions on vodka advertising, and the latest salvo in 2006 outright forbade ads for vodka or beer in prime time. Imagine if the Bush government decided there would be no more Budweiser ads during the Super Bowl!

Nevertheless, a budding oligarch named Roustam Tariko decided to launch a vodka brand called Russian Standard in 1998. Nine years later, *Forbes* magazine's "World's Richest People" ranking placed him at 150, with an estimated personal wealth of $5.4 billion.

---

* In the United States, vodka outsells gin, rum, and tequila, as well as scotch, bourbon, and Canadian whiskey.

The Russian Standard Vodka portfolio has a 60 percent market share of all premium vodka sold in Russia. It is available in over 40 markets worldwide. Two years after launch, Russian Standard Original overtook all imported premium vodkas on the Russian market. This led to the launch of Russian Standard Platinum in 2001 and the company's luxury brand, Imperial Vodka, in 2004.

Just in his early forties, Tariko is unique within the oligarchic hierarchy in that he seems to be untainted by allegations of corruption, extortion, or political shenanigans. A *BusinessWeek* profile in 2004 called him a "born entrepreneur" who made "a good living finding hotel rooms for Italian businessmen" while a Moscow student in the 1980s. He "then became an importer of candy and later upmarket alcoholic drinks such as Martini. From there it was a small step to Russian Standard Vodka."[17]

But it is not his vodka brilliance that put Tariko on that *Forbes* list, nor his Italian connections that garner him a place in this book. Even his innate marketing instincts aren't the true focus of this example, although his launch of Imperial Vodka in the United States merits a mention: in September 2005, Tariko spent $3 million to rent out Liberty Island in New York Harbor for one night to fete over 1,000 people with Beluga caviar, blinis, quail eggs, red borscht, and $35-a-bottle Imperial Vodka.

It is Tariko's marketing skills as a *banker* that are interesting to forward-thinking marketers. When one of the earlier Putin bids for increased restrictions on vodka advertising on TV passed in the legislature in 2000, Tariko was faced with an impossible situation: how could he continue to market a premium brand without the use of a premium advertising channel like TV? How could he reach the growing Russian upper and middle classes without the single most important way to reach them, namely TV? How could he keep the name Russian Standard to mean premium and Russo-focused? And most important, how could he avoid the pesky advertising restrictions coming down from the Kremlin?

The answer was Russian Standard Bank. At a time when the Russian Standard brand connoted good vodka to almost everyone in Russia, Tariko started a bank with the same brand name. The move was a stroke of genius.

Russians hold vodka as a national heritage and an integral part of almost every social rite in the communal consciousness. If the government isn't trusted, a bottle of vodka is. If you celebrate, you drink. If you mourn, you drink. From cradle to grave, the libation runs like a meandering river of life. What better connotation of Russian tradition and cultural continuity? Russian banks were foreclosing and defaulting at alarming rates. But a bank built on the ebb and flow of the most important drink in the country could not fail. After all, it is named after the best vodka in the country.

Everyday Russians flocked to the financial brand in droves. According to the company's press releases, Russian Standard Bank is now Russia's largest consumer finance bank and a pioneer in the consumer lending industry. It has more than 20 million customers and issues more than 77 percent of all credit cards in Russia (the bank is issuing 10,000 credit cards each day). The bank has grown 200 percent since 2001, a short year after Tariko launched it, and has extended $1.1 billion in consumer loans to claim 51 percent of the market. Russian Standard Bank created from scratch the home-lending market in Russia. Another Tariko brainstorm is Russian Standard Insurance, a multi-billion-dollar institution and currently the country's largest life insurance company. *Na zdroviya*, indeed.

In April 2005, Russian Standard became the exclusive issuer and marketer of American Express card products in Russia, issuing the first-ever ruble-denominated American Express card. The vodka brand made it into the big time. (In retrospect, it is a perfect marriage: one is a card that you don't leave home without; the other is a vodka you don't stay home without.)

For Roustam Tariko, the symbiosis between a vodka brand and a financial brand is the result of a unique insight into the Russian marketplace. As he attested in a *BusinessWeek* interview in 2004, "Vodka and banking have one thing in common: they make your dreams come true."[18]

The advertising restriction on vodka did not deter Tariko from doing business. He merely set up a bank to get around the laws. And in doing so, he became one of the most successful bankers in Europe. This is how oligarchs operate in Russia. When one door closes, another can be opened.

The Russian Standard Bank coup became legendary in Russian business circles. Soon, booze and beer brands were setting up their own banks and other financial institutions. Liquor brands unable to advertise on TV or out-of-home launched high-end chocolate products under the same brand lock-up: same name, same font, same brand identity. Vodka brands were able to hawk mineral water with the same brand name, winking at the consumer at each touch point. Why not? Water is an integral part of vodka. One cheeky vodka brand started an eponymous travel agency. The promise was relatively simple for Russians to understand: it takes you to a better place.

Although these types of oligarchic ploys have helped dozens of booze brands to sell product and make millions, the practice has hindered legitimate non-vodka brands from passing muster with the Putin-controlled censors. For instance, TBWA\Russia had an international client that wanted to market a mineral water brand in Russia. The state authorities that monitor advertising content would not air any ads from the legitimate water brand, believing that it was a proxy ad for a new vodka. It took months to convince the authorities that the water being advertised was really water and nothing else.

The concept of "surrogate branding" is firmly in the tradition of the Russian joke. Back in Soviet days, in a society fraught with wiretapping and snitching, the only relatively safe way to criticize the government was through a sly, double entendre– and innuendo-filled anecdote or joke told across tables laden with vodka, whispered in useless meetings or in long lines for bread. This is at the heart of the vodka-as-travel-company advertisement. The people know what's up. They get it. It's really water . . . wink, wink . . . and I love drinking it out of a shot glass.

The Next-Gen Co-Branding: The Branded Brand

Although the machinations employed by Russian vodka marketers may seem dubious at first blush, they truly represent a breakthrough marketing concept. This concept goes beyond mere brand extensions, like when a detergent brand branches out into subcategories of bleach, non-bleach, color, and scent. Rather, it takes its cues from co-branded marketing techniques that are popping up in Europe and North America, and it takes it to another level of business chutzpah and strategic inspiration.

It is now no longer surprising to see two, three, or four separate brands combine their core competencies to launch a so-called "branded brand." Brands in the West are caught in a spiral of brand extensions. In response, maverick marketers seek new ways to leverage their brand equity through unique partnerships and campaigns. For instance, beer brand Heineken has coupled itself to coffee-maker purveyor Krups to come up with the BeerTender, a professional-grade beer tap for the home. Over 1.4 million units of the BeerTender were sold in the Netherlands in less than a year, and now the BeerTender is available for Heineken-owned brands Amstel and Stella Artois.

So a "branded brand" like the BeerTender is indeed forward thinking and experiential, to be sure.* But it pales in comparison to the utter, impudent brilliance of marketing a vodka brand through the platform of a travel agency, or starting a bank to market booze.

Still, the typically Russian and oligarchic outlook on advertising has parallels in the Western market. In the United States, the PepsiCo–bottled water brand Aquafina followed in the footsteps of an oligarch and launched a health and beauty skincare line called Aquafina Advanced Hydration RX. The skincare line, composed of 10 different products, was developed by a licensee and is available at retail, drug, and mass outlets. The Pepsi water brand now competes with Oil of Olay, Neutrogena, and L'Oreal. A water brand.

At the time of writing, it is rumored that in response Coke will partner with L'Oreal to launch Lumaé, a beverage designed to enhance the condition of human skin.[19] This is not a joke. And neither is the increasing proclivity of top brands to engage in some oligarch-like behavior. Corporate brands are getting into the licensing game. Not the brand extension game, mind you. The licensing game. In 2006, in fact, 18.3 percent of licensed items in the United States involved a corporate brand, accounting for $1.1 billion in royalties.[20]

Aquafina—the bestselling water brand in the United States—can "legitimately" license itself to a skincare company on the brand essence of purity and clarity, and in doing so extend the Aquafina brand name from the beverage to the cosmetics aisle. This connection illustrates the marketing mind of the oligarch

---

* Experiential marketing is a philosophy and methodology that seeks to connect brands and consumers in personally relevant and memorable ways. It tries to create branded experiences instead of using traditional features-and-benefits marketing.

and the brand planner and what gives the Russian consumer marketplace its unique character, which Western marketers need to internalize: water and skincare are a fit, and to a typical Russian, so are vodka and banking.

Perhaps another example is in order. In Australia at the tail end of 2005, Unilever's Lynx Body Spray brand (a.k.a. Axe) launched a marketing campaign called Lynx Jet. The premise was simple: imagine an airline staffed solely by nubile and overeager female flight attendants.

The campaign, instigated by Lowe Hunt and Universal McCann, both of Sydney, saw a number of jets being leased from Australian low-fare airline Jetstar and rebranded with the fictitious Lynx Jet logo and color scheme. A television spot for the Lynx Jet campaign featured a babe-laden form of travel that all guys would love—finally, an airline where members of the "mile-high club" are par for the course. What red-blooded Aussie male wouldn't want to sign up?

However, the half-naked hostesses and sexually charged double entendres were too much for the Australian public to bear. A major backlash from the airline stewards' union pressured Jetstar to cancel the lease arrangement it had with Lynx. The Lynx Jet airline—where guys could travel in hot tubs and get in-flight massages—was grounded.

Still, the Lynx target audience—horned-up teenaged guys—loved the idea. And they loved the largesse of the execution. There actually was a jet with hotties on it, ready to take them on the trip of a lifetime. This airline could exist. A marketing campaign—for once—had a level of not-often-seen plausibility that energized the lackadaisical teenage dude.

In the target audience of males 18 to 25, sales of Lynx Body Spray grew by 20 percent in four weeks after the campaign launched, to take an 84 percent share of the Australian deodorant body spray market. Results like these are why the Lynx Jet campaign is globally lauded by marketing and advertising professionals. A simple insight—a hedonistic airline for guys—ended up winning the Grand Prix in the Cannes Media Lions, two Gold Lions in the Lions Direct awards, and a Promo Lion in the sales-promotion category in 2006.

The campaign for Lynx—the deodorant brand—rested on the plausibility and acceptance of Lynx Jet—a surrogate brand. And herein lies the secret to the success of Russian Standard Bank: it rested on the laurels of the vodka brand that preceded it. And to Russians, raised on the inside joke, the marketing proposition was irresistible.

And something else to remember: despite the overwhelming preference and penetration of television, the Russian Standard vodka brand *grew* despite restrictions on TV advertising. The growth and popularity of Russian Standard Bank was better than any advertising money could buy. The vodka brand and its surrogate bank brand achieved marketing symbiosis and rewrote the rules on how a brand can break through and engage a TV-obsessed audience in Russia.

Want another example of oligarchic thinking? How about Microsoft and Mountain Dew? Quite an odd pair, *da*?

Mountain Dew wanted to leverage the most highly anticipated game title launch in Xbox history: Halo 3. The Microsoft-owned video game brand was projected to make millions off this popular game title. In fact, Halo 3 broke practically every record for an entertainment property launch in the fall of 2007. In its first weekend on the market, Halo 3 grossed $350 million, beating out *Titanic* and the *Spiderman* franchise for the top entertainment debut in the history of humankind. The launch of Grand Theft Auto IV from Rockstar Games broke that record in May 2008, grossing over $400 million in first-weekend sales.

PepsiCo North America was prescient enough to hitch its Mountain Dew brand to the game title. Knowing that millions of gamers were going to spend countless hours playing the new game, the company released a red-hued, citrus-cherry-flavored, limited-edition Mountain Dew can and flavor that carried the name of the much-anticipated Halo 3 game. Touted as the first soft drink created for and co-branded with a video game, the new Dew limited edition brand is positioned as Game Fuel.

Amazing. Launching a "game fuel" drink is exactly the type of oligarchic thinking that makes successful branded brands possible. What Red Bull is to clubbing, Mountain Dew is to gamers. It instantly became a gamer's fuel drink of choice. The brand would become the Gatorade of the cyber-athlete. The 20-ounce limited-edition bottle packaging features the game title and its main character, Master Chief, and comes with a whopping 120 milligrams of caffeine.

The Mountain Dew coup for a game fuel brand casts a light on oligarchic thinking. When faced with overwhelming competition in one category, PepsiCo created a completely new one. When the marketplace was poised for a huge product launch, the brand decided to become part of the story instead of buying a seat at the promotional table. Most important, the folks at Pepsi inherently know—much like their bull's-eye consumer—that you'd better go big or go home.

Moreover, oligarchs rarely share their spoils with others, nor do they tread beaten paths. After all, their billions are owed to maverick thinking, a pirate mentality, and a willingness to go it alone. So compare the Mountain Dew's oligarchic thinking for its promotions with the Dr Pepper brand when it announced that it would pay millions to ride the hype of the release of a mega-blockbuster franchise: Lucasfilm's *Indiana Jones*.

For *Indiana Jones and the Kingdom of the Crystal Skull*, the fourth and (presumably) last Indy flick, Dr Pepper rolled out the biggest promotion in the beverage brand's 125-year history. The only other brands that Lucasfilm granted licensing deals to were M&M's, travel site Expedia, Kraft's Lunchables, and Burger King's Indy Whopper. (So much for going it alone.) Dr Pepper's agreement with Lucasfilm allowed it to create a couple of TV spots spoofing the Indiana Jones adventure stories—an Indy archetype is on the hunt for a can of Dr Pepper . . . (yawn)—a couple of print ad executions, a microsite, and the opportunity to be "an official sponsor of" for the movie. Boring.

In reality, Dr Pepper shelled out millions on the deal because *Crystal Skull* was slated to be the biggest movie of summer 2008 in the United States, and grocery stores were wetting themselves with the bundling and cross-selling opportunities that are always at hand when a Hollywood blockbuster comes rolling into their customers' consciousness.* The more ad clutter, PR shenanigans, and marketing bluster around the movie, the more chips and dip get sold. Massive grocery chains like Kroger, Safeway, and Supervalu bundled all of the movie's CPG partners and created larger than usual merchandising displays for the theatrical release starring Harrison Ford and Shia LaBeouf. Naturally, Dr Pepper wanted to be in the same product stack in the aisles of Safeway, along with another half-dozen brands competing for (starving for) the consumer's attention.

Mountain Dew and Dr Pepper. Compare the two beverage brands' use of promotional money and a mass media property. One brand chose to think big, to create something new, to stake a lifestyle marker firmly into the brand's ethos, create a new desire, and then cater to an unmet need. The other chose to create movie-centric ads and get bundled with other brands in a retail promotion.

---

* As of publication, the fourth Indiana Jones movie was the twenty-fifth highest grossing film of all time, and it was the second most successful film of 2008, after *The Dark Knight*.

Most likely, both brands' strategies and tactics sold a lot of soda. But which one better wins the hearts and minds of consumers?

For an oligarch, an "anything goes" brand mentality is well honed and necessary. An overwhelming majority of young Russians aspire to become oligarchs and worship them like celebrities. In other words, they are inspired by their audacity and market expertise. In the Russian economic meltdown that spawned them, the ones who thought big, took chances, and ignored traditional rules and roles in order to acquire thousands of diverse companies and launch thousands of new brands were the ones who came out on top, seasoned and hungry for more. Never resting, a successful oligarchic-bred company continues to uphold an "anything goes" approach to branding. No rule is sacred. No idea is too big. No brand is perfect, and nothing is constant.

Consider the innovative thinking behind Nintendo's Wii gaming console. After initial consumer acceptance of the physical aspect of console gaming, the Wii brand exploded. Christmastime TV coverage on CNN and FOX News was saturated with stories of Wii shortages and innovative consumer attempts to get their hands on one. Even to this day, the most aspirational game console is the Nintendo Wii. There are still shortages. Consumer demand is still incredibly high, a full three years after the initial release of the product. But not resting on their short-term success, the executives at Nintendo seized upon a bigger idea than just gaming.

The Wii wants to transcend the notion of a gaming system, particularly because gaming is stereotyped as a sedentary experience. Its unique technology allows gamers to physically control their onscreen players, revolutionizing the gaming world altogether. The execs at Nintendo fully recognize the potential of a market-wide paradigm shift in gaming acceptance: what is a male-dominated industry could easily become a female-controlled market.

So instead of coming out with more games and licensed titles, Nintendo decided to do something different. It decided to act a bit more like an oligarchy. Why couldn't *it* redefine the gaming industry? The result is Wii Fit: a $90 attachment to the Wii, dubbed the Balance Board, expands the "games" that can be played on the Wii to include yoga and push-ups. The board also acts as a scale that can track a user's weight and body-mass index. Imagine that. A video game whose extension actually motivates players to get *more* active.

But the notion of Wii Fit goes way further than getting players off the couch. This Wii effort is the first of many highly lucrative forays into a fundamental shift in gaming. Wii Fit is a daring attempt to steal a greater share of a vastly underexplored consumer segment, namely, women gamers.

The Wii Fit launch was accompanied by a massive marketing campaign, including PR, TV, print, and outdoor ads. The tagline to the launch, delivered by Goodby Silverstein & Partners, is a simple question: "How Will It Move You?"

It has already moved many. Through a simple accessory, Nintendo is trying to redefine the gaming industry by moving Nintendo—and the entire industry of movement-based gaming—away from its core of young, male gamers and closer to the uncool realm of moms and little sisters. But therein lies the genius. Nintendo is acting like an oligarch. It is making the market. It is redefining its kid-centric brand equity. And it is developing a reputation for innovation that will be remembered by every consumer who has ever played a Wii.

It's important to understand that, on a superficial level, Wii Fit is a brand extension. Many traditional marketers would view it this way. That's understandable, because brands have been overextending themselves with new bells and new whistles for far too long. In trying to break out of the clutter, brands pile on the features. According to a September 15, 2008, article in *Advertising Age*, "Arbor Strategy Group, a new-product consulting firm that has tracked the history of packaged-goods launches for many years, found most categories ultimately spawn a product labeled 'total' or 'complete' at the tail end of a lengthy bout of product and benefit proliferation. Then competitors start all over again with single-benefit claims." In other words, what goes around comes around.

But Wii Fit isn't a brand extension in the traditional sense. It's an entirely new product and service, in the same way that vodka and banks are entirely different. Just as Russian Standard can build its brand equity as both a premium vodka brand and a financial services company, Wii is building a brand based on the conventional notion of gaming (passive and bad for your health) crossed with the notion that millions of people work out at home, and millions more need to. To the Russians, who are accustomed to bold oligarchic moves, both economic and political, the incongruity of the two doesn't come off as outrageous at all. It comes off as inspired marketing.

Taking the notion further, the melding of two totally disparate brands is today at the heart of big-think strategies at leading companies worldwide. When two seemingly incompatible things are combined, new links between the two are likely to be discovered. Psychologists call the result of this process "emergence," and confirm that the more dissimilarity there is between the two products, the more potential there is for emergence.

And behind it all is the almighty Big Idea. Emergence doesn't occur until a "What if?" conversation happens, either internally for an individual or collectively for a group. The Big Idea can surface any time and, more often than not, from anywhere.

Think Differently

The history-making rise of the Russian oligarch class is, for some odd reason, relegated to the past in Western history books and scholarly discussion. The general consensus is that the men and (relatively few) women who seized astronomical wealth during the Soviet state's transition from a planned economy to a capitalist market system are historical figures, rather than people who are still molding the Russian way of doing business. To make such an assumption is a fatal mistake. The appearance of hundreds of billionaires out of the ashes of a superpower meltdown isn't a one-off effect, to be noted but deemed inconsequential by the global marketing and advertising fraternities.

Russian oligarchs—and the countless throngs of über-ambitious, morally loose, and culturally adrift men and women who want to work for them and to be like them—are still in control of the Russian economic landscape and, more important, are still aspirational figures to millions of Russian youth. The opportunists who make up the roll call in *Forbes'* "richest" lists are the ones who seized opportunity and fortune in Russia while Boris Yeltsin was slamming vodka like a Mötley Crüe roadie and selling off entire industrial complexes at the stroke of the presidential pen.

Russian consumers know the oligarchs by name. Actually, they know them by their name and patronymic derivative—the name of the person's father. My name is Maxim. My father's name is Yefim. In Russia, my friends and colleagues address me as Maxim Yefimovich. (If I were a girl, I would be Maxima Yefimova.) To millions of Russians, the oligarchs are as familiar as national war heroes, although not as revered or respected as the war generals and peasant partisans who saved the Motherland. No, Russians know these guys well for a different reason: they may have never met a Hero of the People who was killed in action during World

War II, but they know the oligarchs—and how they made their money—much better.

Remember that Russian consumers were around when factory managers ended up owning the factory, or when neighbors were roughed up by mobsters over unpaid loans. Almost anyone who belonged to the Communist Party in Russia, when the whole Potemkin village came tumbling down, had a chance to make a lot of money. The oligarchs seized that chance. They rolled the dice. And then they fiercely defended their turf. In fact, anecdotal buzz among Russians in everyday conversation confirms the overall opinion that there is blood on the hands of everyone who made more money than they did. If you're rich in Russia, it's assumed that you either did something dirty or did something dirty for Putin's Kremlin.

And yet the oligarchs are admired figures. After decades of Communist rule, a national obsession with material possession is easily understood. So the sheer magnitude of the wealth that Russian oligarchs have acquired naturally elevates the common notion of a better life through material possession. You can't be this successful, the Russians reason, unless you take a chance and bend the rules to suit your needs. You can't pull in this much money without thinking differently.

These guys aren't visionaries. They're hustlers.

The Russian oligarchs—or at least the majority of them—got their big break selling jeans, cigarettes, PCs, and the like on the black market. Of course, as with any black market, official compliance and corruption is instrumental to its success. By the early nineties, the oligarchs who started out by smuggling razors and air conditioners had deep connections in the Russian government during the tumultuous transition from a state-controlled to a market-based economy. Post-Soviet business oligarchs are often relatives or friends of officials in government, or government officials themselves. Many are common criminals and mafia types. All of them were able to acquire massive wealth by getting their hands on government and state assets for bargain-basement prices during the privatization process instigated by the Yeltsin administration.

According to David Satter, author of *Darkness at Dawn*, "what drove the process was not the determination to create a system based on universal values but rather the will to introduce a system of private ownership, which, in the absence of law, opened the way for the criminal pursuit of money and power."[21] This pursuit had everyday Russians up in arms. It's not unfair to say that Putin's popularity among the common folk rests with his determination to bring many of the country's richest men to justice. First-generation oligarchs who have remained in their homeland are often under fire for tax evasion and other state-dictated charges, too.

Boris Berezovsky fled to London. Others, like Mikhail Khodorkovsky, the former owner of energy behemoth Yukos Oil, have been less fortunate. Khodorkovsky was arrested in 2003 when dozens of special forces troops stormed his private jet on the runway as he was fleeing for Europe. The young engineer, who was listed as the twenty-first most wealthy man in Russia only a few short years ago, drew an eight-year sentence for tax evasion in a Siberian maximum-security prison.

The second-wealthiest Russian lives lavishly in London. With the aforementioned estimated personal wealth of $21 billion in 2007, the 41-year-old Roman Abramovich made his fortune selling Sibneft Oil, a major energy concern. According to the *Sunday Times*, Abramovich is the second-wealthiest person in the UK. He qualified by keeping residences in Knightsbridge, London. His 440-acre West Sussex estate was previously owned by King Hussein of Jordan.

To drive the point home, Abramovich owns the 377-foot yacht *Pelorus*. In comparison, Rupert Murdoch, the billionaire chairman of News Corporation, can only muster the 184-foot *Rosehearty*. (It is rumored that Abramovich has ordered a 525-foot vessel, estimated to cost $450 million. It would be the world's largest private yacht.)

While most billionaires have their own Gulfstream private jet, Abramovich owns his own Boeing 767. He also owns a Ferrari FXX, a $2.2 million race car of which only 30 were ever built. He recently bought two Maybach 62 limousines and customized them to be bombproof. Each limo reportedly cost him $2.5 million.

So how did this guy do it? Well, he thought like an oligarch... even though he wasn't one at the time. Between 1992 and 1995, in the midst of market deregulation and privatization, Abramovich founded five companies that acted as intermediaries in the trading of oil and oil products. Together with partner Boris Berezovsky, he acquired controlling interest in Sibneft, a huge oil company. Each paid about $100 million for a company that, in hindsight, should have been valued in the billions of dollars.

But none of his business ventures or acquisitions has garnered more attention than his purchase of Chelsea Football Club, the fabled London side that is currently at the pinnacle of soccer success. Before his takeover of the company that owns the club in 2003, English football (soccer) was a relatively tame affair, with salaries and expectations tempered by the British sense of propriety and reserve. But Abramovich is an oligarch, and an oligarch does not think small.

As soon as he took over, Abramovich poured an estimated $890 million into the club, as well as assuming the $170 million debt the club was carrying. The cash allowed him to go on an international buying spree, attracting the talents of renowned footballers and a Pat Riley–like coach in José Mourinho.

The huge and rapid influx of over $1 billion into a relatively obscure English soccer team meant almost instant success for the club. Chelsea finished second in its first season under Abramovich, from fourth the previous year. The following season they moved into first place and reached the semi-finals of the all-important pan-European Champions League. Since his purchase, Chelsea has dominated its home league in England, as well as trounced all opponents on the international scene.

Many football purists and pundits believe that Abramovich's entrance into the Premier League has fundamentally transformed English football. His wealth, and propensity to use it in staggering amounts, allows him to purchase players at will and at frequently inflated prices. He offered AC Milan striker Andriy Shevchenko a whopping $180 million over four years to join the club. The Ukrainian gleefully accepted, but lasted only two full seasons with the club.

Because of this, Abramovich has single-handedly made the other clubs start doing the same in order to keep up. Teams that cannot handle the spending pressure are forced to look for wealthy ownership overseas, as is evident in the recent purchase of Manchester United by US billionaire Malcolm Glazer and Liverpool's sell-off to the former prime minister of Thailand, who embezzled billions in order to buy the team.

Never mind that Chelsea posted record losses in 2005 and 2006—to the tune of $290 million and $170 million respectively. That doesn't matter. What matters is that his club is winning, while Abramovich's chutzpah and personal wealth are making Chelsea a dominant worldwide football brand.[*] When

---

[*] Abramovich's Sibneft concern signed a three-year, $58 million sponsorship deal with CSKA Moscow. The following year, CSKA won the UEFA Cup. A major Russian magazine called *Pro Sport* named this oligarch the most influential person in Russian football. Not a player or a coach, mind you. An oligarch.

others would rationally fold, Abramovich doubles down. When others would rather write off the investment, the oligarch digs in. When an opportunity presents itself, the oligarch pounces.

The oligarchic character isn't anything new. If you replaced my interpretation of "oligarch" with business writer Adam Morgan's definition of "pirate," you would arrive at a common place.

To think differently, in the context of the Russian oligarch, may erroneously connote an emphasis on violence and aggression. To be sure, the biggest success stories in modern Russian business have participated in violence and aggression. By no means would I imply that this is an example to follow.

Rather, I emphasize the oligarchic archetype as a person or an entity that can fearlessly seize upon new opportunities and diligently protect them as any for-profit concern would. It takes largesse of spirit to be an oligarch. It takes a hustler's mentality to stymie the competition and a free-wheeling will to succeed—with heavy cost if necessary. But most important, oligarchs monetize big ideas because they instinctively know that big ideas pay off.

Take, for instance, India's best version of a hustling oligarch: Vijay Mallya. The owner of United Breweries Group—and six other publicly traded companies in India—has a collection of more than 260 cars. He often sleeps on his 312-foot yacht named the *Indian Empress* to escape the bustle of Mumbai. In 1983, at age 27, he inherited the Bangalore-based UB Group, a liquor company that was third-tier at best. United Spirits, the flagship of the group, is now the world's third-largest liquor company in the world. United Breweries is India's biggest brewer, buoyed by the Kingfisher brand. Mallya's Kingfisher Airlines is expected to become the largest domestic carrier in India after a mere three years in existence. Its first international route is dubbed the Tech Express, as it connects directly between San Francisco and Bangalore. It is said that Mallya started the airline after a ban on beer advertising. Much like Russian

Standard's Tariko, the Indian oligarch parlayed the beer brand to launch a flourishing surrogate one.

In emerging markets, people are looking for aspirations, cachet, affluence, and lifestyle. Mallya is that and more. He has been quoted as saying that "rather than spend millions getting film stars [to market his brands], I am quite happy to be the brand ambassador myself."[22] With more than half the population of India younger than 24, it is safe to say that aspiration is in full abundance there. And the insights gleaned from this country can indeed become the blueprint for the aspirations of youth across the globe.

CHAPTER TWO

Insights Outsourced

(The Need for Global Empathy)

O n my third morning in Mumbai—known then as Bombay—I was sufficiently unjetlagged to enjoy the early morning breakfast offered at the hotel. After negotiating the magnificently meandering halls of the Taj Mahal Palace Hotel, I found the salon where guests were treated to a mishmash of global breakfast fare: from lox, bangers, and croissants to masala, corn flakes, and Camembert.

The Taj Mahal is India's first Indian-owned luxury hotel. It was built in 1902 by Jamsetji Tata, the patriarch of the Tata family, after he was denied entry to a British hotel where he had wanted to entertain his clients. Its seaside breakfast salon is a splendid example of nineteenth-century colonial opulence and etiquette overlooking the Gateway of India, a symbol of British entry to and exit from (both inglorious) this overwhelming country.*

Boiling water was poured over pungent Darjeeling, a tuxedoed waiter lit my first Marlboro of the day, and two local newspapers were placed at my side. It was a perfect way to start a morning.

This trip to Mumbai almost didn't happen. I was supposed to be in the country two weeks prior but had visa hang-ups and was forced to postpone the flight. A few frantic phone calls and a hefty fee to a broker got me the right paperwork for the trip, and after a slight delay, I was in-country.

After a couple of all-day meetings and all-night drinks, I was scheduled for a tour of the Dharavi slum in the early afternoon. (This was an eye-opening experience. Anyone who knows this place will understand what I'm talking about. But more on that later.) The morning was open enough for me to read the two papers cover to cover . . . and I'm glad I did.

The *Times of India* was devoured first. The second—the *Hindustan Times*—was uncorked with my second Marlboro. I found most of the articles echoing the *Times*, until I reached the business section of the *HT*. Delightedly, I stopped at a headline describing something very dear to my heart: experiential marketing.

The headline—"The New-Age Marketing"—certainly caught my attention. But the use of "experiential" in the first paragraph really got me stoked. The article itself was very well written, insightful, contextual, and wholly applicable. And about 85 percent of it was lifted directly from my book *Experience the Message: How Experiential Marketing Is Changing the Brand World*, which had been published a year earlier.

Imagine my surprise when reading this piece, written by Priya Monga, business head at RC&M, a local Indian events and

---

* Tragically, the Taj Mahal Palace Hotel has now become a symbol of global terrorism as well, as it was one of the high-profile targets of the Islamist terrorists who attacked Mumbai in late November 2008.

marketing agency. I laughed out loud, looked around the luscious salon, took a glance at the Gateway of India outside the window, and asked myself:

"What are the odds?"

I was published in India. Well, not me per se. But my words were in print in the *Hindustan Times*. The *Hindustan Times*!

Clearly this was an omen, no? And if so, what could it possibly mean? What are the odds that I would read this in person, physically, and not online? And what are the odds that I would be in the country when the article was published? This is a daily paper, after all. And on the day that I was in Mumbai, the paper published a piece originally written by me.

If I were beholden to my original travel itinerary, I would never have seen this article at all. It took a visa problem to delay the trip. What's the spread on being plagiarized in this daily, I asked myself, when I wasn't even supposed to be here in the first place? What are the odds on that?

Well, actually, they're pretty good.

The reason is that in India, newspaper content is at a premium. Publishers need to fill space. And in their zeal to keep readers reading, they are prone to be more than lax in their editorial standards. The more content, the better. No matter where it's from.

There are more than 45,974 newspapers in India, including 5,364 dailies published in over 100 languages.[1] Despite relatively low literacy figures, these numbers make India the second-largest market for newspapers in the world, with a daily circulation of 99 million copies. Only China has a larger readership, with 107 million copies sold daily. In the United States, 51 million newspapers are sold each day, according to the World Association of Newspapers.

In 2006, newspaper sales in India rose 12.9 percent, and sales have grown by 53.6 percent in the past five years.[2] In comparison, world newspaper circulation rose by 2.3 percent in 2006 and

9.4 percent in the last five years. Even as obits are being written for newspapers in the United States and much of Europe, in India more than 150 million people read a paper every day—compared to 97 million Americans and 48 million Germans.[3] New Delhi has newspapers in 15 different languages, from English to Hindi to Telugu. One reason for the ink-stained boom: the Internet and cable TV have not yet become dominant forms of information dissemination. Only about 8.5 million Indians use the Internet to access news, and most households still can't afford cable. And since a newspaper usually costs less than a cup of tea in India, newspapers are the preferred medium.

As my friend Kaushik Mukherji, general manager of the entertainment media company Hungama, is apt to point out, Mumbai had only one English daily three years ago. Today, there are seven. So it may not be such a coincidence that my book was plagiarized in the *Hindustan Times* (the subsequent retraction and correction blamed a clerical error). In fact, it may not have been plagiarized at all. Instead, it was more probably "outsourced."

For most of us, outsourcing in India means the IT industry. In fact, the rapid modernization of the country can be encapsulated in the extremely brief history of the IT outsourcing industry there. First off, it makes sense to understand just how large the outsourcing market is around the world: according to consultancy A.T. Kearney, 55 countries—from Brazil to Vietnam to Poland—are now actively selling themselves as "remote service locations" to Western multinationals.[4]

What started as a simple industry of offshore call centers has morphed into a potent marketplace for intellectual service offerings like IT and R&D. IDC Research predicts that the world market for offshore IT services will reach $37.8 billion by 2011, more than double the figure reached in 2006. And India is poised to take the majority of this windfall.

According to *Newsweek* magazine, India's outsourcing revenue has increased tenfold in the past decade, accounting for more than 80 percent of the entire offshore IT business. Each of the top three Indian outsource "shops"—Wipro Technologies, Tata Consultancy Services, and Infosys Technologies—has a stock-market value of more than $20 billion. None of these companies was even listed on the market 10 years ago. [5]

The rise of Infosys is a potent example of the offshoring movement in India. The company was started in 1981 by 35-year-old N.R. Narayana Murthy—the so-called Bill Gates of India—when he persuaded five other partners to borrow $250 each from their wives. The idea: to hire Indian software engineers to write computer code for other Indian firms.

By 1991, the company had grown to 176 employees and opened an office in Boston. However, government protectionist policies made life for Infosys a red-tape nightmare. For instance, if an employee wanted to buy a new computer, it would take two years to acquire an import license from the government. By that time, the desired computer would be practically obsolete. If that employee wanted to buy a Microsoft software package, India's import laws levied a 150 percent duty on the software, making a $100 operating system cost $250, a sum unmanageable for a typical Indian programmer.

Once these types of "license raj" policies were abolished, Indian software companies began to flourish. Infosys grew from a $2 million company to a $2 billion company in less than 15 years. The company now employs over 70,000 Indians at impressive salaries and has boasted of creating over 300 employee millionaires through rising stock prices and options. Murthy himself is now worth close to $1.8 billion, according to *Forbes* magazine.

These companies aren't just waiting for Western corporations to come knocking. Their meteoric rise has given them a green light to expand into their clients' backyards. For instance, Wipro paid $600 million in 2007 for an American infrastructure-management firm called Infocrossing, to be closer to its clients and, equally important, to recruit top US talent.

Other countries are getting in on the outsource action, looking to India for guidance and inspiration. The Philippines is emerging as the new hot spot for outsourcing accounting services. Mauritius—a tiny nation in the Indian Ocean—is styling itself as a "cyber island" because of its English- and French-speaking population. European Union parvenus like Bulgaria and Romania are ideally poised to take on some outsourcing work because EU regulations regarding privacy obligate companies to keep certain types of outsourcing services within EU borders.

Still, central European countries can't compete with India on a simple cost basis. Even though white-collar Indian salaries are climbing, an IT operator in Bangalore earns less than one-tenth of his or her counterpart's salary in Baltimore. And if you ask any teenager in Mumbai the quickest way to earn a decent salary in India, he or she will inevitably say "IT."

The growth of the industry has led Indian outsource companies in turn to outsource their work to other countries. Routine and simple jobs are being outsourced to upstarts like Vietnam, where labor is even cheaper than in India. Satyam Computer Services, for instance, is currently outsourcing its work to Malaysia, Brazil, and China and is planning on adding more outsourcing centers in the Czech Republic, Russia, Vietnam, and Thailand.

But only just recently, outsourcing to India has acquired a rather non-IT bent. In fact, in what could be an industry first, India has become a hotbed for outsourcing advertising and marketing, too.

Hello, How May I Help You . . . with Your Advertising?

Imagine a call center filled with copywriters, art directors, and planners instead of customer service reps and salespeople. More and more global ad shops are looking to India as the epicenter of creative assignments for their clients around the world. Recently, a bevy of big-name brands and their respective ad shops have announced major inroads in "outsourcing creative" to Indian firms. Why not? India's advertising business is worth $3.5 billion and will grow massively year after year. And already, according to India's *Business Standard*, the ad outsource industry constitutes almost 10 percent of it.

After witnessing average growth of about 13 percent per annum over the last three years, the Indian advertising industry is now poised to grow another 61 percent by 2010. For every 100 rupees spent by advertisers, 91 rupees goes to TV and print media, while the out-of-home (OOH) category accounts for another 5 rupees. The remaining 4 rupees is divided between cinema, radio, and the Internet. Ad expenditures in India will increase from 0.5 percent of gross domestic product (GDP) to 0.53 percent over the next three years.[6]

The general optimist would look at this figure and see immense growth potential. Not surprisingly, global ad conglomerates are salivating like a Pavlovian mutt at the prospect of shoring up the ad and marketing business in India and outsourcing their global work to the country. London and New York are no longer the creative centers of the world, and the current inexorable trend is a geographical shift in creative and advertising talent toward cities in the emerging economies. Buenos Aires, Shanghai, São Paulo, and Mumbai are cities that nurture hot talent and a hyper-performing marketplace. It is here that the new advertising—a more financially efficient advertising—is being created. Because of this, global communications conglomerates are eyeing these markets lustily, hoping to glean and absorb as much thought leadership and talent in these marketplaces as they can.

For instance, when independent Wieden+Kennedy won the $300 million global creative account for Nokia, it outsourced the India portion to Mudra DDB until it can open up its own office in India—which will take up to a year. But in effect, the Nokia account in India will be handled by Mudra DDB.

In another development in late 2007, PepsiCo announced that BBDO India would handle the global creative account for its 7UP brand, which was previously handled by JWT. When McCann-Erickson pitched for the Intel global account, 60 percent of the contribution came from the India office.[7] In both instances, global accounts of iconic brands have migrated to the offshoring confines of India.

Independent and hot-shot boutique agencies are also flocking to Mumbai and New Delhi. Only recently, Amsterdam-based StrawberryFrog got in the game, along with London's Naked Communications and Bartle Bogle Hegarty, whose Mumbai office will be its seventh largest in the world.

Perhaps one of the biggest outsourced advertising accounts that passed through in 2007 was the Lenovo Group. The Chinese computer maker decided to centralize its global advertising operations out of Bangalore, India. This team will be in charge of creative advertising campaigns for dozens of countries, including the United States, France, and Brazil. Marketing for the IBM ThinkPad brand—the American line of computers that Lenovo acquired in 2005—will be handled by the Bangalore team.

Geographical boundaries no longer exist in advertising and marketing. Since Lenovo sells computers in more than 60 countries, creating ads versatile enough to air in several markets can ease a lot of budgetary pressures. The Bangalore team is charged with working with the marketing teams on the ground in each market.

Indian marketers are already well versed in multicultural and multilingual commercials and ads. Many ad campaigns launched in India are run in 12 different languages, to take advantage of the country's numerous local dialects. In order to achieve efficiencies and a uniform brand messaging, many Indian ads have no dialogue but instead rely on rich imagery and allegory to tell the brand story.

This peculiarity positions the country as an ideal hub for developing worldwide ads, since Indian creative expertise seems to lie in visual storytelling. So for a global brand like Lenovo, establishing a hub in Bangalore instead of Paris, Beijing, New York, or London makes a lot of sense. But the Indian hub won't be doing any creative marketing development for Lenovo's China market. The cultural differences are just too great, according to the company.

Still, many other agencies and brands are outsourcing their global accounts to creatives in India. And the work is paying off. According to the 2007 *Gunn Report*, which ranks countries on the basis of ad awards received each year, India is the world's fifteenth most awarded country. "This represents a sharp jump of six positions from its 21st rank in 2006," the report states. India was ranked ahead of such countries as Mexico, Italy, Malaysia, New Zealand, South Africa, the United Arab Emirates, Norway, and Belgium.[8]

In 2008, at the Cannes Lions International Advertising Festival, India's ad community emphatically announced itself to the world. JWT India accepted the country's first-ever Grand Prix award. Overall, India came away with 23 Lions. Its best tally had so far been 12 Lions, in 2006 and 2007. In one year, as Philip Thomas, the festival's CEO, remarked in his closing ceremony speech, "India is an awakening giant of creativity." Tellingly, although the founder of London-based Naked Communications chose not to participate in the Cannes Lions ad festival in 2008, he didn't miss two of India's major ad awards get-togethers: Goafest and the World Federation of Advertisers conference in Mumbai.

According to Priti Nair, national creative director at Grey Worldwide, the reasons for offshoring creative duties to India are simple: "We work faster. We multi-task. We speak the English language. Our ability to absorb different cultures is higher. Our costs are not as high as in other markets. All of these are very important factors when it comes to advertising in a highly competitive environment."[9]

There is another aspect to the Indian marketing mindset that makes outsourcing creative duties a very tempting proposition: Indian creatives have the expertise and knowledge in understanding and communicating with low-income consumers. India is a market of contradictions, where extreme wealth mixes with millions of consumers who can't afford a packet of shampoo. Indian creatives make campaigns for these spectrums and the myriad other consumer and cultural contradictions that India poses. This is a major advantage, especially when rolling out communication and strategy in the rest of the world, particularly Africa, Latin America, Asia, and eastern Europe. Indian shops "have a wherewithal to understand the pulse of consumers in these markets," says Pratap Bose, CEO of Ogilvy & Mather India. "This is another valuable bargaining chip in helping global clients."[10]

It doesn't hurt that the Indian economy is booming and multinational brands are clamoring at the door to get in on the action. Their respective ad agencies are no exception. There has recently been a spate of mergers and acquisitions for local ad agencies in India by the global conglomerates. IPG consolidated its stake in Indian ad shop Lintas by buying up the remaining 51 percent stake it had previously left on the table. IPG also bought the remaining 49 percent stake in FCB Ulka, another local shop. WPP decided to merge two Indian agencies—Bates and David—in 2007 to create business efficiencies.

The amazing thing about Indian advertising, according to an interview with Sir Martin Sorrell, group chief of WPP, is that "India is a market where while new media are growing, even traditional media are growing."[11] So while mobile advertising is going through the roof, so is revenue from traditional ad placements in newspapers.

Tony Wright, chairman of Lowe Worldwide, echoes the sentiment and places it in the context of where the majority of the marketing offshoring will be done: "Digital and mobile marketing are hugely experiential in nature and we will do a lot of the global work out of India."[12]

I recommend a further extension to the chairman's assertion: I would argue that all marketing—whether experiential in nature or not—could be done in India for global distribution.

Made in . . . Wherever

I've had the glorious honor of working on the Axe brand in the United States as the executive creative director for the brand's experiential agency of record, GMR Marketing. As an integrated agency partner, I was privy to and always impressed by parent Unilever's commitment to a global insight for the Axe brand: helping guys win in the mating game. (In the UK and Australia, the brand is called Lynx.)

The Axe brand is built upon a single premise, a mantra of sorts, that encompasses all advertising and marketing activities: teenage boys want to get laid. By taking deodorant out of the sports and labor categories and putting it smack in the middle of the male teenager's arsenal for a little nookie, the Axe brand has redefined the deodorant and shower gel category, and probably forever influenced the branding ethos of a lot of other consumer packaged goods (CPG).

Because of this singular and timeless insight, Unilever was able to unify its advertising messaging on a global level. Led by creative agency Bartle Bogle Hegarty (BBH)—a maverick agency of sorts that likes to differentiate itself on creativity and planning for its clients—the spots that run for the Axe brand around the world are pretty much the same. For the most part, a guy in Mumbai would see the same Axe ads as a guy in London, Miami, Vancouver, or Buenos Aires.

Take, for instance, the *Billions* spot.[13] In this beautifully ideated and grandly shot TV commercial (and extended-version cinema ad), an isolated and idyllic tropical island is the setting of a massive congregation of wild and half-naked babes, running through the jungle and swimming from all angles toward a single point on the island. Close-ups catch the sweating vixens stopping mid-sprint to smell the air around them and change course accordingly. The women are fanatically hot. The camera moves away from and above the island to display the nubile swarm converging on one point on the paradisiacal archipelago. A quick camera close-up shows that single point to be a shirtless guy spraying himself ecstatically with two cans of Axe body spray. As seemingly millions of hot babes attack him from all angles, the expression of total bliss and acceptance on the face of the guy is truly priceless . . . and global.

In fact, most spots for the Axe brand are developed for a global audience. They hardly ever contain dialogue. Music forms an integral connection with the audience. It, too, is global in nature in that the choice of tunes is not connected to the genre most popular in a particular market but to the nature of the spot itself. The brand insight is so pure and so ingeniously simple that showing guys in typical, archetypal, and hyperbolically successful encounters with hot girls is an easily translatable global message when reaching a teenager anywhere in the world.

Surely, contractual and budgetary considerations can alter

a TV spot significantly. For instance, Unilever paid an impressive (and appropriate, for a category leader) sum of money to US movie star Ben Affleck to star in a Lynx commercial for the international launch of a new variant—a new fragrance in the Axe/Lynx body spray, deodorant, and shower gel product lineup. In the United States, however, the brand used often-photographed singer Nick Lachey to re-create the Affleck ad.

The two commercials are a scene-by-scene, shot-by-shot mirror image of each other. The only difference is that for the North American marketplace, the one major star—Ben Affleck— is replaced by the lesser one, Nick Lachey. (Apparently, Affleck's management thought he was already overexposed in the North American market, given that he was just breaking up with Jennifer Lopez and starring in a string of money-losing films. Therefore, no spot release in the United States.)

In the commercials, both celebrity guys go through their typical day in star-struck and babe-central Los Angeles, count- ing all the "come-hither" and "do-me" glances they get from the ladies. The way they keep their count is with the use of a clicker, the hand-held counter used by bouncers and ushers. At the end of the day, as each star enters an elevator in a swanky hotel, he fishes out his clicker to see the daily tally of flirtations. The number is impressive.

Yet in the elevator with Affleck/Lachey is an Axe guy. He's the average guy. Not geeky, not overly hot. Just confident enough and of-the-time to be an Axe guy. He takes out his clicker. His number trumps the Hollywood heartthrob and the boy-band singer. Badly. The Axe guy's count is five times, ahem, bigger than the star's. The elevator doors close slowly. Affleck/Lachey compares the figures and then looks inquisitively impressed with the Axe protagonist. The satisfied look on our Axe guy is, again, wholly priceless . . . and globally understood.

Whether the spot aired with Affleck in the UK, Hong Kong, and Australia—or Nick Lachey in the United States and Canada—doesn't really matter. (Ben Affleck just didn't want to look like a sellout in the United States; that's why his agent didn't agree to the global rights.) The insight is the same. And so is the creative work. Exactly the same. Different country, different celebrity. That's all.

The notion that creative work can come from anywhere in the world, and then be propagated globally, is entirely profound. And it's more than likely the future of marketing.

The reason is simple: creative work applicable throughout the world connotes victory of human insight over cultural particularities. In other words, cultural differences and nuances should certainly be taken into consideration when creating good ad and marketing campaigns, but more than ever, we marketers need to think beyond these parameters.

Let me give you an example from a story that appeared in *Advertising Age* in the latter half of 2007:[14]

> This summer, executives from Gillette's Puerto Rico division heard pitches from creatives in 21 countries for a campaign to persuade the island's men to trade in their disposable razors for the Fusion shaver. Among the winners were a Slovenian student, a British photographer and an American creative director, all of whom based their submissions on an initial idea from a small agency based in India.
>
> The pitch, despite its strong international flavor, didn't involve any jet-setting or big-agency boondoggling in far-flung lands. It all unfolded over a website called OpenAd.net, a Slovenian-based online marketplace

where ad and design ideas from about 9,000 creatives worldwide are bought and sold. Since it opened for business this past year, OpenAd has served European clients, but a trans-Atlantic expansion is underway. The service is quietly being tested by major US marketers such as Gillette parent Procter & Gamble and plans to establish a physical presence here in coming months.

If it's successful in penetrating the biggest ad market, OpenAd will be yet another potential disruption to the global ad-agency model, and one a long time coming. A dozen years after the internet gained mass appeal, OpenAd represents the ad industry finally taking advantage of flat-earth economics and communications realities to solve one of the marketing business' biggest challenges: finding ideas.*

OpenAd's co-founder, Katarina Skoberne, puts the notion behind the start-up in the clearest of terms: "We are basically doing for advertising what Amazon did for books [and] what iTunes did for music." The members of the site who contribute ideas on a freelance basis represent 116 countries.[15]

Every Indian Is Global

My friend Bobby Pawar is the chief creative officer at the aforementioned Mudra DDB, a shop in India that has a reputation for

---

* Oshiuri, a Japanese site launched in early 2008, is also a place where advertising creatives can share their work. It too has developed an online mechanism by which ideas/pitches can be bought and sold. Creatives can pitch brands, and brands can reach out to creatives directly for spec work. The overall concept behind the site: finding ideas.

outstanding creative work and reliance on home-grown talent. I met Bobby in Chicago when he was group creative director at Energy BBDO, the Chicago arm of the BBDO empire—itself the crown jewel in the Omnicom portfolio.

Bobby has a penchant for wearing fashionable T-shirts under unique blazers, chain-smoking when creating campaigns and pushing his creative teams into uncharted and therefore award-winning areas. He punctuates his sentences with poetic profanity, which endears him to me. And his spot-on insights and strategic thinking endear him to his clients even more.

I met him late one night in the Taj Mahal bar, where we quickly reverted to our old Chicago habits of drinking lots of Johnnie Walker Black and lighting each other's smokes while running our mouths off about the state of the industry. And as the topic of marketing offshoring crept into the conversation, Bobby touched on a very applicable point.

"Every Indian thinks of himself as a global Indian," Bobby said between sips and puffs.

I wasn't sure what he meant at first, because the Indians I saw in Dharavi—the largest slum in Asia—certainly didn't seem to be global citizens in my humble opinion. The two sweating guys in rags pushing an overloaded cart down the busiest street in Mumbai sure didn't look like the epitome of globalization. The street beggars and urchins brushing up against my pockets in the market didn't seem like Thomas Friedman readers.

In fact, if I wanted to epitomize Indian culture—and the myriad denizens that belong to it—I would do so with the analogy of a layer cake. Whereas in the United States the cake is the simple three-layer variety, in India it has 300 layers. Not only are there numerous people but there are numerous ways they communicate, numerous customs and rites they follow, numerous religious and cultural layers, and numerous social mores and sensibilities.

So how do you market to these people?

Let's first slice the cake economically. India has seen average annual GDP growth of 6 percent in the last two decades, and 9 percent in the last three years. The economy is expected to grow by an average of 9 to 11 percent per year over the next 20 years, making it the second fastest-growing economy in the world.* India is the twelfth-largest consumer market globally today and is expected to become the world's fifth-largest consumer market by 2025. Indian consumers have been spending sharply more on consumer durables, apparel, entertainment, vacations, and lifestyle products in recent years. The country's $350 billion retail market is expected to grow 13 percent per annum in the coming years. Why?

Average household incomes in India are expected to grow at a rate of 5.3 percent annually for the next 20 years. Comparatively, incomes in the United States and Japan grew at 1.5 percent and 0.25 percent respectively in the last two decades. The Indian middle class—defined as those households earning between $1,400 and $21,400—stands at 56 million households and will continue to grow unabated. Undoubtedly, prosperity is coming to India.

But let's slice the cake demographically, too. India is composed of 29 states and 6 union territories. There are 18 officially recognized languages in India. About 114 other languages are spoken there, and 900 different dialects.

There are more than 100 million English speakers in India, about twice as many as live in the UK itself. India has 2.7 million collage graduates each year, compared to 1.3 million in the United States. Every year, more engineers graduate with degrees in a single Indian state, Andhra Pradesh, than in the entire United States.[16]

India is the seventh-largest country in the world and the

---

* These projections have obviously been tempered somewhat—but not by much—by the global economic downturn in late 2008.

second-most populous (1.08 billion people). To put it in perspective: one in five people in the world are Indian. Indians are global, indeed.

Each one of the 29 states in India has its own distinct culture. There are, in a sense, multiple countries within India, each with a distinct language, cultural proclivity, education, sartorial style, palette, and entertainment. Then each state can be divided into urban or rural sensibilities and even further segmented into various demographical differences.

So, in effect, India as a nation is somewhat global in nature. With so many different languages and myriad cultural sensibilities, it is a microcosm of a global culture. Never mind that Indians bring global culture back to their shores; we're talking about within the Indian borders themselves. For all intents and purposes, India is a country of countries.

Nevertheless, marketing creative work that relies on human insight over cultural ideas has bridged the differences. As Bobby Pawar continued with his thought, it began to make sense. And the implied emphasis on an experience-based marketing culture started to emerge. "Demographics are tossed out the window. You have to look at mindsets," he insisted. "What are we aspiring to?"

With the types of demographic numbers for middle-class advancement proposed earlier, it wasn't too hard to imagine the aspirations shared by the majority of the emerging Indian middle class. They are not very different from ours:

- a better future for our children
- security from extremism, both domestic and international
- spirituality, or at least a spiritual grounding for existence
- comfort
- food, water, shelter
- a faster way to get to work

- a better place to work
- a world in which the color of our skin is no more significant than the color of our eyes
- dignity
- respect
- admiration and, if we're lucky, love
- peace
- friendship
- community
- compensation for our sweat
- a little bit of hanky-panky
- a little bit of a party

These things are wholly transferable. These are things that as marketers we should celebrate. Rural Indians want the same products that urban Indians have, and the same type of marketing speaks to them all.[17]

"There are certain cultural things that are common for all people," Bobby said. "So you try to reach a human insight, rather than a particular cultural insight."

Most creative directors would disagree. Most would conjure arguments for regionalization and micro-targeting, instead. That makes their job easier, doesn't it? How much harder is it to reach a human insight rather than a cultural one? (I suppose that chasm is amply evident in the political events of the day. If only politicians thought on a human level rather than a regional one.)

Furthermore, the sheer scale of the Indian market makes it imperative to cater to psychographical insights over demographical ones. Naked numbers make human insight more valuable than ever in India. It is a very different game to reach a billion people than to reach millions. Within a billion people are a plethora of cultures, languages, geographies, traditions, and socioeconomic behaviors. It is almost impossible to understand the marketplace with quantitative data and reporting. Understanding the psychological, social, and historical precedents of a target consumer is instrumental to crafting a compelling and contextual campaign.

For instance, Kellogg's saw a goldmine in a billion people when it introduced its Corn Flakes cereal to the Indian marketplace. What the company failed to understand is that Indians think that a cold start to the day is a shock to the system. Breakfast in India—and in China, for that matter—is a hot affair. When warm milk is poured over corn flakes, the result is a cardboard-tasting mush. Kellogg's tried to persuade consumers to add cold milk to the cereal, to no avail. Instead of winning the breakfast market, Kellogg's tried to force-feed cereal to the Indian palette.

In contrast, McDonald's has reorganized and redeveloped 70 percent of its menu to reach Indian consumers who are opposed to eating beef or pork. So the company more or less got rid of its most important ingredient: meat. Instead, it created fare such as McAloo Tikki Burger, McCurry Pans, Paneer Salsa Wraps, Pizza McPuffs, and McVeggie for its Indian clientele. And since drive-throughs are still foreign in the country, scooter and bicycle delivery services get McDonald's food into the mouths of billions.

The Marketing World Is Flat

As *BusinessWeek* pointed out in an article on branding in India, "The best brands are not superficial logos or slogans but organisms that robustly and regularly satisfy some fundamental human need. They are bigger than the sum of their supply chains and storefronts. Their competitive advantage is in knowing, understanding, empathizing, anticipating and serving their customers better that the competition, not just making more copies of the same."[19] And human insight is what will drive global brands of the future. Cultural nuances will certainly take precedence, but the compulsion to be a global citizen will drive the thinking of creatives across the world. The world is flat. And so is the marketing.

According to Scott Goodson, founder of iconic branding agency StrawberryFrog, "India has a clean slate, extremely talented people, the latest technology, and in the next few years it will be on the viewfinder of global agencies to see what it does next." Delivering a keynote speech at Goafest in 2008, India's version of the Cannes Lions, he announced that his agency—with offices in Amsterdam, New York, Brazil, and Tokyo—would open a shop in Mumbai or Delhi within the year. Tellingly, the agency had recently signed Mahindra & Mahindra, a venerable Indian automotive brand, as a client in the United States. The agency was selected over 12 multinationals to create demand for Mahindra pick-up trucks and its Scorpio car brand in the United States. For StrawberryFrog, creative impetus and exchange come from India in more ways than one. "In today's world, ideas are what matter," says Goodson. "This is where Indian creative minds can make a huge, invaluable contribution."[19]

Prasoon Joshi, executive chairman and creative director at McCann-Erickson India, thinks that the Indian creative is perfectly poised for a flattened world. In an editorial in *Advertising Age* magazine, he explains that he sees Indian civilization as "based on introspection and creativity—be it in arts, science, mathematics, spirituality or software—[and one that] has given the world new ideas. Originality and creativity are deeply intrinsic to India. Over the past 5,000 years, India has been a recipient of varied foreign cultures, successfully assimilating them. Diversity is in India's DNA. There is no one India . . . Indians know how to express themselves in more than one language and how to live and communicate in more than one culture. This bicultural global outlook gives Indians unique insight into global trends."[20]

Take, for instance, Bajaj Auto, India's scion brand of two-wheel transportation. In a country where two-wheelers—from mopeds to scooters to motorcycles—account for 80 percent of all vehicles on the road, market leadership is a dogfight between local manufacturers like Tata and foreign entrants like Honda. Bajaj has kept its leadership role with advertising and marketing that pays homage to its roots in Indian society (the family-run company was founded in 1945 and became the dominant scooter manufacturer in the 1960s) while mixing it with a modern and Bollywood-fueled ethos. In a marketplace that up until 2005 still referred to all motorcycles in the country as "Hondas," this positioning has literally transformed the Bajaj brand from a has-been scooter maker to a dominant motorcycle brand in a country that sells 7.1 million two-wheelers each year.[21]

Bajaj's resurgence has been driven in large part by the brand's ability to bridge India's often-contradictory forces of tradition and modernity, austerity and consumerism, conformism and individualism. And it repositioned itself for success in the Indian marketplace with a symbolic and quintessentially Indian TV ad—a beautiful 60-second spot that touched the hearts and minds of millions of youthful Indians.

The commercial opens on a lone, twenty-something rider on a Bajaj Eliminator (a close-up of the fuel tank reveals the model type), who is burning rubber down a rural Indian road. As he nears and passes a roadside Hindu shrine, he lessens the throttle and gestures in piety toward the goddess statue inside the shrine. We cut away to four Bollywood hunks dressed in leather, walking in unison toward their Bajaj Boxers. As one hunk swings his leg to straddle his bike, his foot touches the leg of the guy next to him—an action considered disrespectful in traditional Indian society. The leather-clad stud genuflects in deference to his fellow rider. We then find a young Indian couple together on a Bajaj Caliber. They are both dressed in

T-shirts and jeans, and the girl on the back of the bike has her arms wrapped tightly around the man. (Please note that in India, public kissing can be considered a moral crime. Witness the legal hullaba-loo caused by Richard Gere when he pressed a public kiss on Bolly-wood actress Shilpa Shetty at a fundraising rally.) They are clearly in the bloom of love. She caresses his face and pinches his cheeks. But as they pass an elderly man, she demurely moves her hands away from her beau. The old timer smiles at the chaste couple. We then see a Sikh man in traditional beard and head garment escorting a Western woman through picturesque tourist locations on a Bajaj scooter. When they arrive at a temple, the man joyously places a head-covering scarf on the woman. The spot closes with a shot of two guys riding to a music gig; the guy on the back of the bike has a sitar slung over his shoulder. Their rock outfits certainly clash with the centuries-old instrument, but on a Bajaj bike it seems perfectly natural. Perfectly cool.

Like the Axe spots, the commercial's sentiment is echoed in any country that is in the throes of a cultural and generational transition, with hybrid, global citizen teens flirting between modern consumption, trendy cultural currency, and the traditional mores of their societies. The generational revolutions in hyper-developing countries aren't as swift, abrupt, or nasty as the one witnessed in the United States and Europe during the tumultuous sixties. There is synergy and acceptance for the traditions of the past and the possibilities of the current economies. For teens in emerging markets like India, Russia, Brazil, or China, their future is always somehow rooted in their history.

In all, they are part of the same tribe. Global consumers have many commonalities. Teenagers, in particular, are prone to display common characteristics, purchasing habits, and aspirations across the globe—despite differences in language and nationality. Baby boomers and working mothers with children are also conspicuous global tribes. Those Live Aid hacks were right: we *are* the world. And cutting-edge marketers are now looking ever more closely at tribes rather than nationality or language to efficiently and effectively reach more global customers.

It takes only a few minutes standing outside your hotel in Mumbai to realize that India is a country where tradition is intrinsically wrapped in the aspirational fabric of modernity. I am told that it takes years to understand that the individual Indian citizen—and the collective body—has multiple identities, proclivities, and desires. And it takes a lifetime of observation, as Indian author Shashi Tharoor remarked, to accept that "any truth about India can be equally contradicted by an equally valid truth."

But overall, the astute marketer would quickly ascertain that there are multiple identities and multiple markets in India. Since my all-too-brief stay in Mumbai, I have periodically reminded myself of a quotation that Kaushik Mukherji showed me on our initial meeting, from a first-century traveler named Apollonius Tyanaeus: "In India I found a race of mortals living upon the Earth, but not adhering to it. Inhabiting cities, but not being fixed to them, possessing everything but possessed by nothing."

The obvious contradictions in the identity of the Indian have not been erased by thousands of years of assimilation, imperialism, colonization, or pluralism. Indians are a people who cannot be defined, other than their unassailable will to include tradition, spirituality, and etherealness into their progress through history.

To this effect, a marketing campaign mimicking or mirroring the Indian spot for Bajaj motorcycles could resonate in any country. But it is especially resonant in a poor one. Perhaps this generalization is in fact too regional. Rather, it's valid to state that the spot is resonant for poor people in all countries. The human insight trumps the cultural one. And in doing so, borders get blown open. What does it matter where the spot comes from if it speaks to the human aspirations and trepidations we all share?

In his breakthrough book *A Whole New Mind: Why Right-Brainers Will Rule the Future*, Daniel Pink proposes that the ability to empathize, and consequently the translation of empathy into insights that can be leveraged, will become requisite for all businesses and global brands in the future.

"Empathy is the ability to imagine yourself in someone else's position and to intuit what that person is feeling. It is the ability to stand in others' shoes, to see with their eyes, and to feel with their hearts . . . It is feeling with someone else, sensing what it would be like to be that person. Empathy is a stunning act of imaginative derring-do, the ultimate virtual reality—climbing into another's mind to experience the world from that person's perspective . . . Today, cheap and widespread online access, combined with all those overseas knowledge workers, are making the attributes measurable by IQ much easier to replace—which has meant that aptitudes more difficult to replicate are becoming more valuable. And the one aptitude that's proven impossible for computers to reproduce, and very difficult for faraway workers connected by electrons to match, is empathy."[22]

I believe that, other than the United States, no other country has a greater capacity for empathy than India. It is a nation of social heterogeneity and moral amalgamations. It differs from its BRIC companions in its diversity. Certainly, all hyper-developing nations have their own indigenous and accultur-ated societies, whether it's Tibetans in southwestern China or Mongolians in southeastern Russia. These massive countries all have myriad social and ethnic substrata. But generally speaking, Brazil, Russia, and China are fairly homogenous in their cultural and social composition. India stands alone in its ability to accommodate so many others. And no other hyper-developing nation runs the gamut of contrasts that India does.*

Hungama's Kaushik Mukherji told me over a cup of tea in his office that "the Indian economy is the only economy where we are all mostly *hybrid* human beings, from a mindset perspective." This ability to absorb and acclimate is at the heart of empathy, and also at the heart of marketing insights that will drive global brands. Now a force in supplying IT to the West, India is poised to become a force in providing empathy to markets and economies across the globe.

We All Want to Be Big, Big Stars

When it comes to manufacturing demand in India, winning brands like Bajaj will continue to rely on the unique cultural appropriation of empathy—combined with an extraordinary disposition for heritage and tradition—to create compelling marketing platforms.

No other form of media allows this transition to become manifest better than (arguably) India's greatest export to the world: Bollywood. Bollywood is the informal name for the Mumbai-based Hindu and Urdu film industry. There are a number of other film industries in India, but Bollywood is the best known globally. Without a doubt, India produces more films than any other country in the world. Movie going is a veritable narcotic for every Indian, no matter his or her provenance, ethnicity, language, or caste. Bollywood stars like Rajnikanth, Amitabh Bachchan, or Shahrukh Khan are *literally* deified. There are temples devoted to demi-god actors, and many fans immolate themselves whenever a famous Bollywood star announces her or his retirement. The Indians take their cinema

---

* When I was stuck in Mumbai's notorious traffic inside a chauffeured Mercedes-Benz, the fellow grid-locker to my left wasn't in another car, truck, scooter, motorcycle, or rickshaw. He was simply a guy in rags pushing an overloaded wooden cart.

very seriously. When southern Indian film icon Rajkumar died in April 2006, all commercial and recreational activities ceased across south India and cities like Bangalore. People rioted and committed suicide. A total of eight people died, including a police officer, when a riot broke out upon the news of the actor's demise.

In the West, we tend to discount Bollywood productions as either fascinating ethno-camp or discombobulating quasi-musicals. There is too much panache and melodrama in the productions. Indeed, the genre's formula of combining song-and-dance numbers with a multi-tentacled plotline is a bit too foreign to most of us weaned on Spielberg, Lucas, and Scorsese. Bollywood productions, to the Western taste, are too saccharine and too melodramatic, too overblown and too hard to follow. However, this is changing in the United States. The latest blockbuster appeal of Disney's *High School Musical* film series is testament that the Bollywood formula is indeed translatable into the pop culture milieu of American preteens. According to *Advertising Age* magazine, song-and-dance shows like *Dancing with the Stars* and *American Idol* are the most immune to ad skipping by viewers.[23]

For Indians—both on the subcontinent and abroad—Bollywood is a perfect medium to sustain their heritage, tradition, commonality, and aspirations. The storytelling evident in every Bollywood film harkens back to the deep oral traditions and myths of the majority of Indians throughout millennia. The biggest star of modern-day Bollywood is Shahrukh Khan, a star bigger than Tom Cruise and Brad Pitt combined. He has flourished in today's Bollywood by playing modern anti-heroes and cool guys, "the best of the West and East." As his biographer, Anupama Chopra, writes in *King of Bollywood*, Khan "became all things to all people. He was a yuppie hero whose cool clothes and cooler personal style made him a youth icon. But he also unabashedly celebrated and perpetuated homespun *swadeshi* values."[24]

Swadeshi values, rooted in anticolonial self-sufficiency and communal philanthropy, were first promulgated by Mahatma Gandhi at the beginning of the twentieth century. Literally translated, the term means "of one's own country." Even in modern Bollywood, the urbane skirt-chasing and chain-smoking star extends the deeply ingrained Indian tradition and zeitgeist of Swadeshi. The stories of Bollywood are aspirational and traditional at the same time.

The archetypal plots of love, caste, war, and family are combined with another core Indian tradition: music. Early Bollywood films from the 1930s would have 40 or more songs each. Dream sequences and surrealism were common features in Bollywood scripts, but music and dance still reigned supreme as the genre's unifying theme. Until the 1970s, almost all popular music in India came from movie scores.[25]

The Bollywood formula is an insight goldmine for Indian marketers. For Prasoon Joshi of McCann-Erickson India, Indian marketing should be like its movies: unique and homegrown. "I believe India has the potential to redefine advertising, and do it differently from the way it has been done around the world," he says. "Like what we have done with cinema . . . Take our audio visuals, they are very different. Storytelling elsewhere is very linear. Here we have four or five plots running at the same time. It's like our cinema that inspired movies like Moulin Rouge. In time, they will be inspired by our style of advertising too."[26]

The combination of star power and theatrical pop music has made the Bollywood formula a formidable signpost for marketers looking to tap global cultures and global insights. Simultaneously, Bollywood is being transformed from a local cultural phenomenon into a global marketing machine.

In 2007, a little-known Indian producer began work on a Bollywood film that tried to revolutionize the entire Bollywood film industry. That producer is Ronnie Screwvala and the film he co-produced is *The Happening,* a sci-fi thriller starring Mark Wahlberg and directed by M. Night Shyamalan. Having these two names attached to a film project rocked the Bollywood establishment. But more than the talent, it was the film's budget that had jaws dropping in Mumbai: $57 million. This price tag is higher than that of 10 Bollywood blockbuster films combined.

Unfortunately, the movie tanked in the United States, and its critical panning was especially brutal. Although it turned a profit overall, the Indian-financed Hollywood flick wasn't a brilliant success story. Nonetheless, Screwvala had succeeded in rewriting the accepted norms and rules of Bollywood budgets, and in doing so, created an entirely new vision of Bollywood itself. His company, UTV Software Communications, is setting new standards for Bollywood film production, distribution, and profitability. In effect, his company is taking India's chaotic and fragmented film industry kicking and screaming into the twenty-first century.

It is safe to say that Screwvala's example set the stage for a world-shaking deal between East and West, Bollywood and Hollywood in early 2008. Big Entertainment, the integrated media and entertainment arm of the $75 billion-revenue Reliance – Anil Dhirubhai Ambani Group—owned by the sixth richest man in the world, with a net worth of $40 billion—announced that it would underwrite a slew of development deals with eight Hollywood-based production houses to make at least 10 films in the next two years at a cost of $1 billion. These Hollywood production houses belong to leading Hollywood actors: there's George Clooney's Smokehouse Productions, Nicholas Cage's Saturn Productions, Tom Hanks' Playtone Productions, Brad Pitt's B Entertainment, Chris Columbus's 1492 Pictures, Jim Carrey's JC 23 Entertainment, and Jay Roach's Everyman Pictures.

The announcement prompted the biggest name in Hollywood—namely, Steven Spielberg—to cut a deal with Ambani's
Reliance Entertainment worth close to $600 million for his Dream-
Works SKG imprint. This financing in effect allowed DreamWorks
to split from Viacom's Paramount Pictures. Indian filmmaking
finally has its global spotlight.

Before UTV and the subsequent Hollywood-based deals,
the Indian film industry was closer to a mom-and-pop operation
than a full-fledged studio-based industry. India produces about
1,000 films each year, which is 10 times more than Hollywood's
output. But every one of those films was an independent production run by a producer/director who was more interested in
making cash than making good movies. Backroom deals between
these influential Bollywood "oligarchs" were (are) commonplace,
profits were kept off the books, and actors were blackmailed to
perform at cut-rate salaries. The marketing of the films was left to
individual theater owners. Scenes were written on the spot during
shooting and usually revolved around common themes like cops
and robbers, identity mix-ups between brothers or friends, and
stories about the little guy winning against the rich village landowner. This is how Bollywood has operated since the 1950s, and
until UTV came on the scene, nothing had changed.

To this day, Bollywood is a family-controlled industry.
The mom-and-pop shop analogy is not a flippant description.
Prominent film-producing families would partner with prominent mafia-led families to create entire industries for film production. Consequently, there wasn't much healthy, above-board
competition. This uninspiring environment led to uninspiring
box office results. Although the first 30 years of Bollywood saw
packed theaters every day, the advent and household penetration
of TV in the early 1980s diminished the throngs of Indians who
packed theaters daily. Film revenues stalled between 1985 and

2000, at about $1 billion each year—less than one-third of box office receipts for a single major Hollywood studio.

Yet a new Bollywood has been emerging, one with scripts that don't drone a common theme or depend on lavishly choreographed dance numbers to get butts in seats. Moreover, Indians are getting wealthier and therefore expect more from their entertainment choices. Better scripts, novel plots, more transparent accounting, international investors, and aggressive marketing have dramatically transformed Bollywood, and led to a major domestic boom for Indian films. In 2006, the country's film business grossed roughly $2 billion, up from $1.5 billion in 2004. PricewaterhouseCoopers predicts that Bollywood revenues will jump to $4 billion in the next five years.[27]

These figures are still well below those of Hollywood, and yet Bollywood's 17 percent annual growth rate is something Hollywood hasn't seen since the early 1900s. Moreover, Bollywood revenues are certain to climb dramatically as ticket prices in India—which are a little less than $1 (compared to $10 or more in the United States)—start to climb in response to higher Indian wages and levels of prosperity.

Bollywood movies aren't simply a subcontinental affair. The diaspora of Indians throughout the world has increasingly buoyed the industry. For instance, one of the biggest Bollywood hits of 2007 was Shahrukh Khan's *Om Shanti Om*, which took in $3.6 million in India and $36.2 million overseas.[28] Seven Hindi films earned more that $2 million at the US box office in 2006. Sure, when compared to mainstream earnings, the numbers seem paltry. But there are signs that Bollywood is garnering global appeal. When SRK (as Khan is known to his fans) arrived for a premiere at the Berlinale film festival, he was mobbed by crazed fans. Interestingly, the mob was a mix of ex-pat Indians and native Germans. The melodramatic tone of the Bollywood blockbuster, spiced up with song and dance, is a hit with the Germans. SRK mania travels well beyond the borders of India.

Another Bollywood production, titled *The Namesake*—produced in tandem with Hollywood and Japan's Entertainment Farm—earned $13 million in the United States alone. The typical Bollywood film budget is usually much lower than the $3 million spent on this blockbuster.

The Indian entertainment and media industry is growing at 16.7 percent *annually*, faster than that of Brazil, Russia, or China. The media and entertainment industry in the rest of the world is projected to grow 4.9 percent year over year.[29] Pricewater-houseCoopers estimates that India has the fastest growing media and entertainment industry in the world, growing at a compounded rate of 18.5 percent between 2006 and 2011.[30]

Along with financial growth comes the inevitable growth in talent and expertise. The Indian film industry is producing prodigious talents behind and in front of the camera. Bollywood directors of photography are getting lush gigs to shoot the major multinational brand campaigns won by Mumbai-based ad shops. Bollywood's aesthetic of empathy, its social ethos and humanity—mixed so well with spectacle, absurdity, dance, and song—is getting integrated into the world's advertising as well.

Equally important is how Bollywood-inspired content is being applied to noncinematic media. In particular, the typical Bollywood production—often a three-hour song-and-dance extravaganza centered on unrequited love, a corrupt landlord, or an honor vendetta—has lent itself beautifully to gaming as well as mobile (cell phone) and online video entertainment. In fact, recent press suggests that although the connection between brands and Bollywood today rests with celebrity endorsements and product placement, the real future of the genre and the brands that can draw insight from it will be based on delivering content and experience beyond the TV and cinema screens.

For instance, Rajat Barjatya is ready to capitalize on India's $3 billion film industry with a digital approach to Bollywood. The scion of a well-known film-producing family, Barjatya is developing the first ever serial production for the mobile phone in India. His first foray is a 90-episode comedy that's delivered to millions of Indians in three-minute episodes. On a similar note, Indian game developers are tapping the popularity of Bollywood films to develop games based on the plots and the actors themselves. Developer and publisher FXLab Studios partnered with Yash Rak Films to create a video game called D:2.5, based on the Bollywood blockbuster *Dhoom 2*. The key to the game is to assume the role of a favorite actor in the movie while performing special missions and tasks. This is the first time an Indian movie has been made into a PC computer game.

And why not make games out of movies? After all, about 54 percent of the Indian population is below the age of 25, and the median age is getting younger. The same can be said about a lot of nations across the globe. That's one reason why Bollywood genres like action flicks and comedies are always big box office bonanzas: 35 percent of all moviegoers in India are between 10 and 24 years old. "This segment is completely sold to Bollywood and the latest Hindi releases are the mainstay of their entertainment itinerary," a pundit is quoted as saying in a *Times of India* article.[31]

It is quite amazing how loyal Bollywood fans are to their homegrown content. Despite the widespread availability of dubbed Hollywood blockbusters, 95 percent of all movie tickets sold in India are for Indian films. (This trend is true in the United States as well. About 95 percent of all ticket sales are for US-produced films.)

The youthful consumer is hooked on Bollywood. And although conventional wisdom suggests that the village screen is the preferred way to experience Bollywood, increasingly the cell phone handset is the screen of choice for Indian youth. It makes perfect sense, after all. When you read this, India will have more than 300 million mobile phone users married to the world's largest movie industry. It doesn't take a genius to see where this is heading. India is bound to become a hotbed of new ideas for digital content production and dissemination.

Bollywood execs claim that more people watch their films than people watch Hollywood flicks worldwide. And yet Bollywood's earnings are estimated to be a paltry 2 percent of what Hollywood earns in total: box office, licensing, brand deals, and all the other ancillary revenue sources that Hollywood has perfected. In India, "the eyeballs are there—all that is lacking is the means to cash in ('monetize,' if you must), and those are quickly taking shape."[32]

Here's an example of how powerful the Bollywood system can be, and how interesting the content can get. Some of the more popular digital downloads that occupy the memory chips of Indian cell phones are film dialogue clips from Bollywood movies. Familiar and dramatic dialogues or monologues act as mobile ringtones for millions of Indian teenagers.* In fact, digital music sales in India surpassed CD and cassette sales in 2007. More than 300,000 ringtones are sold in India every day, and they are set to grow at double-digit rates for the rest of this decade. Today, ringtones account for about 40 percent of data revenues for India's major telcos like Bharti Airtel and Reliance Communications. Sony Ericsson's core focus and strategy in India, according to the general manager of operations, is centered on music applications. Much of that music comes from Bollywood flicks.

---

* Another hugely popular cell phone download file is of Indian devotional songs and chants. Can that be said of the typical American teenager?

New Internet-based technologies are helping shape Bollywood into a hotbed of content experimentation, lessons that Hollywood is eager to learn. For instance, the Rajshri Group and Eros Entertainment have created online sites where thousands of Bollywood movies, music videos, and shows are available for a fee or, in many cases, absolutely free. Free is anathema to Hollywood execs, who cling protectively to their content and distribution rights. But in India, online dissemination and consumption of Bollywood content is arguably the future of the film industry worldwide. When Rajshri released the romantic drama *Vivah* for $9.99 on its website the same day it hit theaters, Hollywood looked skeptically on a practice it is loathe to follow. Despite the cheaper cost of theater tickets, within a week of its premiere, the film had been viewed online more than a million times. The Web release would eventually bring in $4.5 million, nearly a quarter of the picture's total earnings. The success of *Vivah* suggests that producers in India are best off releasing their films simultaneously in theaters and online. In doing so, they expose the film to a new market while avoiding the rampant piracy that would accompany its release anyway. Without a doubt, filmmakers and marketers worldwide are closely watching the Indian online film industry, taking invaluable lessons to apply on their home turf.

On the surface, Bollywood is showing the world the star power that it can generate, and the deep loyalty to their favorite movie stars that Indian consumers are apt to develop. Below that surface is a quiet revolution in the production and distribution of Bollywood content. Indian content producers are circumventing the theater screen, learning from the aesthetic of Bollywood films, and adapting its content to new media channels. In the same vein, advertising creatives in India are certainly influenced by the film culture that surrounds them. What's interesting is how they are using new media to deliver the insights and ethos they glean from the movies Indians watch. Whereas US marketers look to the cell phone as a place to deliver "relevant" and "targeted" ads that nobody wants, Indians use it to deliver content that everybody loves.

Create Differently

Of course, the assertion that an Indian commercial for the Bajaj brand would sell motorcycles in the United States is riddled with inconsistencies. It is not a given that any Bollywood film can become an overseas blockbuster. Nor will every mobile ad be influenced by the Indian experience. Every culture has its own beats and impressions. For instance, the Czech car brand Skoda in Europe is on par with the Yugo in the United States. (In 2000, 60 percent of respondents in the UK said they would never consider buying a Skoda.) But in India, the Skoda is targeted as an aspirational brand aimed at high net worth consumers.[33]

This situation is common throughout the world. Certain brands come with certain impressions, and those impressions may vary from one country to another. And yet there is a common denominator to this particular example: rich people don't dig Skoda; those who've been poor do. Yes, this is a generalization. Certainly, I'm guilty of oversimplifying. But that's my job as a creative director: to reach crucial insights that penetrate, complement, or reject a shared human condition.

But however lucrative and satisfying it is to create campaigns for the affluent West, marketers would be hard-pressed for survival if they did not begin creating campaigns for the global poor. This is not just a business imperative based on tapping "the fortune at the bottom of the pyramid." It's a way to tap into a worldview based on shared interest, humanity, and empathy.

India can teach us about the global poor better than many

other hyper-developing countries. Not only does the Indian creative class possess the cultural imperative for empathy, but it is charged with creating demand in a very tight-fisted and skeptical marketplace. Sound familiar? In the forthcoming branding climate, consumers in the West will act more like Third World shoppers than Third World shoppers themselves. It therefore makes sense to start marketing accordingly.

I would not be presumptuous enough to suggest that Bollywood could become the next big player in crafting global stories— or, perhaps, marketing stories. But it cannot be ignored that the insights and plots so expertly rendered in Bollywood productions are globally relevant. Nor can it be ignored that the content Bollywood pumps out is readily and hungrily accepted by an emerging middle class dependent on their mobile handsets to deliver byte-sized content. Bollywood and the mobile revolution gripping India present remarkable opportunities for brands to assimilate and appropriate storytelling and technology in order to produce unrivaled brand experiences.

It is no secret that the Internet has changed the way consumers interact with and learn about brands, companies, and products. The simple fact is that plain data about a brand—and, more important, other people's opinions of it—are readily available at the click of a button. Traditional advertising, therefore, delivers a message that has decreased in value for the new consumer. A 30-second ad—the branded hyperbole—is no longer as important to consumers as the stuff written by other people about it. In other words, a succulent TV commercial that costs a couple million to produce is less beneficial (or desired) than a bare and simple Google search page, or one of millions of blogs that take in no advertising revenue at all. Their opinions and musings are absolutely free, and their influence on brand perception is unmistakable.

The problem with the TV spot is that it's fundamentally a dictum. All commercials are commands; it's just how subtly the command is delivered that changes. The magazine print ad is a command. At the very least, it is an unequivocally unfair enticement. Advertising is an evolved art form (it is indeed art, just like improv comedy or magic) to induce action. Advertising plays upon the sensorial, visceral, rational, and aspirational elements of human decision making. But it has limited itself to doing so on a one-way street. Since its inception, advertising has been a monologue, never a dialogue.

One has only to read *The Cluetrain Manifesto* to understand that the marketplace—applied to the entire world—is predicated on a conversation, or rather, billions of conversations. As brands profitably expand their markets globally, it naturally follows that the conversation is becoming global as well. As the world becomes more networked and connected, pervasive digital tools and technologies are moving the conversations online. Not only are we all talking physically, but we are talking with our fingertips and we are talking with our thumbs.

Either physical or virtual, the notion of establishing a conversation between a brand and its consumer is currently touted by marketers and consumers alike as the best way to communicate a brand message to an increasingly indifferent and disengaged audience. Unfortunately, a majority of mainstay ad shops and branding agencies don't know how to establish a conversation. They know how to shout, for sure. They know the artistic merit of spectacle, and they have fundamentally transformed how we ingest and regurgitate information. But ad agencies aren't so good at listening to consumers. It's not their forte. They want to spark a conversation, not be a part of it.

And therein, perhaps, lies the reason for the (timely, dare I say) demise of the traditional ad agency model. For the majority of future brand campaigns and ideas that are local, national, or international in scope, the underlying brand strategy to engage and influence the consumer will have to be predicated on some sort of a conversation-based experience. Simply put, without personal and human engagement there is little ability to generate empathy. And the ability to discover and leverage global empathy will be at the heart of breakthrough brands, products, and campaigns.

The purposeful commitment by ad creatives, brand planners, and marketers to incorporate empathetic thinking into the creative process—whether applied to a local consumer or to a global citizen—will naturally encourage a spectrum of conversational interactions between brand and consumer from inconsequential banter to impassioned debate. Empathetic thinking—superficially defined as the ability to pick up subtle clues and behavioral patterns in another person and translate them into understandable conversation—will invariably have to be incorporated into all facets of commercial messaging: mass media, below-the-line marketing, digital activation, promotions, product placements, and PR.

Face-to-face interaction between a brand and consumer is the best conduit to discover and parse through empathetic insights coming directly from the consumer. Perhaps this is why experiential marketing is increasingly being utilized by forward-thinking companies to connect with their core customers in a way that traditional media cannot accommodate. Monologue-based marketing, apparently, hasn't been retooled for conversational marketing.

To be clear, a one-on-one interface can include in-store exchanges and interactions, in-field marketing, service personnel, and offerings such as consulting, counseling, and entertainment. All these exchanges and interactions offer opportunities to connect with customers, delight them, provide them with the right information efficiently, and enrich their lives. The methodology is commonly referred to as experiential marketing, which is predicated on one-to-one interactions between marketer and consumer.

Traditional mass media advertising and marketing rely on features-and-benefits positioning, branding, packaging, logos, and retail spaces to push their products and services. These practices are generally static in nature and passive in terms of consumer interaction. Conversely, the one-on-one interface—at a store, on the street, at a hotel check-in, during a sales visit, and even online—is highly dynamic and intangible. The voice, attitude, style, and appearance of the marketer are some of the most obvious intangibles. More important, these exchanges build empathy.

What brands can learn from conversation-based and one-to-one marketing cannot be underestimated. The insight gleaned from such interaction with the consumer can be used to rapidly create more empathetic messaging and a more personal approach. The conversation is also used to acquire qualitative knowledge that is impossible to get with traditional research methodologies.

If done right, a personal marketing experience will change the consumer.* She will have been delighted, touched, or inspired. Her perception of the brand or company will be transformed because she herself has somehow been transformed. This is the power of empathy. It is the connective tissue for our humanity, and it can therefore become the connective tissue that transforms branding into branded experiences.

As stated earlier, traditional marketing developed to efficiently reach as many people as possible with uniform, practically populist, one-way messaging. Focus groups were instrumental

---

* It leaves brands different, too. Avon, a company that relies on face-to-face marketing interactions and peer referrals, reported $2.5 billion in earnings for the first quarter of 2008. The biggest cause of the growth was the recently completed deployment of 15.5 million Avon Ladies in China alone. Not surprisingly, sales in that country increased 29 percent from the year before.

in determining which ideas and marketing campaigns would be acceptable to and influential on a homogenous audience. Marketing wasn't invented to spring breakthrough ideas; it was based on providing selling propositions, couched in creativity, that were watered down enough to appeal to as many people as possible. But now, because of the rising use of experiential marketing and other alternative marketing channels, brand platforms and experiences are being created out of personal conversations—Apple's Genius Bars are a case in point—which reveal universal consumer insights and empathetically transfer them back into the brand ethos. Successful brands are learning that marketing success comes from big ideas that evoke a shared human predisposition for taking action based on our common capacity for empathy.

How else to explain the runaway global marketing success of Unilever's Dove brand, which released a Toronto-created viral video/long-format spot called *Evolution*? This almost-perfect exercise in branding came in the form of a single-camera video that, through time-lapsed photography, shows how a plain-looking model is transformed though Photoshop, makeup, and digital wizardry into a glamorized and extremely inauthentic version of herself. The video was the lynchpin of Dove's brand platform called Campaign for Real Beauty, which used real women—not ideal models or celebrities—in all their advertising.

The idea for the platform was a global insight, brought forth from a concerted effort by the brand to empathize with its core customer. Dove, in effect, implicated the entire beauty industry as inauthentic and manipulative. In doing so, the brand challenged the industry's accepted standard for female beauty. This powerful concept, which emerged from Dove's empathetic ideation process, has since energized the marketing world. It has also sent a wake-up call to industries that are still engaged in a one-way monologue with consumers: their days are numbered.

Companies, brands, products, services—along with the marketers, suppliers, and the ad agencies that work for them—that strive to become more empathetic entities for their customers will invariably have to engage them in a live, face-to-face, or conversational setting. Intuitively, therefore, brands and their advertisers will need to pay more attention to where, when, and how that conversation takes place. Brands will need to devote much more care, thought, and budget to creating the ideal consumer experiences to foster branded conversations. Marketers and creative directors will therefore have to be much better attuned to the subjective cues that provoke empathy in consumers. Marketers must now perfect the exercise of *keeping* consumer attention in addition to their honed and tested practices in *getting* it.

And so in creating brands and the campaigns to support them, marketers will need to hit on key drivers of empathy. Rather than creating meaning in people's lives, forward-thinking companies are now in the business of connecting themselves to the meanings people already know and want. The human yearning for meaning crosses boundaries, cultures, and demographics. In essence, the search for meaning, and therefore for empathy, contains a certain degree of commonality to all people. This is a good thing for companies wishing to do business.

In a book called *Making Meaning*, authors Steve Diller, Nathan Shedroff, and Darrel Rhea outline the major human tendencies and triggers that evoke the indispensable need for meaning, and in doing so, generate a proclivity for insightful empathy.[35] These are, in no particular order,

- Accomplishment—achieving goals and making something of oneself
- Beauty—the appreciation of qualities that give pleasure to the senses or spirit

- Creation—the sense of having produced something new and original, and in doing so, of having made a lasting contribution
- Community—a sense of connection with other human beings
- Duty—the willing application of oneself to a responsibility
- Enlightenment—clear understanding through logic or inspiration
- Freedom—the sense of living without unwanted constraints
- Harmony—the balanced and pleasing relationship of parts to a whole, whether in nature, society, or an individual
- Justice—the assurance of equitable and unbiased treatment
- Oneness—a sense of unity with everything around us
- Redemption—atonement or deliverance from past failure or decline
- Security—the freedom from worry about loss
- Truth—a commitment to honesty and integrity
- Validation—the recognition of oneself as a valued individual worthy of respect
- Wonder—awe in the presence of a creation beyond one's understanding.

Surely, the entries on this list can be shared with each person on the planet. Companies and brands cannot create a uniform experience for any one of these meaning makers because everyone internalizes meaning subjectively. Yet the recognition that these commonalities are indeed drivers of meaning, for people across the globe allows marketers to empathize with their audience, to the point at which companies aren't creating meaning, but *evoking* it through the experiences that they provide their consumers. The future of branding depends on it.

CHAPTER THREE

Bought at Silk Street

(How Pirates Are Making Brands Obsolete)

I shall certainly save my life's grand confessions for a later date, but I can let out a relatively small one in the pages of this book. For quite some time now, I will admit, I have been wearing an exorbitantly expensive Swiss watch—a work of temporal artistry that has been complimented countless times by envious colleagues and strangers alike. This watch is a fake.

The watch in question, a Panerai Luminor Chrono Daylight, is quite a trendy timepiece in the über-chic clubs and boardrooms of L.A. and Paris alike. Erik Hauser, my good friend and founder of Swivel Media, owns a Panerai. A real Panerai. And my knock-off passed all his scrutiny. What should have retailed for close to $9,000 in a high-end boutique in New York, I bought for $18 in a Beijing mall called Silk Street.

The label "mall" is a misnomer. Silk Street is a seven-storey office building in the middle of a nondescript neighborhood in downtown Beijing (which, too, is a misnomer since "downtown Beijing" stretches for miles on end in all directions). This run-down office complex, however, is the epicenter of the finest brand knockoffs in the world.

Each floor consists of a number of areas, each one beholden to a specific high-end consumer good or product segment. The areas house a dozen or more vendors, separated by no more than a cloth curtain or plywood partition. There are over 1,700 such stalls and counters in Silk Street. Each stall holds a brazen polyglot saleswoman—the more shrill, the better—who hawks every imaginable high-end brand fake.

The basement boasts thirty or more vendors selling luggage and handbags (Gucci, Tumi, Versace, Mont Blanc, et cetera), as well as dolls and children's wear (Ralph Lauren, Oililly, Benetton, and so forth). The first floor is occupied by hundreds of stalls selling fashion brands and footwear: Chanel, Hugo Boss, Armani, Bruno Magli, Jimmy Choo, and so on. The floor above that merchandises accessories and perfumes: a veritable duty-free megalopolis. Another floor showcases top-shelf jewelry, such as hundreds of "perfect" Tiffany engagement rings, Hermès pendants, and diamond-studded Rolexes. It is on this floor that I bought my Panerai.

My fake Panerai is no cheap imitation, mind you—the kind you would buy on Canal Street in New York's Chinatown, or from a guy in a trenchcoat on the "L." This knockoff is top-notch. In fact, if I had wanted a cheaper version—for about $5—I would have been directed to another mall. At Silk Street, the knockoffs are genuine.

There is an often-repeated story of workers at a plant producing real goods punching *out* at 5 p.m., and another crew working for counterfeiters punching *in* at 5:15 p.m., working the same lines, churning out the same product. One line goes to the real market, the other finds its way into the "gray" one. So it seems that some knockoffs are just as good as the real thing. (Full disclosure: I don't go swimming with my water-resistant fake Panerai, nor do I shower with it. I'm still skeptical.)

It is at Silk Street, however, that I had my small epiphany. At this crucible of counterfeit goods I caught a glimpse of the future of brands. Granted, this eureka moment was influenced by a steady diet of Vicodin (I had hurt my back playing soccer two days before embarking on a flight to Beijing) and the ungodly din of countless Chinese ladies screaming at me to stop and take a look at their wares. Throw in jet lag and a night of drinking with ex-pats, and the moment was almost destined. In this place, I understood that the future of global brands was being determined by their knockoffs.

My enlightenment came to me in mid-air, actually. As I was walking through the luggage section of the building, an overzealous saleswoman literally grabbed and pulled me into her stall. I am told that Vicodin impairs a person's ability to operate motor vehicles. I can attest that it also impairs a person's ability to withstand the physical onslaught of a vendor selling knockoff garment bags at Silk Street.

I flew through the air, all 250 pounds of me, in a slow-motion combination of gracelessness and horrid spectacle. I was a debacle waiting to happen. I had not been properly prepared for the type of hand-to-hand shopping that is necessary in Silk Street.

As I landed in a cluster of beautifully copied travel accessories, it occurred to me that I was not a dispassionate observer; I was here to get a great deal on a good fake, and I was willing to be physically harmed to do so. Because if it weren't for this 100-pound woman judo-rolling me into a couple dozen carry-ons, I would have suffered at least a couple of bruises from the throngs of brand-frenzied shoppers who clogged the narrow aisles in the building. It was truly a free-for-all.

The intimation of subdued violence that occupies the shopping experience at Silk Street is truly palpable. A mass of people cram into narrow passages, flush with burning cash in their pockets, to be accosted by unabashed retail predators. It is a fascinating consumer game of survival: the buyer who is fully aware of the forgery about him, and the seller who is trying to extract as much real money as possible for it.

The entire place is a microcosm of the new brand world order. Burly, pink Russian businessmen buy massive suitcases on wheels in the basement and then proceed to fill them with so-called Versace, Gucci, and the like as they make their way up to the top floor. Local Chinese middle class and their youthful counterparts come to Silk Street to buy some cut-rate social status. Visiting pop stars and their entourages take over the place, buying up all the best that Chanel, Sean John, and Patek Philippe can offer.

Tourists from every part of the globe make the brand pilgrimage. The *China Daily* newspaper positions Silk Street as the third-best-known tourist destination in Beijing after the Palace Museum and the Great Wall.[1] Most everyone who comes to Silk Street buys something—something they always wanted but couldn't afford. Affluent Chinese bring their European houseguests or colleagues to get a glimpse of "the real China." The irony doesn't escape anyone.

It certainly didn't escape me when I was lying face up on the first floor, with a luggage counterfeiter stooped over me like a counting referee. As I punch-drunkenly tried to dig myself out of the collapsed wall of Tumi all around me, I instinctively readjusted my consumerism. Because although it hurt my pride to go flying into a rack of knockoff luggage in front of hundreds of shocked and amused shoppers, the fall did one good thing for me: it steeled me for the most hyper-shopping experience of my life. The fact that I was shopping for fakes didn't make the experience any more normal.

I'm extremely grateful that my agency colleague was there with me. Adam Troyak, erstwhile senior director at GMR Marketing, is a sharp marketer with a sharper mind for bargaining. But what really mattered was his fluency in spoken Mandarin Chinese. Having spent a few years studying in Beijing during his university days, and majoring in East Asian languages, he was the perfect wingman for a run at Silk Street. Erudite in the cultural nuances of Beijing, he was utterly impervious to the transactional mayhem around him. I, on the other hand, was shocked into survival mode. And I surmise that many brands wishing to break into the Chinese market are shocked into the same state.

When I approached the first of twenty watch counters at Silk Street, I was armed with insider knowledge: always give one-third of the ticket price as your initial offer. That's right. From the get-go, tell the retailer that you will pay one-third the asking price. The negotiation starts from there. In many manufacturing circles, this is referred to as "the China price."

This dance between buyer and seller occurs on the keys of a jumbo calculator, a tool that every vendor in Silk Street wields like a modern-day abacus. Prices are punched into the calculator and passed back and forth, as buyer and seller use the number keys to narrow down a mutually acceptable price. What ensues is a scene that borrows heavily from an absurdist play, superimposed on a quotidian yet profound activity. It's as if Ionesco got drunk with Mamet in a bar run by Adam Smith.

What begins as lackadaisical browsing turns into a death match for an extra 10 yuan. I knew that Panerai was becoming a hot brand in the States, and I asked dubiously to see what kinds of Panerai watches they had. Sure enough, the girl at the counter had every single Panerai model available for sale. We began the dance, as Troyak translated my attempts to haggle and the saleswoman's insistence on a "fair price."

When the bargaining became too much to bear, I nonchalantly switched my glance to the Rolex display. She noticed. And thus the haggling began over a Rolex I innocently spotted. The dance then shifted to a "fair price" on a Cartier, which another saleswoman had brought over in the hopes of making it a "double purchase." We flitted from one ultra-luxe brand to another like slap-happy butterflies. Until we came back to the price of the Panerai.

In the midst of passing the calculator to the overzealous, multilingual saleswoman, I began to recall some of the more egregious examples of forgery and fakery in the markets of Beijing, Shanghai, Guangzhou, Hong Kong—in almost every city in the country.

There's the story of the brewery in Tianjin that makes fake Heineken and Budweiser. About half of all designer eyewear sold in Guangzhou's Renmin Road market is fake, including Louis Vuitton frame designs that the company doesn't even make for real. These frames are available for about $2. The market for Harry Potter books is so hot that Chinese pirates are writing their own Harry stories, many of which are infinitely more popular than the ones written by J.K. Rowling herself. Over 90 percent of all Microsoft products in China are pirated.

Japan's Ministry of Economy, Trade, and Industry estimated that of the 11 million motorcycles produced in China in 2002, 9 million were knockoffs of Japanese bikes. Toyota lost a court case in Beijing when it complained that a local Chinese car manufacturer called Geely actually used a Toyota logo on one of its cars and the Toyota brand name to sell it. Warner Brothers, in a wholehearted effort to bend under the heavy hand of pirates, dropped the price of its DVD releases in China to $2.65, compared to the $25 price tag they normally command in the United States. Alas, this move was futile, because DVDs in any Beijing black market shop sell for about 75 cents. If you find a piece of branded, trademarked, or copyrighted clothing in a local Chinese shop—not in the glitzy malls and retail tourist traps—it is most definitely a knockoff. No matter the price they give you ... it's a fake.*

Pirates Go Legit

There are many markets like Silk Street, where you can buy a perfectly good fake at a perfectly low price. Yao Xiu in Beijing is a market specifically built for fake apparel; the Bai Nao Hui mall specializes in everything electronic. (And no, you have not erred in its pronunciation: the market's name is pronounced "Buy Now.") Whatever you need—a brand new iPod, a motherboard for a PC system, a scanner, the latest Toshiba notebook, any software package that has ever been coded—all can be bought at Bai Nao. In fact, as journalist Ted Fishman contends, "In China anything worth protecting is the first target of pirates and counterfeiters."[2]

And in a move more ironic than anything Alanis Morissette could ever dream of, a press release from the *China Daily* in early 2008 informed the world that the epicenter of counterfeit brands—the ground zero of brand piracy in the world—was going to brand itself.

That's right: Silk Street is becoming a legitimate brand.

According to the press release, "The first items to bear the Silk Street name include apparel such as neckties, shirts and scarves, as well as a few household items such as tablecloths. They are marked 'quality guaranteed' with a label that tells buyers that the goods are certified by the Silk Street market. Anyone using the brand outside the market will be held liable."[3]

This is an incredible statement to make, especially for a market known across the globe for its fake brands. Surely, the

---

* China is not alone. Six of 10 DVDs sold in Brazil are pirated copies.

way that the Chinese marketplace views brands—Western behemoths and local start-ups alike—must be examined and internalized. For the lessons learned in a marketplace like Silk Street are certainly applicable to any brand wishing to build a presence in the global marketplace.

The first question to ask is whether pirated brands are good enough to compete with their genuine counterparts. In many cases, the answer is a resounding "yes." In fact, many of the Microsoft software packages sold at roadside kiosks and back-alley Beijing shops are much better than the code written in Redmond, Washington. Often, the sellers of pirated software will go to the trouble of updating the software with the myriad patches and updates that Microsoft regularly releases online. Whereas those who bought the software legitimately will have to go through the often tedious and laborious process of downloading the additional software themselves, pirates are amenable to updating the pirated code with legitimate updates, saving consumers the trouble.

Even more interestingly for brands, the piracy craze in China has given new life to long-forgotten or ignored software. When entire operating systems are being bought for $2 or $3 a pop, is it any wonder that software packages that didn't make it in the highly competitive Western market are going to get a second life in the highly fecund black market?

Furthermore, the tools that the Chinese have for their computing needs are exponentially greater than those given to their US counterparts. We are beholden to the market positions carved out by the likes of Microsoft, Apple, Adobe, or McAfee. But for the average Chinese, the palette of software options is much more robust. In fact, the Chinese use more than nine bootleg software packages for every legitimate one.[4]

Piracy is changing the way products are developed and brought to market. In fact, there is no real shame in China over using pirated software. The price of a legitimate package is so prohibitive to the average Chinese citizen that it is impossible to buy. If it weren't for piracy in China, the average person on the street would argue, no one would be using Microsoft anyway. At least this way, with bootlegs and cracked code, Microsoft is enjoying immense brand awareness that it otherwise would not have.[*]

In Russia, India, and China, software piracy is a huge problem, one that Adobe had to face at the beginning of 2006 when it decided to release the Photoshop suite of software in those markets. The company knew that no one in those countries was going to dish out roughly $1,200 for the licensed version of the software when a pirated version was available for a fraction of the cost at a local bazaar or through mom-and-pop shops on every corner. So in a move of stunning simplicity and chutzpah, Adobe released it for free to a few billion people. A few billion. Simultaneously, the company shrewdly sold off sponsorship spots in the software to other brands, and made giving something away a very profitable business. How? Well, the "Save" command in Chinese and Russian versions of Adobe Acrobat is sponsored by Citibank, with the company's logo next to the command on the drop-down menu at all times. The "Clear" command is sponsored by Tide. Xerox bought the rights to the "Copy" command. The "Cut" command is branded with the Gillette logo. And so on. In this stroke of marketing genius, Adobe gave away the software in order to establish an advertising channel to billions of consumers whom other brands were eager to reach. And in doing so, Adobe ensured that its product would not be pirated and propagated in inferior versions throughout the developing world.

---

[*] A report by Davenport Lyons and Ledbury Research found that one in eight British shoppers bought a counterfeit watch, handbag, or other product in 2006. Two-thirds of Britons readily admit to peers their counterfeit purchase. And one-third of buyers of fake goods said the experience made them more likely to buy the real thing.

Creative Technology, a Singapore-based consumer electronics manufacturer, saw its patented and highly protected MuVo brand MP3 player knocked-off by over 40 companies within weeks in Shanghai alone. The company has since learned its lesson. It now uses Chinese manufacturers to build bargain versions of its products for the Chinese market, to be sold at much lower prices than its more sophisticated products elsewhere in the world.

If India is the brains of the outsourced world, China is certainly its muscle. Cities we have never heard of have cornered entire global markets. For instance, the city of Wenzhou in Zhejiang province has a population of about 7 million. Yet within its city limits, most of the world's supply of cigarette lighters is produced. Wenzhou's 700 private manufacturers—many are family run—make over 750 million lighters each year, representing about 70 percent of the world market.[5] If you need fake electronics, however, go to Chaosan; in Yuxiao City, it's counterfeit cigarettes. In Jintan City, you can get great knockoff pesticide.

An entire discourse on patents, copyrights, intellectual property, and open-source creation can accompany any glance at the piracy problems confronting global brands. I hope to avoid any intense scrutiny but instead concentrate on piracy as it affects marketing brands and their consequent behavior. Because brands can learn some fundamental lessons from their pirates. And their actions in the face of piracy—and their consumers' progressive acceptance of their forgeries—will be the predominant issue facing brands and branding for the next decade.

It is especially important to understand that brands are being pirated in an environment of hyper-communication and consumerism. The Chinese urban marketplace is a petri dish of new and emerging communication channels, as well as a massive consumer infrastructure that supports a behemoth mass media market.

The Rise of the Commie Bourgeoisie

China has more than 2,000 TV channels delivered by over 600 government-backed broadcasters. There are an unbelievable 192 newspapers in Beijing alone![6] Any anecdotal observation of a visit to Beijing must note that every bus in the city—hundreds of thousands of them—has a TV screen in it, blaring commercials and news stories to the squeezed-in commuters. This is a very screen-centric nation. If it's not TV ads, it's online ads. China's online ad market grew by an astounding 115 percent in 2007, and even greater growth was seen in conjunction with the 2008 Summer Olympics. Moreover, the "third screen" is blossoming like One Hundred Flowers: SMS and mobile communication is an integral part of consumer life in urban China.

Consumerism in China is making Chairman Mao proud. Well, at least it's making his inheritors breathe a little easier. The chairman did espouse flexibility and adaptation in his guerrilla strategies, so why not espouse the same for economic development? I think the Chinese Politburo has learned its lessons from its Slavic neighbors. No one in the Forbidden City wants to be another Boris Yeltsin. And so, consumerism in a Communist nation can be as celebrated as it is in a capitalist one. And the Chinese have taken to consumerism with a passion worthy of a revolutionary.

The urban middle class in China—the bourgeois bane of any socialist—is about to explode. Although much disparity between urban and rural consumers in China will continue to exist, the single most significant evolution will be the urban marketplace. Hundreds of millions of people will migrate from the rural countryside to Tier 3 and Tier 2 cities like Harbin, Wuhan, Nanjing, Chengdu, and Tianjin. The United Nations estimates that, in the first decade of the twenty-first century, 200 million rural Chinese will have become urban consumers. The number of larger-spending consumers in Tier 1 cities like Beijing, Shanghai, and Guangzhou will also explode, and it is estimated that over 1 billion Chinese consumers will be living in urban centers by 2030.[7]

Inevitably, urban households in China will become one of the largest markets in the world. The ever-prosperous urban middle class will be the dominant force and source of aspiration for over 1.3 billion Chinese consumers. The new middle class will also be unusually young. This is an important consideration, because this demographic (25 to 44 years old) is brand savvy enough to be major drivers of brand perception and adoption not only in their market but in the global market as well. With so many budding consumers waiting on the horizon, it is safe to say that the future of global brands can certainly be swayed by such a powerful base.

This base even has a name: "bobo," the bohemian bourgeois. According to Jing Wang, author of *Brand New China*, the urban bobo class is made up of Confucian hyper-consumers who can be seen as both a cultural and a marketing phenomenon, a class of "highly educated folk who have one foot in the bohemian world of creativity and another foot in the bourgeois realm of ambition and worldly success. The members of the new information age elite are bourgeois bohemians . . . They are bobos."[8] They are certainly no yuppies, however. Bobos have a highly attuned spirituality and appreciation for family values, tradition, and balance. They also display brands in order to climb in social circles, considering the ostentatious display of wealth to be an investment in improving one's station in life. Therefore, bobos tend not to buy expensive cars or excessive apartments, as these things are private in nature and may not necessarily be seen by colleagues, but they will spend heavily on more visible things such as dinners with colleagues, vacations, technology gadgets, fashion, and luxury goods. Pouring the world's most expensive brandy isn't seen as showing off; it's simply being a good host.

The Chinese bobo is of the aspirational class. It is this social status that most rural Chinese yearn for, and that's why they are surging into the cities. There they are accosted by eager marketers hoping to entice them into a branded bobo lifestyle. The most prevalent bobo brand messaging is done on TV, but the cities have also spawned a robust alternative media channel that continues to pump branded messages to the receptive Chinese consumer. One such company, Focus Media Holding, has transformed China's advertising landscape with over 190,000 screens scattered throughout the country. No matter where you go in the cities of China—the airport, hospitals, elevators, malls, taxi cabs, buses, karaoke bars—there are video screens selling soft drinks, shampoos, motorcycles, and cell phones.

Focus Media Holding, founded in 2003, is changing the brand perceptions and palettes of the new Chinese consumer. Although state TV is by far the best way to reach China's 450 million households, it is a buckshot approach. However, LCD screens interspersed throughout lifestyle locations—both leisure and business—have become a much more highly attuned and effective channel of brand communication for the bobo class. It's on these screens that new brands are being adopted or rejected, as the bobos who are teeming in front of these screens in office towers and golf clubs are like brand sponges.*

Since the company was founded, 36-year-old owner Jason Jiang has amassed an estimated $1.8 billion fortune. An ex-advertising executive at a Shanghai agency, Jiang bet it all on a

---

* The golden age for digital signage is apparent in North America as well. For instance, GameStop, the world's largest gaming retailer, with more than 4,000 stores in the United States, uses an in-store TV station called (unsurprisingly) GameStop TV. Each store features a screen that showcases game reviews and paid-for product placement, along with integrated advertising such as product mentions and interviews. Nielsen Media Research has revealed that the game titles showcased and advertised on these in-store TVs showed a sales increase of between 19 and 36 percent. Current non-gaming advertisers on the in-store network include the US Navy and the White House Office of National Drug Control Policy (so you know what they think about gamers). Wal-Mart has the world's largest in-store TV network, with over 3,000 stores.

hunch that Chinese consumers wouldn't mind watching ads while waiting for an elevator. (In Beijing, for instance, it's not uncommon to wait over 10 minutes for an elevator car to arrive.) He was right. As of September 2007, Focus Media's digital out-of-home advertising network had 95,400 LCD displays in its commercial (office) network and 43,315 LCD displays in its in-store network, installed in over 90 cities across China. In Shanghai alone, the company owns 200 outdoor LED billboards.[9]

Jiang's media empire—built entirely on re-screening TV commercials on screens outside the home—now includes the second-largest seller of online advertising and is expanding into cell phones, movie theaters, digital TV, and online computer gaming. According to Jiang, China is entering a "golden age for advertising"—an age dominated by his screens.[10] However, within the Chinese advertising screen-topia—annual GDP growth of 9 percent, a middle class growing by the hundreds of millions each year, and a consumer marketplace that accepts and even craves mass media advertising—the inescapable presence of brand piracy makes this emerging hyper-market a unique indicator.

Because if brands are so easily copied, why advertise them? If social status for the bobo class means an obvious display of brand sophistication and brand adoption, how can anyone be sure that the brands are real? When an ad for Gucci is aired in China, who wins: the brand or its pirates?

Well, certainly the pirates. In fact, if it weren't for this damned book, I would seriously consider a career in intellectual property rip-offs. It's a lucrative gig, and China is the leading source of pirated music, film, video games, software, brake pads, heart valves ... whatever. Nintendo estimates that it lost $1 billion in sales in 2007 from piracy of its DS and Wii game lines.[11] The International Federation of the Phonographic Industry estimates that 99 percent of all music files in China are pirated. The trade body of the global record industry accuses China's biggest Internet companies of linking to pirated music sites in order to boost their ad revenue.[12] Baidu, China's leading portal, made its bones on providing pirated music.*

And it's not just digital stuff that's counterfeited. It is all too common for customs officials to seize 800,000 knockoff Oral-B toothbrushes coming through a European port from China, or containers of fake Red Bull drinks labeled Gold Cow. It is estimated that multinational brands like Nestlé, Procter & Gamble, and Unilever lose about 10 percent of sales to counterfeiting—which comes to about $20 billion a year for these three alone.[13] Of increasing concern is that in 2001, nearly 200,000 Chinese were killed by counterfeit medicines.[14]

The Piracy Paradigm

Companies have totally readjusted their operations in order to deal with the pirates. Hollywood blockbuster *Spider-Man 3* debuted in Beijing before it premiered in North America. According to the *Hollywood Reporter*, "The move [was] designed to secure a strong opening at the box office before pirated copies have a chance to flood the market." Pirated DVDs of first-run films are available hours after Hollywood release for about $1 apiece. The Motion Picture Association of America estimates that 93 percent of all optical discs sold in China are pirated.[15] In 2004, China was the sixth-largest market in the world for personal computers, yet only the twenty-sixth largest for software sales. Obviously, this chasm was the work of fleet-footed Chinese pirates.[16]

It's estimated that the video game industry in the United States

---

* For every song bought legally in the United States, around 20 songs are illegally downloaded online, according to Big Champagne, an L.A.–based company that compiles and sells stats about file sharing (*The Economist*, 19 July 2008).

loses over $3 billion from piracy, not counting the pirated games that are played over the Internet.[17] In the stalls of Beijing, in the shadow of the Old Drum Tower, you can find any video game ever made . . . that year. I learned the hard way when I went searching for pirated Xbox games. I happen to own a second-generation Xbox, the model before the Xbox 360, which is Microsoft's relatively up-to-date gaming console. I visited close to a dozen small shops, each one littered with modified gaming consoles and egg-headed Chinese hipsters debating the minutiae of motherboards and Madden.

In each store, I was laughed out the door. No one—and I mean no one—would ever dream of selling counterfeit games for a second-generation Xbox. If I wanted the latest Wii, PlayStation 3, or Xbox 360 game, all I needed to do was browse a couple of photo albums featuring cheaply copied game packaging and front-panel labels. Once I had made my selection, the young shopkeeper would disappear into the back of the store and emerge with the just-burned CDs of the chosen games.

But no games were available for the old Xbox. If I'd had an Xbox 360, I would have had unlimited choice. But I had the old console. The pirates of Beijing had outed my gaming obsolescence.

In my hunt for pirated games in Beijing, I had completely and perhaps foolishly discounted the notion that I was doing something illegal in China. In fact, going out to shop for pirated video games was suggested to me by the concierge at the Grand Hyatt in the same breath as going to Silk Street for fake watches. I had no suspicion of dire consequences as I stood by and haplessly explained to the pirates my outdated gaming needs. And yet some brands in China are protected by dire consequences indeed.

When push comes to shove, the Chinese government has a solution to thwarting piracy, as well as bolstering brand equity: the death penalty. That's right, folks. How about a public execution to build some brand image?

China is renowned as the leader in capital punishment, usually reserved for corrupt and greedy Communist apparatchiks and the outcasts of communist society: drug addicts, criminals, the mentally ill, overzealous human rights activists, traitors, smugglers, and the occasional pirate. In fact, Chinese courts approve more executions than all other nations combined. In a world-famous case of swift retribution, China executed a former director of its food and drug agency for taking $832,000 in bribes to overlook the manufacture of fake drugs and medicines. When China wants to send a signal to the world—in this case, to indicate that it is committed to tackling the issue of shoddy product safety and integrity—it usually comes with an execution notice.

Signals were sent over another one of China's concerns about integrity—this time, brand integrity. The 2008 Beijing Olympics was the Chinese administration's coming-out party. It was the pinnacle of global acceptance of Chinese influence and geopolitical trust. To protect that trust, the Chinese government came down especially hard on brand pirates and counterfeiters who were hoping to make a killing on Olympic knockoffs. As the International Olympic Committee states, the Beijing Games represent the most effective international corporate marketing platform in the world, reaching billions of people in over 200 countries and territories throughout the world. No wonder the Chinese government wanted to keep the pirates out. And so it cracked down hard.

Anecdotal evidence suggested that a number of mid-level counterfeiters of Olympic-themed T-shirts and other logo merchandise were very quickly put up against the wall . . . quite literally. A range of 4,000 products—most featuring the five "Fuwa" mascots—was protected by something more than simple intellectual property law. Anything with an Olympics logo was also protected by criminal law, or to be more specific, capital punishment. Pirating the Olympics would be reason for execution. The reason? Simple.

The Chinese government wasn't willing to share the Olympic pie, or to devalue the global brands that paid billions of dollars to be associated with it. After all, while the 2004 Olympic Games took place in a city of 4 million people (Athens) and a country of 10 million, the audience in 2008 was huge. Beijing has 16 million inhabitants among its 1.3 billion citizens.

It's no wonder how crucial these games are to multinational brands looking to win global equity and local market share. When I was in Beijing in late November 2007, there were already close to 50 government-sponsored Olympic stores in Beijing alone. The government had earlier announced that it planned to open 10,000 Olympic franchise stores by the time the games got underway in August 2008.

Astutely, the Chinese authorities want this billion-dollar quadrennial cash-grab all to themselves. When the world's most prestigious sporting (and marketing) event intersects with one of the world's most hyper-developing and kinetic markets, you know there is money to be made. German sports brand adidas paid $100 million to use the Olympics logo in its marketing in China. This is one logo license—one piece of intellectual property—that the Chinese government would kill for.

Interestingly, however, the piracy game goes both ways. For instance, in 2008, Apple's iPhone was manufactured in China but was not available there. The hottest brand in the world had many admirers in China, however, and millions of handsets made their way back to the mainland. That could explain how Apple sold about 3.7 million iPhones in 2007, but only 2.3 million of them ended up being used by Apple's North American and European wireless partners.[18] It seems that tourists, small entrepreneurs, and smugglers have been buying iPhones in the United States and then shipping them to China, where the software is cracked to work with local wireless providers. This essentially destroys Apple's efforts to launch the iPhone through exclusive partnership deals with wireless network providers in the same way it launched the iPhone with AT&T in the United States. Each iPhone bought in the United States and then cracked in China costs Apple around $120 a year. In fact, this type of reverse migration has cost the company about $1 billion over three years.

A few considerations need to be taken into account. The Chinese market for cracked iPhones is insatiable. There are many iClones in China, all available for about $125. In Shanghai, TV ads hawk the Ai Feng (sounds like iPhone) for $125. Yet the bobos in Beijing want the real thing and are willing to pay handsomely for it. Members of the growing Chinese middle class have been shelling out close to $650—plus another $25 to crack it and add pictograph characters—for an iPhone that costs a little less than $400 in the United States.* The fact that this iconic brand can be smuggled only adds to its cachet.

Many analysts have even openly opined that Apple should unlock its phone system to allow any consumer around the world to use it with any carrier. If brand demand for the iPhone in Beijing is any indication, it is safe to assume that Apple phone sales would explode in China. And they would explode simply because the market has been primed with smuggled goods and cracked software. The Chinese bobo is fully aware of the illegal nature of his or her purchase, and even in the face of it, is that much more proud to be an owner of a real Apple iPhone. So what gives? Why are some brands succumbing to blatant piracy, while others are thriving in the face of it? Wherein does the power of the brand now lie? If pirates are profiting off a brand's strength, how can a brand profit off the pirates?

---

* You can pick up a 30 GB video iPod at the black market Burma Bazaar in Chennai, India, for $280. This is much cheaper than the $440 that authorized dealers sell it for in the country. Industry estimates by Wired magazine suggest that the "gray market" constitutes between 60 and 90 percent of Apple sales in India.

Microsoft, for instance, is using piracy to its advantage by up-selling genuine copies of its software to users at an extremely low price. Furthermore, the fact that its products are so widely distributed and used has in effect trained millions of people how to use operating systems like Windows and application suites like Office without a single dollar in expenses. Because Microsoft makes new upgrades and new operating systems available each year, it can confidently assume that those who are using pirated software now will be willing to pay for the legitimate product at a later time. Massive multiplayer online role-playing games (MMORPGs) that provide free software to play the game but also charge a monthly usage fee—like World of Warcraft, which boasts 10 million world-wide subscribers, each paying a monthly access fee—are actually profiting from pirated versions of the starter desktop software.

Many still remember the VHS versus Betamax saga, in which VHS won in large part because JVC allowed its VHS technology to be widely licensed around the world, whereas Sony dictated that the Beta would run only on Sony machines. In many cases, the success-ful launch of a new piece of technology or software depends on an "open" perspective on intellectual property and copyright. The prime objective at the launch and growth phases is to get mass acceptance, and mass piracy might be the best way to accomplish this. In Micro-soft's case, which is trying to stem the tide of open-source and there-fore "free" operating system software like Linux, piracy allows it to compete with Linux for the time being. As long as Linux is a strong contender in hyper-developing markets such as India, China, and Russia, Microsoft should welcome piracy like a breath of fresh air. It's the only way it can compete against a free open-source system.

The fashion industry has arguably profited greatly from a flourishing pirate marketplace—a global Silk Street, if you will. Piracy of high-end fashion and fashion accessories is at such an all-time high that the Council of Fashion Designers of America has successfully pressured Congress to consider a bill making fashion designs eligible for legal copyright protection. It's as if the stiletto heel could belong only to Dior, or the miniskirt were protected under law for only Gucci to sell.

In fact, for the fashion industry in particular, there exists a "piracy paradox." As law professors Kal Raustiala and Christopher Sprigman suggest in a *New Yorker* article, for the fashion industry to prosper, consumers must like this year's designs enough to buy them, but they must also rather quickly become dissatisfied with them in order to buy the next year's designs.[19] That's a tall order in any business. But piracy in effect makes it happen.

Fashion can't rely on functional improvements like more memory or longer battery life, as most technology products can, to make previously sold products seem obsolete. For fashion, it is copying that induces the obsolescence: "Copying enables designs and styles to move quickly from early adopters to the masses. And since no one cool wants to keep wearing something after everybody else is wearing it, the copying of designs helps fuel the incessant demand for something new."[20]

Certainly, the turbulent world of high fashion is more of a beneficiary than a victim of the piracy boom. Luxury goods makers are recording massive profits, year after year. High-end fashion houses haven't responded to piracy by slashing their prices; they've flourished by increasing them.*

Even more important for the fashion world, piracy has instigated a heady culture of creativity. This is an industry that cannot rest on it laurels, and marketers need to take a heartfelt lesson from this. No longer can a fashion designer hope to hit a home run and

---

* According to the *Financial Times*, shoppers on eBay could choose from more than 2,500 supposedly genuine Louis Vuitton handbags. The company's French site, on the other hand, listed just 80 (Frederick Mostert, "Counterfeits on eBay: Who Is Responsible?" Financial Times, 17 July 2008, www. FT.com).

coast on its multiyear trend. Fashion is a year-by-year business. You're only as good as last season, baby. In this market—and the market in the future—incessant product innovation and speed to market are vital. Consequently, there is more inspiration. There is more innovation. There is more competition, and ultimately, a substantial growth in overall business.

And, parenthetically, there is brand conversion.

I, for one, would love to own a real Panerai after taking meetings and entering pitches with a fake one. The right brand *does* say the right thing. And in fashion, the notion of "aspirational utility"—the enjoyment people get from imitating the lifestyle of the rich and famous—is perhaps its chief up-sell mechanism. James Surowiecki, author of *The Wisdom of Crowds,* wrote tellingly of the allure of knockoffs as being like "gateway drugs: access to the lower-quality version make buyers all the more interested in eventually getting the real stuff."[21] Sometimes, he claims, "imitation isn't just the sincerest form of flattery. It's also the most productive."

Take, for instance, the latest social networking craze (as of the writing of this chapter). It's called Scrabulous, and it's a wildly popular game developed for the Facebook social network site, itself an online property firmly entrenched in the pantheon of Internet idolatry. The virtual knockoff of the popular board game boasts over 700,000 players each day, and 3 million *registered* players. Scrabulous is a social network phenomenon, the perfect product for an interconnected and hyper-developing social ecosystem. And the companies that have the rights to Scrabble*– Hasbro in

---

* Scrabble was born as Lexico in 1931, invented by an unemployed architect named Alfred Mosher Butts, who determined the frequency of each letter in the game and its corresponding value by gleaning over the front page of . . . the *New York Times.* His patent was denied, and it was 17 years before he found a manufacturer, which renamed the game Scrabble (Heather Timmons, "Online Scrabble Craze Leaves Game Sellers at Loss for Words," New York Times, 2 March 2008).

North America and Mattel in the rest of the world—consider it blatant piracy.

They have leveled their litigious sights at the creators of Scrabulous, brothers 26-year-old Rajat and 21-year-old Jayant Agarwalla. They live in Calcutta, India. And they happen to be very avid Scrabble players.

Their Scrabulous game was not created as a money-making enterprise; it was simply an outgrowth of the brothers' penchant for the game. The software developers made a game that replicated the simple rules of the real thing. Although two mainstream gaming companies—Seattle-based Real Networks and Electronic Arts in Redwood City, California—say they have agreements with Hasbro to create an online version of Scrabble, it is Scrabulous that has captured the heart and minds of millions of teenagers and young adults not previously exposed to the original board game. It brought Scrabble an online presence and popularity that the parent company never expected.

So, although Hasbro is suing the brothers from Calcutta, it doesn't want to shut them down. The company doesn't want to alienate the throngs of Scrabulous fans who went out and bought the board game for the first time. Hasbro estimates that it sells 1 to 2 million Scrabble boards each year in North America.[22] Facebook has 3 million people playing Scrabulous. Before the Facebook game, there were only a few thousand rabid fans. I think those Hasbro guys are doing the math.

Anyone who has gone to Facebook's message boards can plainly see the "Help, I'm a Scrabulous Addict" groups populating the social network. Clearly, the Agarwalla brothers have created something truly glorious and "sticky." People love it. It doesn't matter where it came from. And it doesn't matter that it's pirated. People love it anyway.

And here's the rub. Hasbro isn't shutting down the Agarwallas.

It's trying to work with them, and to integrate their licensing partners in sharing the success of a viral runaway. Hasbro's marketers may not be pleased at the piracy, but they are not vindictive. They will ride the opportunity presented to them by crafty and well-intentioned pirates.

Facebook allows independent developers to create applications on the platform and keep the advertising revenue created from those applications. This has led to an explosion of developers—to the tune of over 150,000 in mid-2007—trying to create the killer social network widget or game.[23] How many of those do you think will rip off an idea like Scrabble? And what will the marketers of the copyright do? Exactly what Hasbro has done: ride the opportunity.

Massive social network sites are giving independent developers their platforms. MySpace has followed Facebook's lead. Global social network platforms like hi5 and Orkut are also giving developers the tools to create third-party applications.[24] The Chinese have a saying, roughly transliterated as "Wei-Ji," meaning "crisis equals opportunity." In this case, opportunistic brands have taken advantage of a crisis, namely, a free-for-all for original and not-so-original content to disseminate to Facebook's 150 million active users.

The well-documented demise of the established music industry had its denouement with the popularity of Napster, the free music file-sharing platform, which was rather quickly shut down. But not in time to unleash a total reconsideration of the value of copyrighted material. The Napster revolution has transformed the way that bands—not just listeners—are approaching the music business.

The music world was turned on its head in late 2007 when international multiplatinum band Radiohead announced that it was giving its much-anticipated album away for free as an MP3 download. Well, not exactly for free. The band announced that fans could put their own price to the album. Since piracy and unauthorized downloading has transformed the way people view the value of packaged music—many thinking that the traditional record label model is anti-consumerist and anti-artist—the band decided to give choice to the consumers. They could decide what they wanted to pay for their work, a ten-song album called *In Rainbows*, if they wanted to pay anything at all.

According to an Internet survey following the release, about one-third of people who downloaded the album paid nothing for it, but the average price stabilized at about $8. (A regular CD sells for about $15–$17.) Although the band has not disclosed how much money it made from the Internet release of the album, on its official release in CD and vinyl format it entered the UK Album Chart, United World Chart, and the US Billboard 200 at number one.

The super-group Nine Inch Nails quickly followed the Radiohead example with a pay-what-you-want release of its new album, *Ghosts*. The offerings range from a free nine-song download to a $300 ultra-deluxe limited-edition package of four vinyl albums, limited-edition prints, a data DVD with 36 songs in multitrack format (so that you can create your own songs), a Blu-ray disc with the music in high-definition 96/24 stereo, and an autographed letter from the band's front man, Trent Reznor. The entire work is licensed under Creative Commons, so that fans can remix the songs as they see fit and release them into the marketplace without penalty.

It is obvious that these revolutionary projects were inspired by piracy, with the ability of people to access licensed content for free at its heart.[*] Certainly, the idea that music labels are anachronisms isn't new. For these established artists—they are all mil-

---

[*] In late 2008, filmmaker Michael Moore released his film *Slacker Uprising* online and for free. It is the first major Hollywood film to be released this way.

lionaires, after all—these moves are not designed to cut out the label middleman for monetary reasons. Indeed, as Reznor was quoted on the announcement of the scheme, this is an opportunity "to have a direct relationship with the audience." When artists see labels taking a big cut while their songs are being ripped and released by millions of potential consumers who consider the label business model outdated and one to be ignored, it is no wonder that they want to find more efficient and grassroots channels to have a direct relationship. After all, their fans still buy music. They just don't buy physical music.

Piracy has in a sense contributed to a different dynamic between fan, label, and artist. To emphasize the point, a 2008 Forrester Research paper titled "The End of the Music Industry As We Know It" recommended that record labels forget about CD sales and actually encourage music peer-to-peer sharing, the very thing that ignited pirated music in the first place. The notion that the music can be ripped off and disseminated effortlessly among their fans—their true brand ambassadors—has convinced artists that the best way to capitalize is through fan outreach, novel approaches to distribution formats, added features beyond music, and exclusive content that could come from the artist alone. Major rock acts are realizing that to stay relevant and vibrant, they need to jettison the record label firewall that stands between artist and fan. Bands must come down to the people again. They have to create experiences, not just music, because although a track can be copied digitally, the way that track is delivered and acted upon cannot. Nor can the experience of witnessing it live be replicated on a pirated CD or DVD. Overall these types of schemes are fantastic PR for the bands and are sure to pump up ticket sales for the next Radiohead or Nine Inch Nails world tour.

The Future of (Pirated) Brands

The notion that brands (or, in the above example, bands) must adapt their strategies in a world where consumers are more than willing to access pirated versions is paramount to understanding the future of marketing and advertising. After all, if consumers think that a counterfeit brand helps the real one, then marketers really have to wake up to the future of the brands they are caretaking.

Furthermore, brands that find themselves the target of counterfeiters—studies suggest that only 25 brands make up most of the brands counterfeited—are forced to be innovative about their offerings and marketing more quickly than they normally would.[25] And that's a good thing. In fact, counterfeits in developing markets like China actually add to brand awareness. There is little cannibalization, as most purchasers of fake brands can't afford the real thing anyway.

"If counterfeiting is damaging to brands, how come none of the most commonly counterfeited brands such as Nike, Gucci, adidas, Prada, Chanel or Burberry are suffering?" asks Stuart Whitwell, in an article entitled "Brand Piracy: Faking It Can Be Good." "Turnover at Nike, for example, has increased by 45 percent since 2001. Burberry has seen turnover increase by 68 percent over the same period with operating profit more than doubling. And Microsoft, which accounts for more incidents of intellectual property theft than any other brand, has seen its turnover up by 57 percent."[26]

But because of the speed with which high-quality fakes appear in the marketplace, targeted brands need to take advantage of the unique opportunities that piracy presents. For instance, Spanish brandy Fundador is an extremely popular, and therefore counterfeited, brand in the Philippines. Children would collect the labels and empty bottles of the real thing, sell them to local producers, who would in turn refill the bottles, slap on the labels, and sell the fake brandy back into the marketplace. The brand, however, was able to turn this "problem" into a unique conversion opportunity. It rolled out an enticing promotional campaign that gave away extremely aspirational prizing such as Harley-Davidson bikes and Pajero cars. These prizes were promoted on the real bottles' labels, and the counterfeiters were stymied because the prizes were changed every six weeks. Sales of the genuine Fundador brand quadrupled in three years as a direct result of this strategy.

This type of innovation in the face of piracy—and, indeed, as a direct result of it—is at the heart of future branding across the world. My personal experience at Silk Street with counterfeit brands and the hyper-commerce that surrounds them indicates that brands will need to innovate and adapt at much greater speeds than they are used to, and they will need to reconsider the entire notion of branding altogether if they are to sustain their place on the consumer's radar.

It is my contention that piracy and knockoffs are going to influence brands to eschew brand extensions and concentrate on the master brand instead. Brands will increasingly need to cooperate and co-market themselves with other brands rather than endlessly creating new extensions. They will have to serve up limited-edition products or services targeted to the needs and aspirations of niche consumer groups, in effect becoming more ephemeral. And finally, brands will have to recognize that everything they do and are can be copied except for one thing: the consumer experience they offer at every touch point. The rise of experiential marketing is certainly addressing this issue. So, let's look at some examples of the future of branding.

Brand co-opting takes brand extensions to the next level. Co-opting isn't merely slapping a brand logo on another product. All too often, that's exactly what marketers are doing. Some rather dubious recent brand extensions include a Hooters energy drink, Donald Trump steaks, a Jeff Gordon collection of fine wine, and a *Girls Gone Wild* apparel line.

For decades, the strength of a brand ensured that its extensions would also prove successful, an easy way to respond to consumer fickleness and profit pressures. Since 1991, the number of brands on US grocery store shelves has tripled. Last year, the US Patent and Trademark Office issued an incredible 140,000 trademarks—100,000 more than in 1983. A record-breaking 182,000 consumer packaged goods were launched in 2006, a 17 percent increase over the previous year.[27]

Tostitos comes in 11 different flavors. (Plus the six varieties of Tostitos salsa.) Gatorade comes in 23 different flavors. Kellogg's has 50 types of breakfast cereal. Edge shaving gel comes in 13 different varieties, with product names like Edge Active Care Shave Gel Natural Cool with Eucalyptus. According to famed brand guru and author Al Ries, five years ago the average Coca-Cola bottler handled 200 SKUs; today that number has grown to over 530 SKUs and is expected to grow by more than 65 SKUs a year. As he explains it, "when business is declining, companies tend to respond by introducing new flavors."*

But in a surprising survey of 22,000 cases of brand extension, Research International found that the extensions were more likely to fail than new products. Clearly, brands are not as strong as brand managers and traditional marketers claim. In fact, the proliferation of brands is not a sign of strength but of inherent weakness.

The larger the number of brands in a company's portfolio, the greater the overlap of brands on consumer segments, positioning, price, and distribution channels. Many brands in a portfolio end up competing against each other rather than against those of the competition. A larger brand portfolio also means lower sales volumes for individual brands as they divide the total market share. Brand extensions tend to take up a lot of a com-

---

* SKU stands for "stock keeping unit" and is a unique identifier for a distinct product.

pany's time and energy, as brand managers within the company jockey for ad dollars and other resources. For instance, Diageo sold 35 brands in 170 countries in 1999, but just eight of its brands accounted for 50 percent of its sales and 70 percent of its profits. Unilever had an astounding 1,600 brands in its portfolio in 1999, but more than 90 percent of its profits came from only 400 brands. The rest posted either losses or marginal profits. The Chinese do not prefer brand extensions. Product safety issues and piracy have shifted the focus from individual brands to the parent brand as a whole.

Brands like Lenovo and Haier "have been criticized by transnational marketers for overemphasizing the corporate brand over the product brand," explains Jing Wang, a professor at MIT and the author of *Brand New China: Advertising, Media, and Commercial Culture*.[28] But this type of brand management may be the next big thing in worldwide branding.

Think of a brand like Apple. Everything it does is Apple-branded. When Steve Jobs re-took control of the company, Apple was marketing 40 different types of product, from printers to handhelds to peripherals. The computer portion of the business alone had four different lines—Quadras, Power Macs, Performas, and PowerBooks—each with a dozen different models. Jobs cut the line down to four machines: two laptops and two desktops.*

The piracy and knockoff phenomenon in China is making the corporate brand increasingly important. The bigger the brand, the more it is perceived as safe and therefore attractive. Piracy, in effect, has molded branding in China to focus on a "branded house" approach whereby the master brand acts as an umbrella under which new products are added. No matter what the brand

---

* In the same vein, illycaffè, maker of the illy coffee brand, offers only one espresso blend. Just one. No other major coffee brand comes in one variety. And yet illy is the world's best-selling espresso.

extension, it still puts the master brand front and center. The bigger the master brand, the more brand loyalty it enjoys in China.

Professor Wang makes a distinction between brands in Western markets and those in China. Whereas a firm like Procter & Gamble pursues a "house of brands" strategy whereby myriad stand-alone brands are generally unconnected to each other, Chinese companies prefer a "branded house" strategy. The master brand "serves as the dominant with a large number of sub-brands tugged along under its banner like mere descriptors rather than co-drivers of the overall brand."[29] With this type of branded house structure, willy-nilly proliferation of sub-brands with less-than-appealing personalities and marketing campaigns is a real danger to the master brand. Therefore, the branded house approach is less prone to the type of rampant brand extension climate seen in the West.

There are signs that brand managers are becoming increasingly aware of the consumer demand for more experiential brands and products. Brand caretakers are now bringing different brands and their core competencies together in order to enrich the consumer's brand experience. One such branded experience has reshaped the way people jog and train. Achieving critical mass in early 2007, the Nike+ product is a partnership between two massive brands. The concept is brilliant: combine the two things that are instrumental to a runner's existence, music and metrics. In other words, music has always been a part of a jog for a majority of runners. Also instrumental to the act of jogging or running is measuring how far one has run and at what pace. The Nike+ system does this, and it does much more, too.

Nike partnered with Apple's iPod brand to create a sports kit consisting of a small digital device that is embedded in a Nike shoe and that communicates with a receiver plugged into an iPod. The kit is run by Apple iTunes software and can measure the run from a number of data perspectives. It is able to store information such as the elapsed time of the workout, distance traveled, pace, or calories burned by the individual wearing the shoes, and display it on the screen or broadcast it through the headphones of the iPod. One of the cooler features sees the software figure out the runner's average cadence and then suggest a song list based on the beats-per-minute data for each tune.

An even cooler—and infinitely more important—feature of Nike+ is the community that has sprung up around it. The engagement that runners have found in wearing the shoes is translating into growing social networks. Runners are able to post their Nike+ data to a community site, where evaluation tools help them to become better runners. Other runners share tips and secrets. Running clubs are started. Running contests are born. Running routes are discovered, trail-blazed, and debated. All this engagement builds deep brand loyalty and evangelism.

The success of Nike+ has the partnership looking to expand into other sport categories like basketball, tennis, and soccer. Presumably, these moves would find even more willing participants in the virtual community of dedicated brand evangelists who appreciate the brand's role in their lives. And proving that Nike is still a top experiential brand that knows the power of grassroots activation and long-term engagement, the company is spending millions of dollars on creating more physical interactions between consumers and its brand. Like any visionary company, Nike is now keen to translate its success in creating online communities by staging experiences to gather like-minded communities in the real world, too.

To that end, Nike's flagship store in New York has a Nike Running Club, where runners come in to map out their routes, get training advice from top pros and staff, and attend an evening speaking series on nutrition, conditioning, or whatever—all free and open to anyone. In New York alone, Nike pays five coaches and 17 pacers to lead runs in Central Park three times a week. On

a larger scale, it has created a marathon for women in San Francisco and employs hundreds of street teams to offer free trials of
Nike sneakers at popular early morning running routes across the
country. The idea is to use the community that it created with the
Nike+ product to foster brand love among running enthusiasts and
to generate as many opportunities for product trial as possible.

Perhaps Nike had an experiential marketing strategy all
along, but something tells me that without the introduction of
the Nike+ product and the partnership with Apple, the company's
sales of running shoes and apparel wouldn't be nearly as brisk.
Interestingly, the synergistic partnership between the two brands
has made the sum greater than its parts. Would Apple have tried to
corner the market on runners? And would Nike have got into software and music distribution? A Russian oligarch would throw his
hat in the ring, but for these two brands a partnership provided a
perfect opportunity to create not only some synergies but unique
and market-changing consumer experiences.

The "branded house" approach allows brands to enter new
markets and product categories by carrying the strength of the
master brand. In this regard, the combination of two master
brands like Nike and Apple gives an even greater strength to both
brands. And to take it further, how could pirates ever re-create
such a tandem product offering? Although they could faithfully
reproduce any Nike shoe and any Apple product, how could they
faithfully reproduce the Nike+ experience?

Limit the Edition

Brand extensions do have a place in the Chinese market, however,
in the form of limited-edition products. Not only do they work
to increase brand loyalty but limited editions also turn piracy on
its head. In other words, if a brand knows it is being knocked-off,

it may turn to producing goods that are ephemeral in nature and therefore not easily ripped off. The secret to the success of a limited-edition product rests wholly on the famous brand name that comes with it. This makes limited editions a perfect medium for the Chinese marketplace, which is heavily influenced by brand consciousness and aspirational luxury goods.

The number of limited editions in markets across the globe is indeed growing, led by brands that are frequent targets for pirates. Dolce & Gabbana, known for high-end fashion and accessories, got into the sports shoe market with two limited-edition sneaker styles that sold for about $550 each. Every year, French water brand Evian (owned by Coca-Cola) launches special-edition water bottles designed by world-famous fashion houses like Christian Lacroix. The 750 ml bottles sell for $9.99. Absolut vodka has scored a major marketing coup by releasing limited-edition vodka flavors inspired by US cities. For instance, it released Absolut New Orleans as a mango and black pepper flavor in order to raise money for charity relief efforts in the devastated city. The effort was so popular that Absolut has since released Absolut LA, Absolut Boston, and flavors for other cities.

And if we're talking about beverages, let's not forget the hip independent brand Jones Soda, which has thrived on releasing limited-edition flavors and packaging. Before the 2007 NFL season, Jones Soda debuted its football-inspired flavors, including Dirt Soda, Sports Cream Soda, Perspiration Soda, Natural Field Soda, and Sweet Victory Soda. And in case you are wondering, yes, Dirt Soda does taste a bit like dirt and Perspiration Soda tastes like . . . well, you get the gist.

In Japan, music retailer Tower Records has used a limited-edition strategy to sell CDs. Unlike in the US market, where CD sales are plummeting due to online downloads and piracy, Tower Records has been able to run counter to the trend with a limited-edition strategy that uses co-branding in a unique way. Each limited-edition CD release by a popular Japanese pop artist has been snatched up by throngs of trend-happy Japanese teens. Tower stores have been mobbed by thousands of eager pop enthusiasts, leading to CD sales that would make any US label exec green with envy. The reason? Limited-edition CD covers show pop stars holding a Nike shoe. That's right. The pop star is holding a Nike shoe. One, a singer named Shoko Nakagawa, displays a Court Force sneaker. For another CD cover, the South Korean pop group Tohoshinki took two photos: one with the members of the group with their eyes open and holding Nike shoes, the other with their eyes closed. Both versions of the CD sold out almost immediately. Running contrary to every report of the industry's demise, a music retailer can still sell music outside of the Internet. Not surprisingly, Tower Records Japan is negotiating a similar limited-edition marketing deal with a major global drinks brand.

In the same vein, niche products are becoming a common branding technique. How niche? In 2007, Nike unveiled the first shoe designed specifically for Native Americans in an effort to promote physical fitness in a society with high rates of inactivity and obesity. The Air Native N7 is designed with a wider fit for the distinct foot shape of the Native North American. It will be distributed strictly to Native Americans through tribal wellness programs and tribal schools, which will be able to purchase the shoes at wholesale price and then sell them along to individual consumers. This is the first time Nike has designed a shoe for a specific race or ethnicity. But it's safe to say that it won't be the last.

Nike has also created a shoe called Trash Talk, in partnership with the Phoenix Suns' Steve Nash. The shoe is reportedly made entirely of "trash," mostly leather and synthetic leather waste from the factory floor and scrap foam for the mid-sole.

Reebok is taking on limited editions and "sneakerhead" culture as a company strategy by partnering with brands like Kool-Aid and trendsetting global youth figures such as a Bollywood actress, a Spanish supermodel, and a London DJ. They all got Reebok's blessing to create limited-edition sneakers that sparked buzz and brand equity. One such Reebok collaboration was with MIT Media Lab professor John Maeda. In 2007, the sneaker company paid him to design a sneaker inspired by one of his seven Laws of Simplicity: Time. The Timetanium "was created from scratch utilizing Maeda's original mathematical algorithms and computer codes."[30] Is that limited edition enough for you?

But adidas takes limited edition to its ultimate conclusion. In its use of customization and consumer-generated media, adidas has rolled out an experimental retail concept called Originals, a store that allows consumers to create their own sneakers in a workshop where they choose their own shoe colors, prints, materials, embroidery, and jewels. Every pair of shoes sold in the store is, in effect, a limited edition of one. Adidas understands that the customization experience of a product is in itself a service. And good service means a good brand experience.

The store also features a video wall with an interactive touch-screen display that encourages shoppers to take a photo of themselves and their shoes to be posted on the screens for 24 hours. The first Originals store opened in Berlin in early 2008. A second opened in Beijing later that year.

Coincidence? I think not.

The Authenticity Imperative

Piracy and counterfeiting are making brands more agile and creative, forcing them to become much more cognizant of distinct sub-cultures or tribes in order to customize products catered to their needs, desires, and aspirations.

Joe Pine and James Gilmore have written another paradigm-shifting book. The authors of *The Experience Economy*, their latest opus is called *Authenticity*, and it correctly postulates that "the management of the customer perception of authenticity becomes the primary new source of competitive advantage—the new business imperative . . . In industry after industry, in customer after customer, authenticity has overtaken quality as the prevailing purchasing criterion, just as quality overtook cost, and as cost overtook availability."[31] Their ideas on rendering authenticity—this new branding imperative—made *Time* magazine's cover story: "10 Ideas That Are Changing the World." Authenticity came in at number seven.

So what can be said, and done, about the rampant brand and product fakery that is emerging from the hyper-developing countries like Russia, India, and China? According to Pine and Gilmore, the fact that the market for counterfeits is booming doesn't contradict the consumer's impulse to buy authenticity. Indeed, it may support its value:

> If consumers didn't care about the authenticity of the original articles, then the counterfeiters wouldn't have to pretend to be those originals; they could just supply cheap goods under their own brands . . . In most cases, consumers have no idea they are buying counterfeits . . . In some cases, consumers may even prefer imitations precisely because the quality of the original isn't great enough to offset the higher price. Consumers will pay a premium for authenticity, but there comes a point (which differs, depending on the individual) when they trade off the real for a more available, cheaper substitute with sufficient quality.[32]

In fact, say the authors, a country like China "is now known for fakes but may one day be known for authenticity." For instance, take Chinese shoe and sportswear brand Li Ning.

When I first entered the Li Ning flagship store in Beijing, I almost burst out laughing. The logo for the athletic brand seems to be purposely made to look as close as possible to the iconic Nike swoosh. The brand tagline is also a rip-off: "Anything Is Possible." Opposite the store, adidas billboards supporting the brand's participation in the Beijing Olympics disclose the inspiration for Li Ning's imprimatur: for years, the adidas tagline has been "Impossible Is Nothing."

When it comes to appropriating the best of both brands, Li Ning has found that anything is possible, and that taking global market share from competition like Nike and adidas isn't impossible at all. Named after China's most famous gymnast, Li Ning is now endorsed by Shaquille O'Neal, who signed a five-year deal in 2006, even though the United States accounts for less than 1 percent of the brand's total global sales.*

During the Beijing Olympics, Li Ning was the official sponsor of the medal-winning Chinese table tennis, diving, gymnastics, and shooting teams. The brand also sponsors top-ten-seeded Croatian tennis superstar Ivan Ljubičić. It also signed a deal to outfit the Spanish athletes at the Olympics. When it was outbid by adidas to clothe the Chinese athletes, Li Ning signed a deal to outfit every presenter on CCTV5, the TV network that broadcast the Olympics to a billion Chinese. By the time the top athletes of the world convened in China, Li Ning had over 5,600 outlets across the country.[33] That's not bad for a company that entered the marketplace in 1989.

---

* In a move of sheer marketing brilliance, a Chinese shoe manufacturer named Peak that doesn't sell any shoes outside China has a seven-figure deal with Shane Battier, a basketball player on the Houston Rockets. The only reason for this endorsement deal is that Shane Battier plays with Yao Ming, China's greatest basketball star, and is seen on Chinese TV when Yao plays.

It should not be overlooked, however, that the Li Ning brand is unabashedly predicated on rip-off culture—although no one at the company would ever consider it a rip-off. They would easily explain that the company is simply taking the best from all the great athletic brands in the world and weaving it all back into the Li Ning brand offering. When questions about the disparity in quality between Chinese and Western brands come up, it doesn't go unnoticed that shoes sold in the global marketplace—Nike, adidas, Puma, et cetera—are often made in the same towns and the same factories as Chinese brands.

Even though Nike expects China to be its second-biggest market after the United States by 2009, Li Ning will certainly give it a run both at home and abroad. In 2006, Nike controlled about 16.7 percent of the Chinese sportswear market, and adidas held a 15.6 percent share. Li Ning came in third with a 10.5 percent slice of the pie.[34] So is it unrealistic to predict that a brand like Li Ning could overtake a behemoth like adidas or Nike some time in the near future? (Notice how New Balance, Reebok, Converse, and Puma aren't even considered.) Is it in fact hard to believe that Li Ning could be the number-one sportswear brand in markets outside China? Of course not. In fact, Li Ning is already planting seeds in the United States.

It is telling that Li Ning chose Portland for its first US office. Nike is based in Beaverton, just outside the city. Adidas America, although based in Germany, has its US headquarters in Portland. And now, Li Ning joins the gang. As the *Seattle Times* reported on January 22, 2008, "Opening the US outpost . . . indicates the fast-growing sporting-goods company wants to tap the pool of creative talent in the region, home to an increasing number of smaller outdoor and athletic-wear brands and supporting services."

A Chinese brand like Li Ning may currently be associated with fakery, but is striving to be known for authenticity. As Pine and Gilmore note, the crucial criterion for the future success or failure of a company or a brand is whether it is perceived as "real" or "fake"—as authentic or inauthentic.

This transition in perception can no longer be influenced or accomplished by traditional advertising. Once consumer perception of the inauthentic has been instilled, it is extremely difficult to reverse it through mass media. People know which way the wind blows.

The authors of Authenticity are (rightfully) proclaiming that the brand authenticity rests with the creative spaces—real or virtual—that can be built to deliver the brand experience. Since an individual's experience cannot be replicated, an experiential approach to products, services, and brands seems to be a natural countermeasure to the rise of brand piracy. It's what Ray Kroc, the founder of McDonald's, would impart to all his executives: anyone can sell hamburgers, but only McDonald's can sell an experience. Would Starbucks say the same thing about coffee?

In the context of marketing and (less so) of advertising, brand experiences must become customer-centric, instead of the current emphasis on the product or brand. In the case of the adidas Originals store concept, the consumer experience was predicated on a crucial tenet of promoting brand authenticity: let people define and even create their own offerings.

Through this process of creation and customization—the idea that limited-edition products try to harness—"the output automatically qualifies as authentic for the consumer." This process renders authenticity through customization, and turns the consumer into a "prosumer," a proactive consumer. Therefore, "consumer-controlled production, offering a prosumer platform rather than a finished product, shifts attention from the supplier's moneymaking motives to the buyer's self-defining pursuits . . . There is no need to avoid staging experiences, even virtual experiences, now that authenticity is the foremost consumer sensibility."[35]

The experience is the message. It's the marketing. It's what makes a brand authentic. What the Chinese (Indian, Russian, Nigerian) pirates have taught global brands is wholly simple: whereas brands once relied on a visual but intangible promise, today's global consumer wants something more than that. In other words, "the best way to generate demand for any offering— whether a commodity, good, service, other experience or even a transformation—is for potential (and current) customers to experience that offering in a place so engaging that they can't help but pay attention, and then pay up as a result by buying that offering. Stop *saying* what your offerings are through advertising and start creating places—permanent or temporary, physical or virtual, fee-based or free—where people can experience what those offerings, as well as your enterprise, *actually* are."[36]

Once the emphasis is placed on the consumer experience with a product or brand, invariably the marketing and advertising become more experiential. The brand itself becomes as fluid as the personal experiences that it can deliver at touch points beyond traditional media.

Allow me a seemingly odd parallel. Bruce Lee, the famed martial artist and inventor of the Jeet Kune Do (Intercepting Fist) fighting philosophy, explained his adaptive approach to combat and training: "Be like water making its way through cracks. Do not be assertive, but adjust to the object, and you shall find a way round or through it. If nothing within you stays rigid, outward things will disclose themselves. Empty your mind, be formless. Shapeless, like water. If you put water into a cup, it becomes the cup. You put water into a bottle and it becomes the bottle. You put it in a teapot it becomes the teapot. Now, water can flow or it can crash. Be like water, my friend."[37] Be like water. That was the secret to Lee's masterful and revolutionary vision for martial arts, and kung fu in general. It naturally assumed that the best defense is a good offense, one that is as fluid and powerful as the inexorable flow of water.

Brands must learn to be like water. They will have to become part of a flow of shared brand experiences disseminated by their customers. The successful and cutting-edge brands, and the marketers who serve them, understand that in the emerging global marketplace, brands must evolve into a new branding paradigm, one that doesn't necessarily depend on the brand itself.

A manifestation of such an evolution occurred in early 2008 when an ad agency called Modernista!* redesigned and launched its website, and in doing so, redesigned the agency's existence in a world of brand fluidity. It decided not to design a website at all. Instead, the agency simply made itself accessible to the digital landscape and moved along with it. Instead of showing off its creativity with complex Flash programming, stimulating visuals, awesome soundtracks, and the growing list of cool bells and whistles, Modernista! simply created a navigation bar.

Users who type "Modernista" into their web browser are redirected to their preferred search engine, where the Modernista! site "exists." From wherever you are online, clicking through to Modernista! does only one thing: it pops up a red navigation bar at the top left corner of the page. All the links on the navigation bar are Modernista!-centric, but none of the content that comes up is truly controlled by the agency. In another words, the agency simply put itself out there in the marketplace using branding tools that are as fluid as they are powerful.**

For instance, clicking on the "about" link in the navigation bar gives the user the option of bookmarking Modernista! and

---

* Modernista!'s clients include Hummer, Avon, Cadillac, TIIA-CREF, Product Red, and Stop Handgun Violence. It has done award-winning work for Converse, MTV, Gap, and Anheuser-Busch. It is headquartered in Boston, with offices in Detroit and Amsterdam.

** This is what it says the first time a user clicks through to Modernista.com: "Do not be alarmed. You are viewing Modernista! through the eyes of the Web. The menu on the left is our homepage. Everything behind it is beyond our control."

visiting the agency's page on open-source site Wikipedia or on Facebook, where the agency literally joins in the social networks that interest it. The link to a description of the work Modernista! does takes the user to a Flickr page that organizes the client work by category or medium. The news function on the navigation bar clicks through to a Google News search page for Modernista! The contact function downloads the agency's global contact list into the user's clipboard and automatically links him or her to available employment opportunities at the agency.

In effect, Modernista! has gone siteless. It has adopted this fluidity to create a unique brand experience for the user and position itself on a platform of constant change and openness. And presumably, this philosophy will permeate the work it does for its clients. (The only tagline to the Modernista! experiment is "Modernista! isn't for everyone. Is it for you?")

Adrants marveled at the cool audacity of the idea: "Considering most anybody in the digital space can pretty much be defined by what appears in a vanity search, we don't just find the Modernista! approach inspired. We think it paints a picture of the inevitable: near total transparency, and the taken-for-granted notion that you are what the world says you are. That's scary, but powerful, and it's the direction the online world has increasingly chosen to take."[38]

I would venture to add that it's the direction for many major global brands as well. The premium nature of the logoed brand is losing its luster. Counterfeiting has fundamentally transformed the way brands are viewed by the global consumer. It's not the brand that matters any more but the consumer's experience with it. How else to explain the glut of fake Louis Vuitton handbags on the one hand and skyrocketing profits for the brand on the other? To compete and thrive in such a new environment, brands will have to become like water.

I don't mean to suggest that brands should infiltrate or flood our daily lives in even greater scope and depth. Brands will cease to be so overt and instead become more ambient. The fluidity of future brands ensures their effectiveness. As Bruce Lee would often remind his pupils about his revolutionary style, "Absorb what is useful; disregard that which is useless." The future of brand marketing rests with this maxim.

Brand Differently

With the unparalleled proliferation of new products and brand extensions—coupled with the advent of massive communications networks and online markets—the perceived value of a brand seems to be at an all-time premium. With so many me-too products out there, "the brand" has for two decades become more important than ever. Once there was a time on Madison Avenue when the emphasis was on "the client"—or rather, the company. Today, marketers are much more likely to name the brand rather than the company when asked who they are working for.

The primacy of the brand—as intoned in MBA classrooms and swanky boardrooms alike—is a fundamental anchor for both established and upstart companies. Without a strong brand, it is often repeated, how would consumers recognize, trust, and ultimately buy your product? In a global marketplace awash in a sea of product parity and squeezed by increasingly frequent price wars, "the brand," and the practice of branding in general, has become one the most closely protected, frequently changed, and obsessively examined aspects of running a modern business and commanding consumer perception.

So how does a brand like Wal-Mart succeed in a massively lucrative market in which the collective consumer viewpoint is that there is absolutely nothing wrong with calling a competitive retail chain Wu-Mart, even if it is modeled almost identically to a typical Wal-Mart and sells the same stuff? How does BlackBerry protect its brand and company image when there exists in China a wireless email service called RedBerry? What power and equity do the BlackBerry or Wal-Mart brands possess when a billion potential consumers have already had an experience with their nearly indistinguishable "counterfeit" doppelgängers?

The explosion of brand, product, and intellectual property piracy—and the implicit global consumer acceptance of it—has brand managers worried that their seemingly untouchable equity is dissipating as fast as Chinese factories can churn out their counterfeited (but impressively mirrored) versions. However—and this is a big point—experiential marketing methodologies have so far proved to be the best bulwark and likely savior for brands that are endemically and profitably pirated.

In fact, a Wharton School of Business professor and former chief economist for the Federal Communications Commission bluntly reveals that "in the business world, when you talk to consumers about protecting copyrights, it's a dead issue. It's gone. If you have a business model based on copyright, forget it."[39] Piracy has made it that simple.

Piracy, however, has led to brand innovation as well. In efforts to minimize their exposure to counterfeits, marketers are redefining the notion of branding , and by extension, the value of a global brand that is easily and often ripped off. In doing so, they are coming up with some innovative brands and products, something that probably would not have occurred without rampant pirating and the consumer ambivalence toward it.

For example, the sale of counterfeit vodka in Russia is a social crisis that the government has put on par with AIDS and cancer. Perhaps the term "counterfeit vodka" is too sophisticated. What I mean to convey is that the vodka is homemade.

All it takes to make homemade—or fake—vodka is a supply of empty bottles bought from street collectors, a simple capping machine, tap water, and pure alcohol. Mix up the water with alcohol—sometimes anti-freeze or simply gasoline—and you've got a vodka line in your kitchen. What may seem like a ludicrous joke is nothing of the sort: 550,000 to 700,000 people die in Russia every year of alcohol poisoning and related illnesses.[40]

The fake-vodka epidemic has reached such acute proportions that a Russian lobby group for the drinks manufacturing industry has called on the government to subsidize or outright produce a "people's vodka" as a cheap and regulated brand, to allow poor Russians to buy genuine vodka. The head of Russia's Union of Wine and Spirits Producers, Osman Paragulgov, wants the government to own and sell a "social vodka" brand that is "neither eye-catching enough to attract better-off drinkers nor so wretched as to embarrass its poorer consumers."[41] This is indeed a bold position for a man whose sole job is to protect the market share of his members' brands—none of which, notably, are as yet government owned.

Imagine if Anheuser-Busch directed its teams of counselors and directors to publicly call for the US government to create a beer brand that would be practically given away to the rural and urban poor! Or if the main alcohol lobby in Washington called on the Oval Office to start a proprietary hooch brand called Capitalist Elixir. Or maybe Democracy's Drink is a better brand name.

In another typically Russian move, Deputy Finance Minister Sergei Shatalov proposed abolishing tax breaks for all alcohol-based products, perfumes, and drugs. You see, some unscrupulous booze producers market their liquid as perfume, but everyone knows it's for drinking, not spraying. Some counterfeit booze is sold openly as a form of cold medication. Everyone who buys it knows what kind of remedy it provides. According to the minister, this rather sinister "surrogate branding" has instigated a proposed change in law because "the current laws give an advantage to those alcoholic beverage producers who mask their products by putting them into the category of pharmaceuticals."[42] So, when was the last time you took Jim Beam's Nighttime Sniffling Coughing Sneezing So You Can Rest medicine?

Obviously, if these are the actions of responsible legislators and lobbyists, the fake-vodka epidemic is dire in Russia. For discerning vodka drinkers, a real mistrust of quality control in the production and treatment of the national libation is a valid consumer attitude. To be sure, savvy Russian marketers have capitalized on the fear of imitation vodka and its dangerously poor quality.* But all evidence suggests that Russians just don't care. It doesn't matter what brand is on the bottle, as long as there's a bottle to finish.

The function of branding as we currently know it will inevitably change. How can it not? We are currently in a consumer world where knockoffs of top-notch and top-dollar fashion brands are eagerly bought by influential and trendsetting consumers, who then mix and match their fake brands with real ones. In fact, scoring a "good" fake is a common reason to show it off to friends and peers.

Consequently, young consumers who, almost since infancy, have been taught the notion of brand primacy by the innumerable campaigns and brand launches, now have absolutely no qualms or shame in announcing that they are wearing a counterfeit. This seemingly counterintuitive and anti-marketing consumer disposition not only to buy fake brands but also to assign equal (or near equal) value to them is a seismic shift in how brands are perceived now and how they will be perceived in the future.

Brands are no longer infallible. They are no longer unassailable. And most important, brands are no longer brands. Instead,

---

* Premium Ukrainian vodka brand Nemiroff is packaged with a proprietary red ring around the neck of each bottle. If someone opens the bottle between the production plant and the retailer, the ring automatically dissolves and cannot be restored.

they are becoming milestones in an evolving consumer ecosystem that leverages consumer touch points and creates experiences that bring the brand to life in a contextual and relevant way. These experiences, by their temporal and subjective nature, cannot be replicated. They, and the brand impressions (both quantitative and qualitative) generated by them, are wholly unique to the consumer.

Brands therefore no longer need to play the role of consumer consolidator. Branding campaigns no longer need to appeal to as many people as possible, most often at the expense of a good creative idea. Brands no longer have to singularly carry the burden of determining and directing mass-based messaging. There's no such thing any more. Instead, a brand will evolve to become many things to a single person.

This is an important and industry-changing prediction because it incorporates the power of word-of-mouth messaging. In this market climate, top-down messaging loses much of its effectiveness in creating, sustaining, and repositioning brands. That job now belongs to you and me. The brand, in effect, is no longer delivered to consumers via marketing and advertising. It constantly mutates with the needs, wants, opinions, and pocketbooks of its customers, and in this transformation, the brand moves from a construct designed to talk at the consumer and shout louder than the competition to one that is part of the conversation itself.

Equally important, the rise of piracy comes at a time when "authenticity" in branding is as important as ever. It is ironic that one of the most significant and endemic social paradigms for the people of China, the biggest producer of counterfeit goods, is the Confucian idea of *guanxi* (pronounced "gwanshee"). This interpersonal system is a prominent mainstay in Chinese society and shapes the way that marketing takes root in the country. In fact, *guanxi* is the predominant social gauge of success in China, as well as a source of personal and quasi-spiritual satisfaction.

Guanxi is a concept of personal connection that goes beyond simple social networking. While North Americans put a premium on networking, information, and institutions, the Chinese place a premium on an individual's social capital within a group of friends, relatives, and close associates. It's not what you know, it's who you know. But knowing as many people as possible is not the point of *guanxi.* The point is to project a professional and personal image of someone who has good *guanxi*: not only do you know many influential people but you use your relationships with them to hook up your friends, family, and business partners. In exchange, you build up your *guanxi* credit with the ones you connect. *Guanxi* is based on the notion that what goes around comes around, and the concept's everyday use is integral to life and business in China. It is like a real-life karmic interpretation of LinkedIn or Facebook on steroids.

Therefore, in a consumer society that deeply values honesty, transparency, social networking, and personal relationships, the practice of inauthentic marketing and fake branding negatively influences the way consumers view the brands. Moreover, brands that attempt to overstate their benefits or underdeliver their services are organically pushed out of business by consumers who hold the brand to ever-increasing standards of authenticity. Simply put, if brands are no longer perceived to be authentic, their marketing will no longer be welcomed by the discerning and emergent consumer.

CHAPTER FOUR

No Logo Metropolis

(How Much Advertising Is Too Much?)

São Paulo is a metropolis. It's as much a metropolis as any other teeming city on this planet. After all, any city of (unofficially) 20 million people deserves such a moniker. This place is massive. It is sprawling. From the air-conditioned tower of my gleaming hotel, the city stretches, literally, as far as the eye can see. It is a wonderful testament to the propensity of human congregation, and an indictment of the windfalls that come from the sheer scale of this gathering.

The traffic that comes from 20 million people is monstrous and oppressive. It is no wonder that São Paulo boasts the world's second-largest fleet of private helicopters. Road travel is just too inefficient for the newfangled *paulistano* businessman or business-woman. And although the air quality may not be as noxious as that of Beijing, São Paulo has some serious environmental problems because of its expanse and density.

There are tall buildings everywhere but none more than 35 storeys or so. A strange city ordinance that prohibits skyscrapers has led to seemingly unending urban sprawl. If any city resembles the metropolis in *Blade Runner*, São Paulo is a strong contender. There are innumerable languages and dialects here; there is a Korean town and a Japanese town, an Italian town and a German town. São Paolo streets teem with traffic and commerce, and the evenings don't start until late . . . really late. Deep into the wee hours *paulistanos* start their dinner, their after-dinner drinks, and their dancing. The city comes to life at night. At one time, the impact of advertising out in the streets of São Paulo—where all the action goes down—was undeniable and inescapable. There is no limit to the creativity of outdoor advertisement in the urban jungle of Third World countries.*

Much like the city envisioned by Philip K. Dick—or director Ridley Scott—São Paulo was teeming with advertisements, neon, and overcommercialized street life. There was media detritus everywhere. Everything was for sale: jeans, cell phones, automobiles, credit lines, and phone sex. Messaging overkill was present at every vantage point. Kiosks, shops, clubs, taxis, and myriad brands competed for space within the sprawl. The messaging that accompanied the street media—billboards, building wraps, bus stops, screens and ads in buses and taxis, ads on public benches and stop lights, street signs, flyers, posters, commercial graffiti, and storefront signage—was as provocative as it was pervasive.

---

* The streets and commercial districts in Bangkok are characterized by a maze of thousands of legal and illegal electrical cables and telephone wires that criss-cross overhead for miles in all directions. The entanglement of wires, cables, and hook-ups presented a unique opportunity for a hair conditioner that promised to untangle unmanageable hair. The brand, called Rejoice, installed huge combs in the wires, high above the barrios. The stunt proved a huge success, and now Rejoice combs and brushes are "beautifying" the ubiquitous sight of knotted wires throughout the city. In a country where household TV penetration is still comparably low, this simply ingenious marketing ploy is seen by millions of Thais every day.

The Brazilian zest for life is often exhibited through sexuality, and the creative applications of this zest constantly pushed new limits within the Brazilian marketplace. Most of the billboards featured bikini-clad women and men—this is Brazil, remember—and many were simply lascivious.

It is said that at the end of every month, millions of Brazilian men stuck in traffic would be found ogling massive billboards at main intersections and ads on the sides of buses. The end of the month is when the Brazilian edition of *Playboy* always advertised its next cover. And there it would be, in its full glory: a threesome of thong-clad stewardesses, a Rio beach babe posing au naturel, or a well-known soap star in a topless (but tasteful!) pose. What many US states force *Playboy* to wrap up and conceal, Brazilian publishers were splashing on massive billboards 100 meters (330 ft) long. The city may not have been just the metropolis inspiration in *Blade Runner*. It could've been Babylon too.

But not any more. That was the old São Paulo. The new São Paulo is very different.

In 2007, the populist right-wing mayor of the fourth-largest city in the world instituted a total ban on out-of-home (OOH) media. No outdoor signs. No posters. No outdoor ads, period. Mayor Gilberto Kassab called his city's onslaught of street-level product and brand promotion "visual pollution." And much as noise pollution, water pollution, and air pollution could diminish the quality of life for the city dweller, so the pollution of commercial messaging had begun to oppress the populace.

In response he outlawed outdoor ads. He had over 15,000 billboards in the city taken down. It is estimated that advertisers lost more than 1 million display opportunities in São Paulo. The mayor made leaflet distribution illegal. He criminalized postering. No ads on buses. No sandwich boards on the sidewalks. No posters of upcoming movie premieres or album launches.

No neon on restaurants. And storefront signage—the words that let people know what business you are in—had to be really, really tiny. Shops have to limit their signs to 1.5 meters (five ft) per every 10 meters (33 ft) of frontage.*

The elimination of "visual pollution" was radical by any measure. But the mayor thought it was necessary for the benefit of the city. And remarkably, over 70 percent of *paulistanos* agreed with him.

In an NPR interview, Vinicius Galvão, a reporter for *Folha de São Paulo*, Brazil's largest newspaper, explained the almost immediate effect of the ban: "São Paulo's a very vertical city. That makes it very frenetic. You couldn't even realize the architecture of the old buildings, because all the buildings, all the houses were just covered with billboards and logos and propaganda. And there was no criteria. And now it's amazing. They uncovered a lot of problems the city had that we never realized. For example, there are some *favelas*, which are the shantytowns. I wrote a big story in my newspaper today that in a lot of parts of the city we never realized there was a big shantytown. People were shocked because they never saw that before, just because there were a lot of billboards covering the area."[1]

It is hard to imagine how an entire slum can be hidden by hoardings, placards, billboards, and corrugated posters. The *favelas* are unmistakable in the vast urban landscape of São Paulo, an archipelago of poverty and destitution randomly strewn through an ever-expanding sea of modernity. My *paulistano* friend, a great-natured twenty-something chap named Reggie, would not accept responsibility for my well-being and refused to go into the slums with me. He would rather show off

---

* In his book *Ogilvy on Advertising* (New York: Vintage, 1983), legendary ad man David Ogilvy prophesized more than 25 years ago that billboards would eventually be abolished.

the wealth and beauty of a neighborhood like Jardins, where the lack of advertisements opened up beautiful, tree-lined streets flanked by the latest and trendiest fashion boutiques. He would rather get us into a taxi to see the Das Lu mall, where one can stroll in and buy a helicopter.

Admittedly, the lack of advertisements around a picturesque neighborhood like Jardins—named for its abundance of flora, mansions, and tree shade—and its neighboring downtown and financial center does transform the experience of being there. The absence of advertisements is palpable to a casual observer, and downright stunning to an ad man like myself. It is, dare I say, liberating. In the São Paulo streets, the yoke of consumerism has loosened considerably.

Without the constant barrage of ads and visual pollution, Reggie explained, his everyday behavior has changed for the better. For instance, when he was running to class and had a thirst, the ads along his commute would remind him to buy a Coke. Now, he grabs an all-natural juice from one of the thousands of corner fruit vendors in the city. He notices architecture more now, and has uncovered shortcuts he never knew existed in the back streets of the urban behemoth. Most of all, Reggie said, he can breathe a little easier for some reason. Perhaps visual pollution is nothing to sneeze at after all.

Blame It on the Ads

The mayor of São Paulo may have had visual pollution to blame for his crackdown on outdoor media, but the central government of China had a reality check in mind when it began tearing down billboards in Beijing—the fourteenth-largest city in the world by population. The reason was simply and outrageously Communist: too many billboards touting luxury goods and high-end housing were "using exaggerated terms that encourage luxury and self-indulgence which are beyond the reach of low-income groups and are therefore not conductive to harmony in the capital."[2]

What an excuse to ban advertising! If this reasoning were applied to American ads it would drive the entire industry out of business.* And yet here was a government kicking the stuffing out of the out-of-home advertising industry. Of course, one must recognize that Chinese monolithic state rule makes such dictums easy to pass. And this is precisely why the São Paulo ban is so significant.

The giant Nestlé logo on top of the company's Brazilian offices is gone. Microsoft's headquarters is indistinguishable from the myriad other drab corporate buildings in the city, since there is no big sign to announce the world's best-known company. São Paulo's new law dictates that no sign may be more than five meters (16 ft) off the ground, whether on the side of a building or on poles, like McDonald's golden arches.

But the ban in São Paulo was not rubber stamped by an aging Politburo; it was an overwhelmingly popular move by a shrewd, up-and-coming politician with eyes for a larger pulpit. The mayor is no dummy. He still has some city advertising to dole out. In fact, spared from the draconian ban was the media of street furniture controlled by the city: bus shelters, public toilets, and newsstands being the most prevalent. Over 14,000 of these installations are still controlled by the city of São Paulo, and the bidding for a 20-year contract on those pieces of street furniture went up as soon as the ban went into effect.

A lot of politicians around the world are singing the praises (and copying the strategy) of mayor Gilberto Kassab. Other cities

---

* The Beijing Municipal Committee of the Chinese People's Political Consultative Conference, China's top advisory body, has proposed that advertisements should not overstate wealth and luxury.

in Brazil are exploring the option of imposing similar bans. The mayor of Buenos Aires is contemplating legislation as well—so far, he has already removed over 40,000 billboards, amounting to 60 percent of total outdoor advertising, from the beautiful city. Moreover, it was reported in June 2007 that the mayor of Moscow was mulling over a ruling to outlaw advertising in the Russian capital, the fastest-growing metropolis in the world.* The Norwegian town of Bergen outlaws outdoor advertising. In the United States, although Maine, Vermont, Hawaii, and Alaska are the only four states that ban outdoor advertising, cities like San Francisco and Austin are exploring similar prohibitions. In the United States alone, 1,500 towns have bans on outdoor advertising.[3] Quebec City is set to phase out all billboards in the next five years. The honorable mayor of São Paulo is a widely copied politician.

Almost fittingly, the law that Kassab signed into effect—the so-called Clean City Act—was inaugurated on April 1. Far from being a joke, the law was meant to be "a complete change of culture" for the city, a beacon for new urban planning and social activism. It was certainly seen as a new development in the rights of consumers to block out commercial messaging, and interestingly, it created the impetus for the traditional agencies to get more innovative. As one creative director for an Omnicom shop explained, "There is one thing the ban has brought . . . People at all the agencies are thinking about how to develop outdoor media that do not interfere so much in the physical structure of the city."[4]

The sentiment went a little further with Robert Weissman, managing director of Commercial Alert, a consumer rights watchdog in the United States. According to him, "advertising is so pervasive in the outdoor environment, so our perspective is

---

* Rumors of an impending decision forced News Corporation to sell its stake in News Outdoor Russia.

that things that push back, restrict or restrain outdoor advertising is good. [Bans] make the public landscape more enjoyable, less cluttered and essentially more public in nature. They enable more civic interaction and civic claims to space rather than commercial points."

Yeah, well, maybe. But in any case, a billboard ban will not occur in the United States of America. The laws on commercial expression and small business protection are too entrenched for a maverick American politician to challenge. And many Brazilian marketers, for that matter, didn't panic when the outdoor ban came into effect. Most Brazilian product introductions and branding is done on TV. Still, for global outdoor media companies like Clear Channel Communication and JCDecaux, the ban in a city like São Paulo is something to not take lightly.

Out and About: The New OOH

Let's not discount the importance of outdoor media in emerging economies. Indian marketers rely on murals in small towns and villages to convey both the product promise and the way to use it. Pictorial stories about hygiene and cellular service presented on wall-sized billboards are a staple in India and Pakistan. For hyper-developing urban centers like Mumbai and Moscow, outdoor advertising is a highly effective mechanism to reach a potential consumer. Especially when you're bumper to bumper.

Hey, traffic is traffic. It's the same everywhere. In Canada for instance—surely a stretch from Calcutta or São Paulo—the Out-of-Home Marketing Association says that urbanites spend an average of 9.3 hours outside the home on a weekday and 6.2 hours on a weekend day. During that time, they are exposed to 3.8 hours of advertising on a weekday and 4.7 hours on a Saturday or Sunday: "That's more exposure in a week to out-of-home than to ads delivered by TV, Internet, radio, newspaper and magazines."[5]

OOH is an eyeball business. And it works. Nothing is better at getting people to look at an ad (how are you going to TiVo the billboard when you are stuck in gridlock?) than out-of-home media. It is the second fastest-growing ad segment, behind only the Internet. In 2006, it grew at an impressive 8 percent clip to reach $6.8 billion in the United States, according to the Outdoor Advertising Association of America.[6] The overall ad business could scramble up only 4 percent growth. In fact, across the world, out-of-home media is a booming business as more people move into cities and begin to drive cars or take public transportation. The OOH market is expected to hit $30 billion by 2010 worldwide.[7]

Plenty of creativity is applied to out-of-home campaigns. A fine book called *Advertising Is Dead, Long Live Advertising* presents a near-future for mainstream advertising that leans heavily on the outdoor media scene for inspiration and activation. Will Collin, founding partner at Naked Communications, writes in the book's foreword that "advertisers can no longer rely on consumers to behave like the passive receivers they once were. We are harder to pin down, more demanding, less predictable. So professionals have responded by looking for new forms of communication that are more noticeable and that engage with consumers more actively than the mass communication of old . . . By harnessing our natural curiosity for surprising new forms of communication, brands are compensating for the declining impact of traditional advertising."

Many techniques for new forms of communication have been blossoming with the explosion of the OOH marketplace. One can't help but wonder whether the medium is growing because of the creative executions for it, or because ad agencies are becoming more adept at using the medium as it grows into a viable communication channel. Among the techniques is one called "intrusion," which makes use of places and objects to carry a brand's message. France's Carrefour shopping marts marketed their books in the grocery sections. For instance, a copy of *Snow White* was merchandised in the apple produce section, a book about *Jack the Ripper* was next to the butcher, and a copy of *Moby Dick* was displayed in the seafood aisle. Physical spaces can be altered to deliver branded communication, as Mini has done by installing a photo of its car next to an oversized phone book or newspaper box, driving the point home about its diminutive nature.

Street installations have become effective tools to create branded environments, as when Ikea began installing life-sized and seemingly working living rooms and bedrooms on street corners and billboards across the globe. Publicity stunts use the outdoor arena to cause widespread gawking and buzz, a technique Virgin's Richard Branson has perfected. GMR Marketing staged a vertical catwalk—a real fashion show on the side of a building 10 storeys high—for the grand reopening of Marshall Field's department store in Chicago. OOH media is becoming increasingly interactive as well, with creative applications inviting passersby to press a button, pull a lever, or text a short code. Solo, a national telco brand in Canada, promoted the launch of its walkie-talkie phones by connecting bus stop shelters in Montreal, Toronto, and Vancouver to each other with the actual phones. People would push a button and be randomly connected to another bus shelter across the country.

Clearly, brands are using OOH media to make statements, generate massive publicity, and garner bragging rights against their competition. Jim Beam partnered with the Rio All-Suite Hotel and Casino in Las Vegas to place a 32,000-square-foot (10,000 m²) ad on the side of the hotel to celebrate National Bourbon Heritage Month. The ad covered 40 storeys of the hotel. Advertising space is now being sold by Ad-Air for ads that cover more than three football fields. Measuring more than 60,000 square feet (18,000 m²), the ads will be placed on the grounds around the world's busiest airports, including those in Heathrow, Abu Dhabi, Tokyo, Los Angeles, and Atlanta. Passengers with nothing to look at on take-off or landing will be able to make out the ads from thousands of feet away. Marketers can take advantage of "clutter-free environments and moments free of any other commercial messages" to reach flyers with their own.[8]

Clearly, out-of-home media is an increasingly integral part of a marketer's arsenal. The medium is essentially the same all over the world and can be greatly effective with top-notch creative and placement. Furthermore, as digital technology revolutionizes the medium, the growth of out-of-home will only continue its rapid ascent. Imagine when all the world's billboards look and function like big LCD screens or jumbotrons. Each message can be easily changed by the minute through a digital network that manages the communication for thousands of brands and businesses. Throw in Bluetooth technology—so the billboard can interact and interface with a mobile device—and you have a veritable advertising revolution. Advertising is dead. Long live advertising. Indeed.

So, if out-of-home media is so important to the future of advertising, why ban it in São Paulo? The city is a business hub for the country. Over a third of all ad spending in Brazil goes down in São Paulo, followed by 14 percent in Rio.[9] So why would you neuter it with an outdoor ad ban? Because the sheer number of messages had reached a tipping point.

Admittedly, many of the posters and flyers in São Paulo had been posted illegally. It is easy for a marketer to hire a street team in the slums and *favelas* of the city. The thousands of street urchins and Ronaldhino wannabes could within hours blanket an entire neighborhood with flyers for dubious offers. Above-board campaigns therefore needed to crowd out the DIY pamphleteering, and so added to the message overload.

The visual pollution in São Paulo became unbearable, and the mayor decided to clean it up. Some *paulistanos* grumble that he just wanted the revenue from fines levied on companies, ad firms, and shops that disobeyed the regulations: within a year of the law, over $8 million in fines had been collected. Monetary motivations aside, the municipality of São Paulo showed the world that visual pollution caused by out-of-home media could be synonymous with the mental pollution caused by advertising media in general.

Faith Popcorn, an astute futurist and consumer consultant, has almost prophetically predicted paradigm shifts in consumer behavior and social trends, especially for kids, teens, and young adults. "Like the movement to combat environmental pollution, the next consumer-led reaction will be against the mental pollution caused by marketers," she said. "With every corner of the world—both real and virtual—becoming plastered with marketing messages, bombarded consumers are starting to say they've had enough. The current attack on marketing to kids is just the beginning."[10]

Advertising Age estimates that the average consumer sees anywhere between 254 and 5,000 commercial messages each day. That's a pretty wide range, a spectrum so broad that only a magazine devoted to promoting the ad industry could pull it off. And yet without taking the low end too seriously, an average of 3,000 or more commercial messages a day is a fairly shocking amount. The staggering number of competing messages coming from ever-increasing sources—online, in-game ads, SMS messages, taxi cabs, virtual worlds, in-store POS, radio, TV, print, outdoor, coffee cups, dry cleaning bags, your best friend being paid to tell you about Netflix—is perhaps, just perhaps, causing an epidemic in mental pollution, the so-called problem of clutter gripping the advertising business in North America and abroad.

Let's take a few more examples of the marketing clutter that pollutes the mental environment, from the January–February 2007 issue of *Mother Jones* magazine:

- The 2005 season of NBC's reality show *The Contender* had 7,502 instances of product placement—adding up to 11 hours and 57 minutes of screen time.
- CBS hired a company called EggFusion to print its eyeball logo on 35 million eggs.
- Clear Channel radio, the largest radio conglomerate in the United States, has started to air one-second (yes, one second) ad spots called "blinks."
- After Israel bombed the Lebanese infrastructure in an escalation of violence with an Islamist organization, Johnny Walker put up billboards in Beirut that depicted a broken bridge with the slogan "Keep Walking" next to it. A spokesperson for the brand said the ad was meant to "capture a popular mood about moving forward."
- In the top 20 chart-topping songs of 2005, Mercedes-Benz was mentioned 100 times, Nike 63, Cadillac 62, Bentley 51, and Rolls-Royce 46.
- Wizmark's Interactive Urinal Communicator plays 10-second commercial messages to the "ever-elusive targeted male audience you are constantly aiming for."
- In 2005, Target bought all the ad space in the August 22 issue of *New Yorker* magazine; its logo appears more than 1,200 times in the issue.
- In 2008, the Chinese central government promised a vigorous crackdown on mobile phone spam after seven ad agencies sent unsolicited commercial messages to half of China's cell phone population—about 350 million people.[11]

And the more of it, the more people start noticing. Just like smog in L.A., mental pollution is a shared burden. As *Advertising Age* heroically pointed out, "Attempts to beat clutter only end up yielding more of it, a bitter irony bound to have dire consequences for a business already struggling with questions of relevance and effectiveness. Put simply, the ad business is crushing itself under the weight of its own messaging, squeezing the effectiveness out of its product as consumers get more and more inured to the commercialization of their culture and surroundings."[12]

And perhaps therein lies the abstract definition of a person suffering from "mental pollution": someone who is inured to the commercialization of their culture and surroundings. And much like a true epidemic, the problem is certain to accelerate precipitously. As advertisers find their audience more and more discombobulated by the ad barrage—a situation leading to a lower recall rate for advertisements—they decide to increase the barrage, hoping to break through. And the cycle continues.[*]

The most conspicuous sector of mental pollution, according to the mayor of São Paulo, was the visual one. Out-of-home media was something everyone had to put up with, so it would be the first to go. The question, of course, is: What contributor to mental pollution will be targeted next?

There are certainly myriad contenders. In our zeal to reach elusive consumers, marketers and advertisers alike have been inventing, appropriating, and repurposing media channels and technology to deliver branded messaging at any possible moment and place: online branded videos, in-store TV networks, lobby elevator screens, TV and film product placements, cellular ads,

---

[*] Nearly 80 percent of Asians believe there should be more regulations and limitations on what is communicated. The figure rises to over 95 percent in China, where mistrust is high. Comparable figures in the West average only 68 percent (Vivian Wai-yin Kwok, "China Looks into the Case of the Mobile Spam," Forbes, 24 March 2008).

sponsored events, online search, video games, street furniture, and interactive billboards. Overall, a total of 18 of these emerging channels—now bundled as alternative media—is expected to garner over $160 billion in 2012, up 82 percent from 2008 and accounting for 27 percent of all ad marketing spent in the United States. As one executive stated bluntly, "Americans are spending more time out of the home, working late hours, communicating via wireless devices, shopping in malls and stuck in traffic. There has to be some change in the advertising and marketing strategies to reach these people."[13]

Depressing ontology aside, this statement does seem to drive the incredible growth of alternative media channels, all accumulating in a messaging din never heard before by the modern consumer. The cumulative effect of the new and increasingly savvy ways that advertisers will reach billions of global consumers is bound to amplify calls for a curb on the prevalence of visual and mental pollution.[*]

Brazilian Bellwether

In a *Wall Street Journal* article, John Borthwick, CEO of Fotolog and a former top technology executive at Time Warner Inc. and AOL, called Brazil "a leading indicator of future trends." Brazil is well known in media circles as an early adopter of new technology and digital social networking tools. Moreover, ZenithOptimedia ranks Brazil as the seventh-largest online advertising market

---

[*] One interesting measure of visual pollution is the number of stars in the nighttime sky that can be seen by the naked eye. One common measure rates the darkness of the sky on a scale of one to nine, with one as the darkest. Galileo's sky was a one. New York City is a nine. The typical US suburb is between five and seven. Standing on top of the Empire State Building on a clear night, one would see only 1 percent of what Galileo would have seen with the naked eye (The Next Wave, 24 September 2007, www.thenextwave.biz).

in the world.[14] This is a country that incubates social networking trends and properties. For instance, Microsoft estimates that Brazilians account for 12 percent of all users of MSN Messenger—more than any other country. Orkut, the country's most popular social networking site, is the fifth-most visited site in the world, behind Yahoo, MySpace, Google, and Facebook.[15] Interestingly, it is popular only in Brazil, unlike the global dominance of the other behemoths. In Brazil, Orkut has simply dominated the social network space, with 15.6 billion page views every month.

So if Brazil is such a bellwether for major social networking tools, could it also promulgate an entirely new way to deal with mental pollution? Why not? If São Paulo can outlaw outdoor ads, why couldn't Paris outlaw corporate sponsorships of events and venues, something that is valued at more than $33 billion in the United States?[16] Why couldn't London work with telecom companies and handset manufacturers to severely restrict ads on cell phones, something that the Chinese government is threatening to do?

The lessons marketers learn from experiences in hyper-developing marketplaces like Brazil and its marketing hub of São Paulo should not simply be about finding new ways to reach hyper-consumers. They should also include the realization that these emerging markets could be windows into the future of a massive consumer revolt against brands and companies that are perceived to be major contributors to the mental pollution of a marketplace. A consumer-led corrective reaction to ever-intrusive marketing is not only possible, it is a hard reality in the world's fourth-largest city.

A landmark survey published by Yankelovich Partners in 2004 found that 65 percent of consumers believed more regulations and limits should be imposed on marketing because they were "constantly bombarded with too much advertising," and 61 percent thought that advertising was "out of control." Clutter, product placement, and publicity stunts were named as the primary reasons for this dissatisfaction, leading 60 percent of poll takers to state that their view of advertising was "much more negative than just a few years ago."[17] These figures are hard to ignore, and yet so many marketers continue to ignore them. If consumers are cynical about our messages and put up higher barriers, marketers reason, then more extreme efforts are needed to break through.

One of the first pundits to bring attention to the excesses of marketing and the social impact of mental pollution was writer, thinker, and activist Bill McKibben. Writing in the anti-consumption and anti-corporate magazine *Adbusters* in late 2001, he expounded,

> The modern consumer economy sends up an almost infinite blitz of information and enticement, till the air is so thick with it that every feature of our society is changed. It is not pollution in the usual sense, easily cleaned with a smokestack filter or combated with a more wholesome image. Instead, it's a volume problem. In the case of the so-called information society, it may be the largest psychological experiment in history.

> Here's another way of saying it: We are the first few generations to receive most of our senses of the world mediated rather than direct, to have it arrive through one screen or another instead of from contact with other human beings or with nature.

> So far, in one sense, this experiment is working. That is, people manage to consume more stuff with each passing year, keeping the economy expanding. And

since nations have taken that expansion as their sole goal ("It's the economy, stupid.") we count this as a success. In fact, we now spread this experiment around the world, by persuasion and by force. And yet by most other measures, cracks are appearing. Just as the physical world is sending warning signals about rising temperatures (disappearing glaciers, more powerful storms, changing migration patterns), so the culture is sending ever-louder signals about the side-effects of this experiment."[18]

Clearly, the cultural signals coming from the forces working to curtail mental pollution are hard to ignore for marketers and consumers alike. The São Paulo outdoor ban is a harbinger of other steps to come around the world. In the UK, the promotion of QSR (quick service restaurant) food to children under 16 is banned. The anti-obesity lobby has successfully banned one of the most famous TV ad slogans in Britain: "Go to work on an egg." The UK's ad clearance board refused to run the 50-year-old slogan for the British Egg Information Service because "eating an egg every day was not nutritionally sound."[19] In Sweden, no advertising to children under 12 is allowed. No advertising at all. Imagine how Disney or Nickelodeon must feel about that kind of law.

Russia, one of the world's top markets for cigarettes, is threatening to ban all tobacco advertising comprehensively. According to Nielsen Media Research, more than 300 billion cigarettes are sold each year in the country, accounting for about $10 billion in sales. This massive market has been thriving despite the fact that Russia had already banned all cigarette advertising on TV, radio, and out-of-home in 2002. The cigarette brands figured out other ways to market their products, enough to grow sales by 4 percent year over year.[20]

In early 2008, the French president—in a move to benefit his private media mogul friends as well as appease anti-commercial groups—banned all advertisements from national TV stations in the name of a "cultural revolution in public service television."[21] In all cases, the underlying hymn from the activists who cajoled or forced governments into action was predicated on the notion of curtailing mental pollution.

The curtailment is most often a government-sanctioned or -directed action. Throughout the world, the ad industry has been on the defensive for certain product categories, like tobacco, and for media channels like TV and out-of-home. Some European states are mulling over the ban on personal loan ads, in an effort to address the hot topic of consumer debt and the housing crisis. In China, all "sexually suggestive" ads have been banned from TV and radio because they are considered harmful to society.

Imagine that! Imagine if "sexually suggestive" advertising was pulled from network and cable TV in the United States. What would the ad industry be left with? To paraphrase the latest tagline from Dunkin' Donuts—America runs on Dunkin'—American media runs on porn and violence. But as implausible as it seems for the US market, a similar ban on ad detritus in Europe or South America isn't so improbable.

China has also made domestic websites sign a "voluntary" pact to exercise self-censorship in order to ensure "a healthy and orderly cyberspace."[22] The Chinese government, it seems, wants to eradicate porn and violence from the Internet. (Good luck with that.) It has already launched a national campaign to limit the hours teenagers spend online playing games. Under the new rules, Chinese Internet gaming companies must install code into the game that requires players to enter an ID card number. After three hours, players under 18 are prompted to stop playing and instead "do suitable physical exercise."* If they continue, the new software cuts in half any points earned in the game. All points are deleted if the underage player keeps playing for more than five hours. China's two largest online gaming portals, The9 and Tencent, have implemented the screening software.

The Mental Pollution Solution

At the 2008 annual conference for the Promotional Marketing Association, a keynote speech warned the marketing industry of the regulatory crackdown that invariably comes in times of economic downturn, as state and federal administrators and politicians look to recoup lost tax revenue by fining companies that overpromise, overclaim, underdeliver, or egregiously add to the mental pollution of the populace. The media-savvy mayor of São Paulo was certainly playing populist politics to curry favor with overwhelmed and fed-up *Paulistanos*. The same could be said of cash-strapped governors and federal district attorneys looking for a bit of national airtime and the support of the constituency. Who wouldn't applaud a ban on spam or street posters?

Kalle Lasn, the founder of *Adbusters* and author of the books *Culture Jam* and *Design Anarchy*, describes the current consumer culture very convincingly. "Our mental environment is a common-property resource like the air or the water," he explains. "We need to protect ourselves from unwanted incursions into it, much the same way that we lobbied for non-smoking areas 10 years ago." When anti-consumerism is tied to both environmentalism and public health, it is clear to see how populist the notion of mental pollution can become.

---

* The government explanation for the three-hour cut-off is that it is based on the time it takes to play an archetypal chess-like game called Go.

Furthermore, the effects from the political expediency of cracking down on thriving marketing practices and emerging ad media are exacerbated by the seemingly self-defeating reasoning employed by the ad industry. Steve Hall, the founder of industry-gadfly blog *Adrants*, puts the current state of the industry thus: "In some respects, advertising is a never-ending cycle of idiocy. People ignore ads so marketers just create more. People block ads so marketers just come up with more methods to circumvent that blockage. Most of us just ignore the proliferation of advertising and go on with our daily lives. Others fight back by creating anti-advertising cause groups that aim to point out the proliferation of ad creep insanity . . . There's really no end to this cycle. Marketers need to sell stuff so they advertise. People don't want to be over-loaded by commercial messages so they will do what they can to avoid them. It's that simple. So the battle rages on."[23]

It's unclear when and how a winner will be declared. However, it is safe to say that the battle can only get hotter. Without delving into the anti-consumer movements and the anti-brand activists who sustain them, the tactics employed against mainstream brands are becoming increasingly sophisticated. "Buy Nothing Day" is a massive social statement against hyper-consumerism that has grown in reaction to the proliferation of digital media, social networks, and mobile technology. Activist "flash mobs" can be organized practically instantaneously using text messaging, to "hijack" a store or marketing campaign.*

In the case of billboards and other out-of-home media, the obvious weapon is the spray paint can. For billboard media companies and brand marketers who thought the graffiti problem would

---

* A tactic called "shopdropping" is in effect the opposite of shoplifting. Culture jammers surreptitiously place products that resemble the real thing into the displays and racks of retail stores. Along with fake bar codes and altered tags, these dropped products are meant to derail the checkout and inventory process of the store and cause havoc for the low-paid staff.

go away with the advent of digital billboards, a hijacker codenamed Skullphone has single-handedly kept them up at night with his shenanigans. At the beginning of 2008, Skullphone was the number-one enemy of Clear Channel Communication in southern California because he had managed to hack into 10 of the most prominent and lucrative digital billboards around L.A. He (or she) inserted a digital calling card—a skull talking on a cell phone—between the array of movie, TV, and auto company ads that make up the normal advertising displayed on the giant digital boards. By hacking into Clear Channel's most lucrative and forward-thinking medium, Skullphone created his (or her) own brand. The irony of such culture jamming is inescapable: adulterating commercial advertisements in order to advertise a personal brand.

But let's take another example of creative billboard usage. Let's see how a medium vilified in Brazil can be lauded in France, and how a campaign to eradicate billboards can be counteracted by the creative employed on them.

In 2007, the top prize for the Outdoor Category at the Cannes Lions International Advertising Festival—which highlights the best ad work on the planet—went to a billboard campaign done in South Africa. Specifically, the top prize, called the Grand Prix, went to a billboard, just one billboard, tucked away from the bustling commercial downtown of Johannesburg in a low-income neighborhood called Alexandria. The Cannes jury decided that this particular billboard, created by Network BBDO, "was more than advertising" and displayed the type of "corporate responsibility and advertising that supports social responsibility." The jury awarded the Grand Prix because it wanted to set a creative example for the future of the industry.

The white billboard was created for a local bank called NedBank. It displayed one line of copy: "What if a bank really did give power to the people?" Solar panels around the billboard collected enough energy to power several community buildings around it, including a schoolhouse. The billboard, and therefore the bank, literally *did* give power to the people.

The solar panels also happen to feed power directly into the kitchens of the MC Weiler School in Alexandria, on whose property the billboard rests. Because of the bank's billboard, the school saves about $300 each month, which it can then put toward feeding 1,100 kids every day. In other words, with one simple idea for a billboard, NedBank has introduced an entirely new way for a financial brand to make a public and measurable contribution to "good" while still communicating a highly relevant and contextual brand message. "Why shouldn't advertising pioneer ways of putting something back into the community?" asked Mike Schalit, creative chief at Network BBDO.[24]

This single billboard will continue to give off power. This piece of out-of-home media is now an integral part of the community. At a time when marketers are fixated on short-term promotions, NedBank's billboard—and tagline—will extend its presence in that community for years. And the community, as well as all the other poor neighborhoods in a hyper-growing urban city center, will always connote the NedBank brand as something that does indeed give power to the people.

Interestingly, the contest for the Grand Prix was quite intense. The runner-up billboard campaign was called "Liberator/ Occupier," produced by BBDO New York for BBC World. The billboard featured a single photo of a platoon of US soldiers on patrol in (presumably) Iraq. Flanking the image on either side were two words: "Liberator" and "Occupier." Beneath each title was a giant LCD counter, with a short code for people to text message displayed next to it. Much like the voting on *American Idol*, passersby in Times Square could text in their vote—Liberator or Occupier— and the billboard would keep a running tally of votes. The same creative thematic and vote-by-text mechanic was applied on other billboards: to a photo of the Chinese flag ("Befriend" or "Beware"), a photo of the culling of bird-flu-infected poultry ("Imminent" or "Preventable"), and a shot of Mexican laborers confronted by US border officials ("Citizens" or "Criminals").

This piece of outdoor creative shows how new technologies and appropriation of mobile communication allow greater engagement between brand and consumer, marketer and audience. Both billboard creatives are experiential in nature, for both deliver a relevant and visceral experience through the media. The experience is the message, if you will. For the BBC creative execution, mobile technology made the passive medium of a flat billboard into a shared experience and a personal forum for consumers, and clearly showed a media brand as covering both sides of the issues facing our world. The NedBank campaign was experiential as well—extremely so—because it literally delivered a clear and meaningful benefit. And as a popular *Advertising Age* article pointed out at the tail end of 2007, "Consumers are willing to pay more for purchases from a company they know to be doing good."[25]

In fact, we as consumers are willing to pay, on average, a 6 percent premium for a product we see as doing good. As the article points out, "Good corporate citizenship takes many forms, ranging from charitable funds derived from sales of a particular product to progressive corporate policies. However, the consumer does not distinguish among the many terms marketers use to describe a company's efforts to be a force for positive change: corporate social responsibility, pro-social marketing, cause marketing. For her, they all fall under the rubric of doing Good."[26]

It is significant for the advertising industry that companies that market their good credentials to their consumers and potential consumers are better able to reap the rewards of being a socially responsible brand. This notion certainly applies to

T-shirt brand American Apparel, which has combined committed and transparent social altruism with sexy advertising to become the third-largest T-shirt maker in the United States after Hanes and Fruit of the Loom in less than a decade. Whirlpool has partnered with Habitat for Humanity since 1999 through employee participation programs and appliance donations—two appliances for every home built by Habitat for Humanity. When consumers were made aware of the partnership between brand and cause, brand loyalty increased an average of 160 percent. Yoplait uses its packaging for an experience-based campaign with its Save Lids to Save Lives program: for every pink lid consumers send back to the company, Yoplait donates 10 cents to a breast cancer cure foundation. So far, this single program has raised more than $18 million for the breast cancer cause.[27]

The NedBank billboard is rightly a Grand Prix winner, for it simultaneously does something good and tells people about it. It is a committed campaign, and experiential in its benefit to the consumers it is trying to engage. It is causal and it is buzz worthy. And if this idea had been introduced in São Paulo instead of Johannesburg, would the mayor have taken a second look at the mental pollution claims that framed the ban debate?

Maybe. Maybe not.

But a significant number of marketers, advertisers, and creatives are taking a second look at the way brands are being communicated in the marketplace. The radical move in São Paulo has only reinforced that "branded utility" must be inherent in progressive marketing.

One of the promulgators of "branded utility" is Benjamin Palmer, cofounder of Boston-based progressive digital shop Barbarian Group. This shop is leading the charge for an entirely new way of looking at the brand-to-consumer relationship by developing digital applications and campaigns that are truly "first-ever." To him, branded utility occurs when "the brand creates a commitment to a relationship. It's where the brand creates something useful to you, something that's a utility in your life. The consumer will feel more confident with the relationship if the brand will continue to be part of your life. Branding has been about cultural relevance," he states. "What we're saying is that it's not so much about relevance as usefulness. Brand messages need to be in a useful format." Would this argument convince the São Paulo municipality, and the *paulistanos* who were fed up with non-utilitarian brand messaging? "The key is to create something that is of fundamental difference," he continues. "Not making more spin." Tellingly, Palmer is considered a maverick in the ad business.[28]

Simply put, a marketing experience that doesn't deliver an inherent benefit to the consumer—physically, emotionally, viscerally, or mentally—may never be accepted. If there is no brand utility to the campaign, then it's just more white noise and clutter. More important, if consumer experiences are the next big battleground for customers and their loyalty, then companies cannot afford to engage in unbeneficial experiences. Adding to the clutter will only turn more people off.

Another star in the new agency world is Johnny Vulcan of New York–based Anomaly, a channel-agnostic and idea-centric planning agency that is at the forefront of the new marketing and advertising landscape emerging from the ashes of the old agency model. Vulcan's perception of the future of marketing centers on the idea that "brands [have to be] genuinely useful to their customers, employees, suppliers and the people they touch . . . [We start] with what would be good for people, then what this brand/product/company do to be a part of that, then how we can help that brand/product/company deliver that. It has led us to get involved in highly technical R&D conversations with our clients and to be present at the birth of new products and intellectual property ... We go far deeper into our client's organizations then we ever used to, and it's not only highly stimulating work, it also leads to fundamentally better solutions."[29]

A Better World Is Better Business

In the case of out-of home media, could a better solution be the one adopted by JCDecaux throughout the world? Has the world's third-largest outdoor media company embraced the notion of brand utility? The Paris-based outdoor media concern, in an effort to win a contract in cities throughout the world, offered mayors and city councils the use of hundreds of thousands of free bicycles in exchange for the cities' outdoor media contracts.

Let the company explain: "Cyclocity is a cost-effective, sustainable transport option that helps minimize the impact of traffic and congestion in towns and cities. The easy-to-use system allows the hire of a bicycle from one location and its return to another. It has proven to be a viable alternative to private vehicles and complementary to public transport."[30] In the offer made to Paris, JCDecaux would set up a bicycle-lending business in exchange for exclusive rights to the city's 1,628 billboards.* In France, JCDecaux's free-bicycle scheme has taken off.

The Cyclocity service in Paris is called Vélib—a word play on *vélo* (bike) and *libre* (free)—and since its inception has provided more than 20,600 bikes at 1,540 stations—or about one station every 250 yards across the entire city. Although longer rides involve a rental fee, most of the bike rides are free for *les Parisiens*.

---

* At the time of the offer, JCDecaux already operated 20,000 bikes in Lyon. A similar offer was also extended to the mayors of Moscow and Chicago, who were seriously considering it.

It is estimated that more than 100,000 rides are conducted every day in the capital, and that more than 4 million people have so far used the bicycles. Cyclocity/Vélib is entirely financed by JCDecaux, which is counting on rental fees from longer rides and the sale of billboard advertising to cover the costs of running such a massive bike service. Clear Channel Communication, its main rival, has set up similar operations in Barcelona. The city pays the media company to run its public bike rental operations, which has more than 6,000 bicycles in use and over 90,000 paying customers.[31]

The Cyclocity concept is modeled on Amsterdam's famous "white bicycle" plan from the sixties, in which idealistic hippies repaired scores of bicycles, painted them white, and left them on the streets for anyone to use for free. But in the end, the bikes were stolen or became too beaten up to ride. However, JCDecaux has been able to create a vandal-proof bike design that is much sturdier than that of typical street bikes. Furthermore, the company is running a rental business, not a commune: Each rider must leave a credit card or refundable deposit of about $195, along with personal information.[32] The company pays all the start-up costs of about $115 million and employs over 280 people full time to operate the system and repair the bikes—for 10 years. All revenue from the program will go to the city, and the company will also pay Paris a fee of about $4.3 million a year.

Despite the seemingly steep price tag, brand utility is a way to build JCDecaux's business. In the outdoor ad industry, because of multiyear city contracts, it is very difficult for a company like JCDecaux or Clear Channel to grow organically. But a strategy to capture share through brand utility is proving to be a stroke of genius for these companies. It may be as simple as public bicycles, but brand utility will become mandatory for companies seeking to capture the sensibilities of both hyper-developing countries and established markets in North America and Europe.

The brand utility strategy goes beyond simple business tactics for acquiring city contracts. The notion is not merely a cynical quid pro quo between governance and capitalism. Cyclocity is a way for the weary and mistrustful consumer to acquiesce to the mental pollution surrounding her. It's a way for JCDecaux to "pay back" city dwellers for the opportunity to direct commercial messages their way. The scheme, again cynically speaking, is a way to offset marketing's clutter footprint, the way polluting corporations can buy credits against their carbon footprint. But so what?* It works. In Lyon, the city's 3,000 rental bikes have logged about 10 million miles (16 million km) since the program started in May 2005, saving an estimated 3,000 tons of carbon dioxide from being spewed into the air. That type of success in curbing air pollution gets a lot of consumers much more comfortable with their mental pollution problems.

Furthermore, the Cyclocity project gets consumers believing in brands again. That's the magic in the bottle for a concept like brand utility. And the growth of alternative marketing—digital, event, experiential, outdoor, and so on—can trigger the necessary growth spurt of campaigns that revolve around the concept. Experiential marketing methodologies and new technological applications to outdoor media will most likely become the main drivers for brand utility, allowing advertising and marketing to transcend themselves and becoming their raison d'être, something that traditional media like TV and print simply can't pull itself to do.

Take, for instance, the city of New Orleans in the aftermath of Hurricane Katrina. After a natural disaster devastated the area, bureaucratic disaster stepped in to finish the job. The total and almost treasonous failure of the federal government to deal with

---

* A suburb in the city of Manila announced that it would convert its police cars to run on a mixture of diesel and used cooking oil obtained from the city's McDonald's franchises.

the rescue and humanitarian mission should not be forgotten by any Americans, not just our brethren in the wards and towns of Louisiana. It was certainly noticed by the rest of the world as another glitch in the Matrix, a small peek behind the curtain of America's supposed superiority and magnanimity. It was during that time of total inadequacy and ineptitude from the state and federal levels that the private sector decided to step in. The fourth estate poured coverage into the city of New Orleans with almost as much ferocity as the pounding hurricane poured rain into the swollen levees. CEOs and celebrities took out 30- and 60-second spots to offer solace, hope, and community to those affected by the disaster. They added that a sizable corporate contribution would be made to some hastily formed charity.

One brand, however, decided to become utilitarian for the people of New Orleans. That brand is Tide. In less than three weeks, the brand was physically present in the city and directly engaged in doing good things.

The brand's parent, Procter & Gamble, created the Clean Start program, and in doing so transformed the way people in New Orleans will forever remember Tide. The concept was extremely simple: a mobile laundromat placed on the back of a massive semi-truck and driven directly into the hardest-hit areas so that people could wash their clothes. The truck, created by New Hampshire–based Gigunda Group, housed 14 washing machines and 18 dryers, and would run 24 hours a day. The average US family does about 300 loads of laundry each year. The Clean Start truck was averaging 600 loads each day.

But apart from providing clean clothes, the Clean Start program provided dignity. Everyone who brought in their dirty and moldy clothes would return the next day to find them neatly bundled, wrapped, tied off, and signed off for pick-up. The care with which the clothes were washed and packaged spoke volumes about the care the brand had for the people of New Orleans.

Once the mood in New Orleans shifted from survival to reconstruction, the hierarchy of needs shifted from food, shelter, and safety toward dignity, hope, and self-esteem. The program transcended utility. It became a symbol of humanity. After all the promise and bluster from politicians and corporate donors, what will the people who experienced the Clean Start program remember most? And what about their friends, cousins, and coworkers? What will they think about when told of Tide's campaign? Will they think it was a symptom of mental pollution? I think not. And I guarantee you that all the thousands of people who experienced the brand campaign will never buy anything but Tide detergent.

Let's state the obvious: this is a truck campaign. It's no blockbuster TV commercial or celebrity endorsement. It's simply a bunch of washers and dryers on a truck. As Ryan FitzSimons, founder of Gigunda Group told me, "The idea behind the Clean Start program was to put the brand in ultimate proof-point environments—the epicenter of dirt and destruction—for the sole mission of delivering dignity and delight." Wherever the Clean Start truck is needed—for example, near the wildfires that ravaged the residential areas of San Diego the following year—consumers now find the Tide brand. How awesome is that?

This type of marketing fearlessness will be at the heart of future campaigns. It will be something that consumers demand from the brands that are trying to reach them. And it will be a major brand differentiator in increasingly competitive goods and services segments.

But above that, we want marketers to realize our mutual humanity. We want branding campaigns to be more than hype, spin, or pithy slogan. We want substance over style. We want marketing to deliver on its promise of making the world a slightly better place to live.

Sadly, it takes disasters and calamities to get the industry talking about its evolution. After the September 11 tragedy, many marketers and economists began talking about charity and community in earnest, not just as a marketing ploy but as a realignment of corporate values. Writing in *Marketing* magazine shortly after the attacks, business ethics consultant John Dalla Costa declared that "all of our learning about brand equity has taught us that great brands are not the product of marketing alone, but of operations and culture, of designers and manufacturing people, of sales and service support. Brands live in companies, express their companies to customers, and are carriers of vision and values. If companies are going to become as focused on human development as on profits, and on social impacts as on competitive positioning, then by necessity if not by default brands, too, will become catalysts for human development and conduits for community building."[33] If brands are to assume this stance, then the marketing of these brands must do the same.

Dalla Costa organizes the history of brand marketing into five periods. In the 1960s, branding was characterized by awareness and convenience; in the 1970s, branding evolved into parity and pricing; in the 1980s, it was all about quality and status; in the 1990s it was generalized by technology and globalization; and now, "it looks like branding will . . . be about human development and community building."

Emerging markets are coming out of something, in the same way that New Yorkers and other Americans came out of the repercussions of the attack on the World Trade Center and the hurricane that destroyed New Orleans. For hyper-developing countries, that something is very often severe poverty or political repression. These consumers, the people of the hyper-developing world, are all too painfully aware of the hardships they have experienced in the recent past. They are acutely sensitive to the notion that in order for brands to influence their forged sensibilities, they will have to create a clear and meaningful benefit to their existence.

In its own altruistic endeavor, electronics maker Philips took its medical technology to shopping malls in Argentina, Chile, Brazil, and Mexico and offered all pregnant women in the area ultrasounds. The images were captured and sent off by email to family and friends, or printed out on the spot. To some, this may seem like a cynical marketing campaign. But consider that most women in these developing countries had probably never had an ultrasound and had not yet seen their own babies. They had for the first time experienced what we take for granted in most of North America. Of course, Philips was there to market its technology and increase brand awareness, but it did so by providing a clear benefit to the women in those malls.

Successful brands sustain their relevance by discerning, understanding, and delivering what consumers value and prioritize. More often than not, consumers appreciate and prioritize brands that balance their inevitable complicity in mental pollution with a concerted and authentic effort to be a force of good in the lives of their consumers. Consequently, the forward-thinking agencies that serve these brands are also challenging the status quo of mental pollution.

For instance, a campaign called Tap Project, spearheaded by Publicis Groupe–held Droga5—a much-lauded creative agency—is helping (perhaps inadvertently) to undo the decades of branding and brainwashing that have accompanied the $12 billion-a-year bottled water industry. That's right. An agency, along with a number of corporate sponsors, partnered with thousands of restaurants to encourage patrons to donate $1 every time they ordered tap water. The servers who participated in the campaign would explain that the money went to UNICEF efforts to provide clean drinking water for kids in

Third World countries. The idea is both simple and powerful. It immediately makes it clear how good we have it and how consumerist we have become. By suggesting that consumers order tap water instead of the branded and bottled kind, the promotion simply stated the obvious: you have the option to drink regular tap water. The campaign certainly wasn't anti-bottled water; rather, it was an ingenious way to increase awareness of UNICEF efforts to provide water to the wider world. Because of the strong and omnipresent marketing that bottled water brands have employed in recent years, the message was much more potent. Somehow, and certainly without direct intent, Tap Project became an anti-marketing marketing campaign created by an anti-advertising advertising agency.

The unique circumstances behind the campaign deserve mention. As first reported by Stuart Elliot, the long-time advertising columnist for the *New York Times*, the idea for the Tap Project was born out of a feature article that *Esquire* magazine was compiling for its "Best and Brightest" issue for 2006. One of those shining lights to be nominated by the monthly was David Droga, head of Droga5. In order to do the profile, the magazine's editors asked Droga to "show, not tell" how his agency was different from the rest. Droga responded by offering them a campaign to give more drinking water to destitute people across this planet.

The editors were ecstatic. They offered Droga two pages to "pitch" his idea to readers with a couple of print ads for the still-fictional campaign. One ad featured a number of fancy packages and familiar bottle shapes, all branded with a bare-bones label spelling out "N.Y. Tap Water" instead of the expected Perrier, Evian, or Aquafina logos. The tag next to the product shots was "Now with added karma." Another ad with the same photo came with this tagline: "What if every glass of water you drank quenched someone else's thirst?"[34]

The description from the Tap Project website indicates just how powerful the idea has become since the magazine first published it. The success of the Tap Project shows a glimpse of how corporate brands, creative agencies, and private businesses can come together to create paradigm-busting social messages and movements:

> From March 16 to March 22, thousands of patrons visited over 2,350 restaurants in 46 states, all for one unified cause: to help provide clean water to kids around the world.
>
> We are grateful to the over 2,350 restaurants, over 2,200 volunteers, Ambassadors Lucy Liu and Marcus Samulesson, proud national supporter American Express and our many partners, including 13 renowned advertising agencies, *Esquire Magazine*, Turner Broadcasting, Opentable.com, MSN, WASRAG (Water and Sanitation Rotarian Action Group), the Empire State Building, the Sundance Channel and others for joining the Tap Project and helping UNICEF address this critical issue. We hope you enjoyed being a part of the Tap Project and please stay tuned to learn about the amazing results of the campaign.
>
> On behalf of the world's children, thank you for raising your glass of water during World Water Week! We hope you will join us again next year![35]

In Elliot's *Times* article, Droga describes his agency as one in which "our core business is still advertising, but not in the traditional way." And so in crafting a philanthropic cause to encourage drinking tap water, Droga decided to brand tap water just as an ad agency would brand bottled water. In doing so, he created a branded concept that is inherently utilitarian. That's fearless marketing.

So is the marketing that Italian fashion brand Benetton embarked on in early 2008. Remember Benetton? This is the brand that introduced the world in the 1990s to a print and outdoor campaign of controversial, often brutal, and always thought-provoking images of dying AIDS patients, kissing nuns, and death row inmates. The fashion house, a direct influence on fashion brands like American Apparel, is operating in 120 countries and includes the brands United Colors of Benetton, Sisley, Playlife, and Killer Loop. Each year, Benetton turns over about $4 billion and produces about 150 million pieces of clothing.[36]

At the swankiest hotel in Dakar, Senegal, the Italian brand announced a partnership with African superstar Youssou N'Dour to create a micro-financing company called Birima—in honor of a former Senegalese king. Micro-financing is the practice of giving small loans to impoverished people with no credit or collateral. The loans are approved only after a thorough interview of the applicants and an evaluation of the applicant's prospective project or small business plan. To get into the micro-finance business is a groundbreaking move for any company, let alone a fashion-focused one. Although Benetton has never shirked from attaching its brand to shocking global imagery and Third World plight, this is the first time the brand has dived into direct action. This direct action is set to cost it millions of dollars each year, yet this is the business that the brand wants to be in.* It's an experiment for sure, but the scion of the Benetton family wants

---

* Benetton isn't the only big company that is seeing the brand utility future. A March 2008 article in *Advertising Age* titled "Unilever, P&G War over Which Is Most Ethical" began with the following sentence: "Procter & Gamble Co. and Unilever have battled over many things over the decades, from soap shares to spy scandals. But the latest battleground may be the most surprising and intriguing—a race to show who's best at saving the world."

to make a statement for the future of his company. That future includes funding projects, offering hope, and ultimately saving the lives of millions of impoverished Senegalese who have never heard of the brand.

Believe Differently

Brands and companies are increasingly at the mercy of their consumers. Therefore, they must now serve the interests of their core customers—to provide them with a benefit beyond a logo and a product—in order to exist and profit. In fact, we are witnessing a profound change in consumer mindsets and core values. We are beginning to actively reject intrusive, mindless, and me-too marketing campaigns, and in the process, stop supporting the brands that launch them.

At the same time, we as consumers are slowly but surely developing a new belief system that focuses on trying to make our world a better place. Could there be a link here? Certainly, the newfound ability of consumers to block out, customize, or "mash up" the advertising and marketing messages directed toward them confirm that they are evolving into "prosumers"—active and eager participants in a brand's marketing mix. So if consumers are increasingly empowered to influence the way in which companies market to them, they are more confident than ever in thinking that this empowerment can also command, or at least instigate, a brand's involvement in altruistic causes.

That involvement should, in theory, be voluntary. Instead, companies are getting into "cause marketing" because their consumers are asking for it, not because the CEO had a Jerry McGuire moment about rainforest conservation.

According to a study released by Boston-based companies Cone and Amp Insights, a majority of Generation Y consumers—

about 78 million of them in the United States, for instance—
cares about social causes and is more than willing to reward or
punish a company based on its commitment to a cause. In the
study, 61 percent of Gen Y consumers agreed that they were personally responsible for making a difference in the world. More
tellingly, 78 percent of them said that companies had a responsibility to join them in this effort.[37]

Companies need to join their consumers in a common cause
that goes beyond a strictly transactional relationship. Causal marketing is becoming an indispensable tactic in creating deeper consumer relationships. And in order to authentically and effectively
establish this relationship between a brand and a consumer, the
consumer must be convinced that the brand or company in question is a force of good. By doing good, brands look good. And if
they look good—even if it is perception more than reality—their
consumers will notice.

The causes themselves—or the marketing campaigns centered on them—do not need to be Greenpeace or Amnesty International. It could be a bit more fun. For instance, a South African
convenience store chain called Supa Quick staged an auction of a
30-second advertising spot, with the winning bidder able to screen
his commercial at halftime during the 2007 Rugby World Cup
match between South Africa and England. After a 25-hour auction,
Supa Quick received a bid of R151,000—making the spot the most
expensive ad in South African TV history. The brand immediately
announced that the value of the ad would be donated to a charitable
foundation for severely injured rugby players. For this effort, Supa
Quick garnered massive public approval and brand love.

Almost every global brand supports a cause or a charity.
Corporate citizenry has never been more popular. Corporate
causal efforts tally into the millions—if not billions—of dollars
each year. From the Ronald McDonald House Charities to Procter

& Gamble's support of the Special Olympics, major global players are seemingly doing their bit to help the world and its occupants in need. Global concerns are also paying close attention to ethical issues like deforestation, animal testing, pollution, child labor, and global poverty. They are doing so not because the CEOs and boards are turning over a new leaf. Companies are becoming ethical because there's money in it for them. A recent global survey found that nearly a third of respondents said that buying an ethical product made them feel good, but more important, another third said they were willing to pay a 5 to 10 percent premium for these ethical products.[38]

But if consumers are willing to pay more for ethical brands and products, the companies behind them must deliver the goods. If companies are jumping on the ethical bandwagon, we reason, they must therefore be held more accountable for their practices and standards.

Sadly, many companies leave much to be desired. And consumers notice. Almost half of the consumers surveyed in the United States, the UK, France, Spain, and Germany think that corporate ethical behavior has declined. In Germany and the United States, moreover, over two-thirds of consumers think that companies are out only for themselves.[39]

We as consumers are now less interested in the charities that companies support but instead look to how they act toward their customers, their employees, and their communities. We think that if companies are doing a good job, they should actively promote their ethical credentials and accomplishments to the public. But we don't think they should advertise them. Instead, studies have shown that a company's ethical accreditation is built on blogs, online consumer chat forums, and simple word of mouth. So in effect, major companies that have built their brands squarely on the reach of mass advertisement can no longer communicate one of the most important and compelling stories about themselves in the media they are most accustomed to using.

This is most likely going to change. Companies will wise up and begin to weave their ethical grounding into their mass communications. Consumers will begin to take their chatter about brands into the mainstream and expect the brands they support to become much more overt in their ethical marketing campaigns. In the near future, marketing will most likely be based on some sort of altruistic bent espoused by a brand or its parent company. A survey reported in *Advertising Age* found that 90 percent of millennials—those born between 1979 and 2001—said they were "very likely" to switch from one brand to another that had a strong association with a good cause.[40] With consumer tendencies like that, how can brands afford *not* to base their marketing on social consciousness?

They cannot, and will not. But the notion of social consciousness doesn't start and end with altruistic causes or ethics-based marketing campaigns. The consumer demand for an untried type of brand behavior is an early manifestation of a profound transformation of the practice of advertising and marketing: believing differently.

Believing differently isn't solely about being altruistic. Companies cannot believe differently if their leaders continue to think that altruism is a profit center, however roundabout those profits may be. It's no novelty to think that doing good does a bottom line good. Believing differently means rethinking the notion of marketing altogether. Believing differently isn't about crafting better messages or creating better branded products, services, or experiences. Believing differently isn't about entering emerging marketplaces with high hopes and deep pockets. Believing differently isn't a better business model. It means more than that.

It means faith.

That's right. Faith.

Emerging economies, emergent consumers, and their booming markets are thriving on the premise of "not knowing" rather than "knowing." In contrast, the marketing and advertising industry in North America and Europe is stubbornly clinging to what it knows rather than embracing what it doesn't.

Traditional agencies and their offshoots can't cope with the reality that consumers and the marketplaces they inhabit are increasingly immune to their charms and come-ons. In fact, they are more than ever mistrustful of the messages that regularly emanate from brands and their agencies. For a growing population of über-consumers, brand information comes from social networks, blogs, and word of mouth, while intrusive and non-contextual brand messages are easily blocked by technology and software.

In response to this tectonic consumer shift in personal and communal empowerment, successful ad agencies of the near future will be organized around communities of like-minded people, not the various disciplines like TV, print, PR, or digital employed by agencies engaged in the persuasion industry. In other words, ad agencies will no longer be the promulgators of brand messages. Instead, they will be like creative sherpas to the brand marketers trying to reach communities formed by mutual interests.

Most senior ad execs—the brand managers and the veeps they kowtow to—are much more comfortable with traditional channels built on the bedrock of mass media. Their role is either to produce messages or to distribute them as widely as possible. To believe that they can do anything other than that is still considered heresy.

But all they have to do is look around. Get on a plane and disembark in Moscow or Manila, Mumbai or Dubai. They would quickly ascertain what the term "media agnosticism" really means. All they have to do is realize that close to half of the people on this planet don't give a rat's ass about the bedrock of mass media and that the people who are now emerging as the consumers of the future are, quite literally, massive blocs of communities formed by mutual interest and not by mass messaging.

Forward-thinking companies are now radically rethinking (re-believing?) their role and responsibility in the global marketplace. And they are taking their cues from emerging markets. According to a 2008 article in the *New York Times*, Nokia is cementing its place as a paragon of new business and new thinking by employing what it calls a "human behavior researcher" or a "user anthropologist" to travel the world so that the company can accumulate as much experiential knowledge as possible about human behavior globally. This knowledge—not gleaned through sales data or consumer focus groups—comes from the Nokia ambassador living, eating, sleeping, and partying with people who may or may not want to buy a Nokia phone.

For instance, hanging out in a bowling alley in Tupelo, Mississippi, revealed a real-life social hub where Nokia could learn how people communicated and rumors spread. Living with a family in Mumbai's Dharavi slum showed Nokia how ingeniously a father earning less than $3 a day took care of his cell phone during the monsoon season. The hooker ads in Brazilian phone booths— where the names are fake but the phone numbers work—led to an insight that "in an increasingly transitory world, the cell phone is becoming the one fixed piece of our identity."[41] These unique and empathetic insights are then reported back to the designers and technologists who create Nokia's products and services.

Rather than send in salespeople rife with product pitches, sales kits, and glossy branding, as traditional marketers are apt to do, Nokia reversed the process. The marketer goes out into the marketplace to listen. The brand enters into communities and observes them, ingratiating itself and building trust and credibility through its ethical and transparent modus operandi. Instead of simply tweaking an existing marketing campaign for existing products in a new market, Nokia has chosen to know its potential customer optimally, and only then does it create a cell phone product specifically catering to them. This is an example of believing differently; a massive multinational company believes that it can't thrive without turning the conventional marketing paradigm on its head. Marketers in North America and Europe—along with the ad agencies that service them—need to believe it too.

And I believe that marketers in the so-called developed world can believe again. All they have to do is look to countries like India and China—or Bangladesh and the Philippines—to get their belief back. At a time when Western audiences are seeking new ways to avoid commercial messages and intrusive brand campaigns, the marketing and advertising industry must unquestionably look to the developing world for inspiration.

Causal marketing is still essentially quite rudimentary in that it uses a perceived commitment to a social cause in order to improve brand sales. Causal marketing is a tactic, not a belief system. Instead, the marketing itself has to be a benefit to the world. Many products—too many to count—offer up the proposition that they can improve people's lives. Why shouldn't the marketing of those products do the same?

Steve Jobs used to tell all new hires that their job was "to make a dent in the world." That's exactly what we can do, for the first time in history. We have to believe in marketing again, to create better agencies and to act as sherpas on unknown peaks. To do so, we have to reinvent it for a higher purpose. This will ultimately achieve a better level of acceptance by the marketplace, so that consumers and marketers alike can believe again.

CHAPTER FIVE

The World Is Poor

(And the Meek Shall Inherit the Mall)

When we talk about global consumers, let's get one thing straight: we're talking about poor people. And when we talk about marketing in India, we are really talking about marketing to poor people. So understanding the dynamics and paradoxes of that subcontinent can open up insights into those in other parts of the world.

There are more poor people in India than in any other country. An estimated 350 to 400 million people live below the poverty line—more than the entire population of the United States.[1] Many factors contribute to this: primitive agricultural methods; dilapidated or lacking infrastructure; a high birth rate; a shameful illiteracy rate, especially among women; past protectionist policies; and the millennium-old caste system. Whatever the factors, the Indian mindset revolves around the notion of poverty and how to survive within it.

The easiest way for me to understand this was to walk out of the plush Taj Mahal Palace hotel and hop into a car with Kedar Kurdikar, general manager of Virtual Marketing India. We were headed to Dharavi, the largest slum in Asia. I had imagined an hour-long drive to the outskirts of vast Mumbai; instead we got out of the cab in the heart of the city after a mere 20 minutes in traffic.

Before us lay the slum, a "working slum" of (officially) 600,000 people—about the size of Seattle; Washington, DC; or Frankfurt. An unofficial count puts the number close to 1 million people, occupying about 1.75 square kilometers, or 0.675 square miles. Anyone want to do the math?

We were met at the slum's perimeter by Dvendra, our teen-aged guide from Reality Tours and Travel, one of only a handful of tour companies that take Westerners into Dharavi. Not solely because the slum is very dangerous—it is—but more significantly because the community is tightly knit, caste- and religion-based and, quite simply, too appalling for an unguided experince.

The narrow streets are strewn with waste, animal and human. There are so many origins of stench in the place, it's hard to tell which one is the worst. On some streets, no sun ever penetrates. At night, people sleep literally on top of each other. A family of 12 usually shares about a 90-square-foot (27 m²) room: aunts, uncles, fathers and mothers, brothers and their wives, unmarried sisters, and a bunch of kids all live together in squats and rooms in Dharavi. Families have been known to occupy a 45-square-foot (14 m²) space for decades, passing it on to siblings and offspring after arriving from some rural village decades ago. Nighttime in Dharavi can prove to be quite a sleepless affair, as throngs of people try to get some nonexistent space and nonexistent privacy. But it is the daytime in Dharavi that is truly illuminating.

Early every morning, the inhabitants wake up to begin work in one of the slum's 15,000 hutment factories. That's right: 15,000 factories in the midst of a million people shuttered in an area smaller than a mall and its parking lot. These hutment factories are jerry-rigged, usually two-storey sweatboxes that see hundreds of thousands of slum dwellers tan hide, melt plastic, weave baskets, work cotton, mold clay, collect scrap, and reshape iron. Regardless of Dharavi's poverty, its residents produce clothes, toys, containers, and recycled material that earn them millions of dollars. Dvendra, the guide, reckons close to $675 million each year comes into the slum.

Dharavi is a microcosm of the growing opportunity and commercialism in India and the rest of the hyper-developing world. The superiority complex that Westerners display when confronted with Third World entrepreneurialism can be easily shattered by the experience of close to a million Indians—Tamils, Bengalis, Maharatis, Muslims, Dhalits, Assamese, and Biharis—living together and prospering. This is hyper-capitalism at its finest, unburdened by regulation and policy. This slum is serving the global economy. One belt maker in Dharavi delivered an order for 25,000 belts to Wal-Mart in 2007.

This is a place where the son of a vagrant ragpicker can own several small businesses—a co-op bank, a mobile phone shop, a printing press—all within the Dharavi marketplace. As an article in *The Economist* in late 2007 described Dharavi,

> Everyone is working hard and everyone is moving up. All of Mr. Korde's friends—or their fathers—arrived in Dharavi much poorer than they are now. Most own at least one business. Some of these slum-dwellers employ several hundred people.

> Aftab Khan is typical. A tailor with a trim moustache, and scholarly wire-rimmed spectacles, he arrived from Uttar Pradesh 20 years ago, with little more than a

needle. He now employs a dozen youths—all recruited in his native village—to turn out 150 items of children's clothing a day. In workhouse fashion, they eat and sleep where they labour, in the upper two floors of a hutment. Reachable only by a ladder and rope, this resembles nothing so much as a tree-house with sewing-machines. Yet for their drudgery, the apprentices earn 200 rupees a day—about four times a rural wage in Uttar Pradesh.[2]

In a place like Dharavi, and in dozens of places just like it around the hyper-developing world, the future of the global consumer marketplace is being built. The process, without a doubt, is tumultuous. In Dharavi, it was outright pungent. Neither Kedar nor I was prepared for the olfactory onslaught. (I was even less prepared for the simplest of things: don't wear flip-flops to the largest slum in Asia during monsoon season.)[*]

In Dharavi, 85 percent of the households own a TV, 75 percent own a pressure cooker and blender, 56 percent own a gas stove, and 21 percent have phones.[3] But to many in Mumbai, even a slum like Dharavi is out of reach. It is estimated that there are 25,000 families living in the streets—literally in the streets—around the city's airport.

Blessedly, according to Forecasting International, an estimated 300 million Indians are now in the middle class, as one-third of them have escaped poverty in the last 10 years. India is adding 40 million people to its middle class each year. At this rate, a majority of Indians will be middle class by 2025. Here's a country that has switched on the middle-class button. The drive to escape poverty has finally reached a tipping point in India. Is it

---

[*] Although I had endured enough open sewage during my time in the Peace Corps, stationed in N'Djamena, Chad, I had not really expected such a deluge of doodie.

any wonder that it can serve as a model for the rest of the world seeking to do the same? And doesn't the advertising and marketing mindset follow suit? In other words, the aspirations and consumption patterns of an Indian can closely mimic those of any other poverty-stricken world citizen looking to make a better life for his or her family.

There are 4 billion people in this world who live on less than $2 per day.[4] *Four billion people.* That in itself should make anyone—marketer or not—stop and think . . . and shudder. And yet the real story is more dynamic and awe inspiring than the extent of the poverty—the billions who are part of the so-called bottom of the pyramid (BOP).* The real story is that these people, these teeming masses yearning to be free consumers, are emerging slowly but surely out of the morass of poverty. And when the trickle becomes a flood, marketers will be faced with a new consumer entirely: a price-conscious and brand-cognizant global citizen who needs to be catered to with mass offerings that bear deeply ingrained and aspirational value.

This new developing-world consumer needs a bit of evaluation by global marketers. And no country can better illustrate the potential of the global consumer of the future than India.

The Poor Prosumer

In the cooler-than-thou offices of Western marketing and advertising agencies, the term *prosumer* has been bandied around for a few years now. And although it may seem to be an ad-speak twist on the conventional term *consumer*, its accepted definitions can be seen as

---

* Coined from the seminal work by C.K. Prahalad, who postulated in his book, *The Fortune at the Bottom of the Pyramid*, that the BOP is a formidable group that marketers must understand and engage, and that the future of the world's economy depends on corporate involvement from a capitalist—rather that a strictly altruistic—approach.

manifestations of never-before-seen consumer behavior in mature marketing milieus like North America, Europe, Japan, and South Korea. The definitions of a prosumer are as follows:

1. A consumer who is an amateur in a particular field but who is knowledgeable enough to require equipment that has some professional features (professional + consumer).
2. A person who helps to design or customize the products he or she purchases (producer + consumer).
3. A person who creates goods for his or her own use and also possibly to sell (producing + consumer).
4. A person who takes steps to correct difficulties with consumer companies or markets and to anticipate future problems (proactive + consumer).

Let's take the first definition: this is all about that kid with two turntables and a microphone DJing to his friends in the basement, who's using the same technical equipment as the top London DJ.

The second definition is applied to the so-called mod movement of online gaming. Programmers and gaming experts are frequently able to access the code for a published game and modify the play. In many instances, the "mod" game is better than the original published game and is often available as a free download on gamer networks, wikis, and boards.

The third definition is perfectly embodied by the so-called sneakerheads, consumers who customize mainstream sneaker brands like Nike Air Force Ones and turn them into works of art. Nike recognized this trendy market years ago and created Nike iD, an online shop and service to personalize its sneakers. Many designers create highly sought-after niche sneaker lines around brands like Nike (the perennial favorite), Puma, or adidas. These are extremely pricey shoes and are treated as esteemed cultural currency by those "in the know". One has only to watch an episode of HBO's *Entourage* to appreciate the cultural importance that sneakers, especially customized and sub-branded sneakers, have on the youth in both cities and suburbs alike.

And the fourth definition of a prosumer is probably the most bitter pill to swallow for those who are oblivious to the fundamental shifts in consumer behavior: consumers are pissed and they are not going to take it any more. More important, they have the tools to deal massive body blows—if not death strokes—to any brand that gets in their way.

Simply search for "iPod's Dirty Secret" on YouTube for an example. The short video will illustrate how two brothers, $40 of spray paint, and a video camera fundamentally challenged and changed one of the most popular product launches in the history of consumerism.

The prosumer class is what marketers need to engage in the immediate future. Much like the quick and seamless transition from Neanderthal to Homo sapiens, the advanced consumer will be an evolutionary leap. And although the prosumer is being catered to now with forward-thinking consumer-generated ad campaigns, social networking, and viral platforms, with gaming placements and experience-based marketing, savvy marketers would be wise to prepare for the next-generation consumer's arrival. It is just around the corner.

For instance, India is currently the twelfth-largest consumer market in the world but predicted to be ranked fifth by 2025. Total consumption by Indians is expected to quadruple in real terms from $420.7 billion in 2006 to $1.73 trillion in 2025. In this time, the middle class is expected to grow almost twelve-fold (12 times!). And over 23 million Indians will join the ranks of the country's wealthiest—rivaling the total population of Australia.[5]

When mobile phones were introduced in India, conventional wisdom dictated that only the über-rich would be able to flash a Nokia. Fees were about 16 rupees (50 cents) for both incoming and outgoing calls. Considering the *average* daily wage for an Indian is about $4.20, the telecommunication revolution looked certain to bypass the subcontinent. Yet in 2007, India tallied over 250 million mobile phone users (still only about 20 percent of the entire population). On average, 6 million customers are added every month.[6] In November 2007, 8.32 million Indians subscribed to a cell phone. In December, 8.17 million signed a contract. And today, India enjoys the lowest call rates in the world, at about $0.01 per minute. Fixed lines are declining, to about 39 million, as Indians turn to cheaper mobile phones for their telephonic needs. (And yet only 23.9 percent of Indians have a phone—fixed line or mobile.)[7]

What has prompted this improbable mobile naissance? As Captain G.R. Gopinath, the founder of India's Air Deccan—which provides no-frills connections between India's far-flung towns and cities—reportedly stated at The Marketing Summit 2007 trade show in Delhi, "India is no more a country of a billion hungry people; it is now a country of a billion hungry consumers." And about 70 percent of India's 1.1 billion population—or 770 million people—live in villages and rural areas.

Mobile Marketing in the Boonies

Squalid villages, ox-trodden farmland, and isolated farming cooperatives are the hotbed—the ground zero—for the new global consumer. This is where he or she enters the brand-sphere. In villages, rural hinterlands, and urban slums, the consumers of the future are found. New products catering to the rural and ultra-poor Indian consumer are redefining and revolutionizing entire global industry categories. Tata Motors—India's auto giant—has reinvented the concept of a car with the Nano. Hindustan Unilever has ignited a consumer packaged goods boom. And micro-lending is teaching the world a new way to finance enterprise.

For mobile phone companies, the biggest innovations have involved delivering state-of-the-art technology at a cut-rate price. Motorola's offering for the Indian market, called Motofone, costs around $40. Nokia unveiled seven models in mid-2007 that start at $45. Indian mobile operator Reliance, however, took the cake when it began selling a Chinese-made phone for 777 rupees, or about $19.

Another ingenious plan is helping make India the world's fastest-growing mobile phone market. Mobile operators are offering a one-time payment of $25 for a lifetime of free incoming calls. That's right. Never pay for incoming calls again. Would a US operator ever dream of such a scheme?

There is a veritable gold-rush mentality for mobile operators in India. In 2007, Indian cellular operators invested $20 billion to penetrate the rural marketplace for the next two years. That was 50 percent higher than the total investments over the past 12 years. The huge outlay is to be covered by the growing mobile revenues, estimated to reach $43.6 billion by 2011, from $22.5 billion in 2006. In rural India, mobile penetration is at a mouth-watering 1 percent, whereas the urban marketplace is at about 40 percent.[8]

As most of the current growth in mobile service is still concentrated in urban areas, Indian telcos are undoubtedly eager to penetrate the impoverished heartland. And so are international concerns like the giant Vodafone, which purchased a controlling stake in Hutchison Essar, an Indian–Hong Kong mobile venture. In late 2007, US giant AT&T applied for a license to operate in India through a local partnership.

Speaking at the same marketing conference as Gopinath, the CEO and president of Reliance Retail Lifestyle, Bijou Kurien, amply delivered the marching orders for brands and their marketers seeking to win in the Indian market: "Marketers are reaching only the first 1,000 of India's 4,500 towns."[9]

Only a few years ago, each one of those 1,000 towns that have now been touched by the "modernity" of branded services and products had only one landline phone to connect it to the rest of the world. Small town businesspeople—weavers, farmers, tradespeople, and shopkeepers—had to rely either on the postal service or on the single line in town to do business. A deal that normally takes minutes in the modern world would take weeks, if not months, in an Indian village. As Hungama's Kaushik Mukherji pointedly reminded me in his boardroom, surrounded by teams working on code and content, "Less than 10 years ago, having a home phone line was as much of a status symbol as having a car in India." Indeed.

Now, a mobile phone allows a fruit vendor to connect with wholesalers directly in order to set prices and put in orders, while calls from a few choice customers can get them fruit more efficiently and at a lower cost, leaving time and money for reinvestment into the small business. It is common to hear how small village vendors and traders have doubled their incomes almost immediately after getting a cell phone. For the rural poor of India, a mobile phone has become the fifth-most important household expenditure item after food, clothing, shelter, and education.[10] (I wonder how the ranking of an illiterate farmer in Chhattisgarh state compares to that of a highly connected teenager in Tokyo's trendy Harajuku district. Pretty close, I bet.)

Undoubtedly, the demand for a mobile handset in rural India has produced a boon for handset marketers. Nokia is the clear winner, with a 74 percent market share. And operators are mushrooming: at last count, there were 13 mobile phone operators, and Bharti Airtel was leading the pack with a 24 percent share.[11]

How does one stay ahead of the field in such a competitive marketplace? If you are Bharti Airtel, you innovate your products and services to provide an experiential differentiation from your competitors. For instance, the mobile leader runs a project for farmers in the state of Uttar Oradesh that provides tips on farming and animal husbandry delivered by mobile handset. The farmer's phone can also access information on the availability of micro-loans, as well as twice-daily weather forecasts, all delivered into the palm of the guy with a patch of land and dreams of a better life for his family. As one colleague put it bluntly, "this is the real digital revolution" in India.

Motorola is servicing the Indian rural farmer with its Motofone model, which sells for about $32. And although margins on low-end handsets like the Motofone barely squeak over 3 percent, the sheer number of sales keeps manufacturers and providers coming up with unique and rural-driven features. For instance, the Motofone's screen remains visible even at high noon (the Indian midday sun is truly radiant), perfect for use in the unsheltered fields and country roads. For customers who can't read, Motorola developed an icon-based menu for its phones. Even better, the handset comes preloaded with voice prompts recorded in a variety of regional languages and dialects. Of course, the phone also boasts an enhanced battery life, as charging opportunities are few and far between in a farm town during monsoon season. Even Mumbai, India's most industrialized megacity, often goes up to 15 hours daily without electricity during the summer. In such circumstances, you'd better believe battery life is important to the Indian consumer, urban or rural.

Experience the Message

But features and benefits aside, the battle among marketers and service providers for Indian market share of handsets will be waged through experiential strategies and tactics.*

Nokia has built its leadership in the Indian mobile handset market by going deep in-country to connect the unconnected. It has sent 25 vans into the countryside on continuous six-month treks to visit long-forgotten and remote villages. These modern-day explorers aren't selling phones, however. They don't even take orders for Nokia phones. Instead, it is their job to explain to their audience why a peasant in a tiny farming community would want a mobile phone and why it should be a Nokia. The feet-on-the-street marketing campaign is necessary to first establish the *idea* of a mobile phone, and only then explain why that idea is a good one for a farmer.

That's why it's imperative that the marketing outreach use an experience-focused approach. Nokia's vans aren't your typical Sprinter or Econoline variety. Each one resembles a carnival truck, the kind that transforms into a shooting gallery or ring toss. Instead of balloons and dolls behind the counter, Nokia displays its handsets. When the van appears in the center of town, it creates a carnival-like spectacle that gets the villagers running to see the commotion.

Before the van throws open its doors to the panoply of Nokia products and blasts popular Bollywood songs from its speakers, the villagers are treated to a skit acted out by the brand ambassadors. The skit usually invokes a Bollywood storyline that all villagers can relate to and presents scenarios in which a mobile phone is necessary to save the day. The skits more or less present a Nokia handset as the dashing hero of the drama.

In fact, these skits are a key component to getting villagers to understand the product and the role it can play in their lives. Sure, TV advertising penetrates the hinterland. But only an

---

* On another note, a recent anti-AIDS campaign in India featured the release of a free ringtone that chants "Condom, condom!" The campaign was financed by the Bill & Melinda Gates Foundation.

experiential outreach like the Nokia van—and the live spectacle that accompanies it—is doing the trick for the brand. It is branded entertainment at its finest.

Scores of attentive and lucrative potential consumers are immersed in a branded play before they are presented with the products. This not only drives understanding and relevance to the consumer but also engages him in a long-term brand experience that a TV spot could not accomplish.

In fact, many Indian brands seeking to reach the rural poor are dramatizing their TV spots as live skits acted out in front of an attentive audience. The live presentation of the TV commercials is becoming an integral communication strategy in rural markets. And the audience for these commercial plays can number in the hundreds of thousands. (This should give any marketer in the United States faced with millions of ad skippers and ad blockers a case of serious envy.)

Religious and regional festivals are numerous in India, as are national holidays. Certain religious pilgrimages and local festivals attract millions of people to one place at one time. Diwali, the Festival of Lights, is celebrated for six days and is marked by firecrackers and festivities. It is part of the rich, tradition-soaked, colorful, and fragrant social fabric of India. This significant holiday, and the thousands of years of spiritual connection to it, has an even greater variety of interpretations and celebrations in southern India, in the central state of Maharashtra, and in West Bengal—where a five-day festival called Durga Pujo is dedicated to a 10-armed warrior goddess, represented in effigy with countless statues, floats, and pavilions in Calcutta. The purpose of the holiday is a simple one: to celebrate the victory of good over evil.

Hundreds more holidays and religious observances occur frequently throughout different locales and neighborhoods across India. Such major holidays drive millions of people to first- and second-tier cities, as well as to tiny villages that swell with human-ity on the shores of a sacred river or at the temple of a holy relic.

These holidays are especially celebrated at the *melas,* loosely translated as country fairs, in countless villages and towns in rural India. Usually a *mela* is held on the market days of a small town or agricultural hub, when farmers bring in their produce and shepherds their livestock. About 25,000 *melas* are held each year, with another 42,000 *haats*—or produce market days—scattered throughout India.[12]

During these *melas* and *haats,* villagers are dazzled by snake charmers, fortune-tellers, swamis, and acrobats. Food vendors fill the village air with spice, and bakers sell sweets to the throngs of kids running ragged through the town. There may be horse rides. A bigger village might get a dilapidated carousel or Ferris wheel. But among the most popular attractions for the villagers at a *mela* are the daily puppet shows and theatrical re-enactments of folk-lore, scripture, or pop culture.

There is rich storytelling in these shows, and the Bolly-wood spirit of the average Indian is easily swayed by the love story doomed by caste or the tale of the greedy landowner, poor but pious father, and vengeful son. The audience is ready for a story. And even if it's branded with a Nokia message or a Motorola tuto-rial, it's still a good story.

"One-on-one marketing is beginning to take off in India, because to this day not everyone has a TV set in their home," Mudra's Bobby Pawar explained to me that night at the bar, prob-ably on the third or fourth round. "Village fairs are very big. So the opportunity to do something face to face is driving a lot of interesting things in this country."

A division of his company called Mudra MMS specializes in rural marketing and has pioneered the live theater technique in this marketplace. As Bobby explains, "Each region has two or three major fairs, where literally there are hundreds of thousands of people. And this is a great opportunity for a brand to interact with its audience." Knowing that the rural populace is much less likely to be affected by TV commercials than their urban cousins, Mudra and other forward-thinking agencies in India have appropriated the time-tested tradition of village theater in order to create a unique application of branded entertainment.

"You take the sense of what you are communicating in the mass media campaign, and you make it into a folk art," says Bobby. "Folk arts have always been a major component in every region. So you can adapt your message region by region with a live theater interaction. People are familiar with the folk art tradition. They have seen plays put on in the village before. So with a brand coming in and doing it, it familiarizes the brand with the villagers that much more. It makes the brand the salt of the earth."

Imagine the possibilities of a contextual and compelling message delivered live to hundreds of thousands of people. If done at festivals where millions of people congregate—and then tell stories of their pilgrimage to their fellow villagers back home—this theater-based way of delivering a branded message can rival any traditional TV spot in terms of reach. But it accomplishes so much more than a 30-second spot ever can. On a base level, it is the retelling of a TV spot, but in a more contextual light, it is Bollywood and experiential marketing mixed into a formidable and "sticky" content delivery and media channel. It is live theater that captures the heart, not just the eye.

Branded Entertainment on Wheels

But if you think that branding a theater performance at a *mela* is borderline tacky (or genius, as I do), you may want to consider this example: "traditional entertainers" make their living by piercing various body parts in front of large crowds on the streets of Mumbai and Calcutta and at the thousands of village *melas*. A reported guerrilla marketing craze in India is to hire these fakirs, yogis, swamis, and mystics to promote commercial products and services.

One enterprising marketer paid body piercers to advertise Zonex-P, an analgesic tablet, by painting their backs with the company's logo and brand promise—"Instant Pain Relief"—and to perform their act for hundreds of thousands of consumers. Again: tackily pandering to the obvious, or a very effective marketing campaign? I'm eager to go with the latter.*

In early 2008, the New York–based Advertising Research Foundation released a report stating that in-person events could boost purchase intent as much as 52 percent. In other words, a customer's stated interest in buying a product skyrocketed after participating in a brand-sponsored event.[13] Is it so hard to believe that a captive audience wouldn't sit through a branded show or theatrical production "brought to you by Nokia" in a village *mela* or at a *nagar* truckstop on a major Indian highway?

North American TV watchers consume hours of branded entertainment every night. In fact, a report by PQ Media in early 2008 stated that paid product placement in the United States ballooned by 34 percent to $2.9 billion in 2007, representing a compound annual growth rate of 41 percent between 2002 and 2007. Advergaming (ads in video games) and webisodes (branded Web content) drew another $217 million in marketing dollars, up 35 percent annually.[14]

The difference, of course, is that the Indian version of branded entertainment is *live*. There is an element of theatrical-

---

* Parenthetically, GoldenPalace.com pioneered the practice of "back-vertising" when it paid a professional boxer to paint the company's URL on his back for a televised boxing title bout in the mid-1990s.

ity in a branded event that an in-show product placement can never simulate. The "touch and feel" of the brand at an event is exponentially more visceral. Maybe that's why the same report by PQ Media showed that event sponsorship in the United States, by far the biggest segment of branded entertainment, climbed to $19.2 billion in 2007, rising 12 percent over the year before.[15]

These events allow brands to tell their story more compellingly and contextually than a TV spot could. These branded stories, no matter how they are communicated, get people to understand the brand's product attributes and accept it in their lives.

Indians love a good narrative. They love the flow of language, especially if it's in their own dialect and of their own provenance. And they love to share stories. They love to share their humanity with each other. These festivals and *melas* present a ready audience, and branded entertainment is interwoven with the other festivities in the village. Essential to branded theater, however, is the emphasis on the product. The theater for Nokia must be demonstrative as much as it is lyrical.

It's as easy to understand the performances as "try before you buy." The play does not fail to demonstrate how the features of a particular Nokia phone model saved the day for the impoverished farmer or was integral to the saccharine reunion of the lovers. This type of marketing is based on simple demonstration encased in a theatrical delivery to a receptive audience. And it lies at the heart of the experience-based marketing that Western brands are increasingly employing to woo a reclusive or alienated consumer.

Or to examine this statement another way, let's propose a question: Are the marketing tactics used to sell insurance to an Indian farmer different from the marketing tactics used to persuade a US teenager to join the army at a time of war? As a matter of fact, there is little difference in the tactical philosophy.

In rural India, I am told, the only time one sees loud-speakers on a car is when they are blaring political propaganda or Bollywood soundtracks. So it must have been quite a surprise for villagers to be greeted with a branded van rigged with loudspeakers and announcing an offer of an entirely different nature: insurance.

A majority of the rural populace has never even heard of insurance. In villages and farm towns across thousands of miles of scorched earth and monsoon seasonality, paying for a promise is a tenuous proposition. Money is hard to come by. So why would a farmer buy something and get nothing on his plate for it?

Potential customers aren't really potential customers if they have no idea what you are selling them. You therefore have to start from scratch. To sell insurance policies in such a climate is arduous at best, and finding cost-effective ways of selling them is imperative to success. One Indian insurance company, Alegion Insurance Broking, may have figured out a way to do just that. The idea is simple: create a mobile office and take it to the villages and towns.

By retrofitting a Maruti Omni van—about the size of a VW bus—with a desk, computer, printer, and forms, the company began selling insurance on the spot in villages in the southern states. It quickly realized that the way to reach 600,000 villages efficiently, and to sell insurance to people who had never heard of it, was with a mobile office. It's called fishing where the fish are. This simple insight allowed the company to expand quickly, from one van to a planned 500 in 18 months.*

A mobile office does two things tactically: it allows a marketer to take a branded message to the consumer rather than

---

* India's insurance industry is set to grow from $12.8 billion in 2008 to more than $60 billion by 2010, according to the Associated Chambers of Commerce and Industry of India. Two-thirds of the growth in insurance is expected to come from rural and semi-urban areas.

expecting him or her to come to it, and therefore extends the time for dialogue; and it provides a place to conclude the transaction quickly from brand impression to close, thereby shrinking the sales cycle considerably.

For Alegion, the mobile office provided a cost-effective way to explain and sell insurance services to a massive rural market. For the villagers, the mobile office was something more. It gave the concept of insurance its much-needed perception of formality and service. The mobile office, and the courteous and knowledgeable insurance salesman in the back of the van, became an experiential way to convince a mistrustful and frugal customer.

For the US Army, a mobile, experience-based campaign called the Virtual Army Experience (VAE) has been designed to explain a complex proposition like a stint in the armed forces to a skeptical teenager. More interesting, the VAE allows the Army to identify and engage potential recruits, and then sell itself to a highly skeptical and resistant consumer faced with the prospect of actual deployment into war.[*]

The Virtual Army Experience is a branded "footprint" that rolls out of trailer trucks at amusement parks, air shows, hot-rod races, and gaming conferences. This footprint—like a small-scale carnival attraction—features a real Humvee and real Army equipment, which consumers can use in a simulated combat mission. Using digital technology, large screens, and life-sized replicas of Army-issued weapons, consumers enter a simulated world of shoot 'em-up against a desert-dwelling insurgent. The production value is as good as any high-end Disney ride or 3D flight simulator. It's IMAX mixed with Xbox.

---

[*] At the tail end of 2008, the US Army opened a 14,500-square-foot Army Experience Center in Philadelphia's Franklin Mills Mall in order to test and refine various marketing techniques for broader use in its national recruiting campaigns. The "store," right across from the Sam Ash music store, an indoor skate park, and a Dave & Buster's, cost the Army about $12 million.

In fact, the simulation game is basically a real-life version of the Army's highly successful video game series called America's Army, which also acts as a recruitment tool.[*]

The other obvious distinction to the live experience is that recruiters are able to gather personal information about each real-life gamer and then use it to customize the recruitment pitch during the experience. Before participants enter the VAE, they fill out an online questionnaire and are issued a tracking device with their stored answers. The device lets recruiters monitor which attractions the participant visited and lingered at. The questionnaire also addresses some of the goals of the participants—combat, financial aid, college, job training, and so forth. Based on those answers, recruiters are able to frame the conversation in the appropriate context for the participant.

This type of customization extends the "branded" interaction as well as making the sales pitch more palatable to a prospective recruit. The experiential campaign also allows the Army's brand to enhance a consumer's engagement with it—over 73,000 people have so far participated in the VAE—and to build a relationship that is more in line with a prosumer's perspective. It's try before you buy. And it works.

It can be broken down more simply, in terms of "sales." (And remember, the sale involves a major—MAJOR—life-altering decision.) It is estimated that the cost per visitor is about $110, and the budget for the VAE so far is close to $8 million. The Army guesses that about 10 percent of the visitors are enlistment material, making the price tag for each potential recruit roughly $1,000 per prospect. However, the Army currently spends about $18,000

---

[*] According to the director of the program, Colonel Casey Wardynski, 20 percent of those matriculating at West Point in 2005 had played [the video game] America's Army, along with 20 to 40 percent of enlisted soldiers recruited that year" (B. Joseph Pine and James Gilmore, Authenticity [Boston, MA: Harvard Business School Press, 2007]).

per recruit—after advertising costs, direct mail campaigns, and recruiter salaries are accounted for. This kind of price-tag difference gets the Army very excited.

Creating an Experience Place

The rural Indian and the rural American may have something deeply in common as consumers of brands and media: they have to try out the brand or product in order to like it. They have to lay their hands on it. They need an experience-based relationship with it. Whether it's Uncle Sam or insurance, the emergence of the prosumer class demands that marketers begin considering themselves experience providers rather than messengers.

Amway, for instance, is hungrily eyeing the Indian marketplace and the primed middle-class explosion that it contains. It is so hungry, in fact, that it is willing to alter its long-held and successful strategy especially for the Indian marketplace. Instead of the now-famous home delivery model that Amway employs all over the world—business owners place orders for their products on the Internet, or by phone or fax, and the products get delivered to their doorsteps—the multinational has decided to open up hundreds of Amway Touch Points (ATPs) throughout towns and villages in order to woo the "rural and consuming class."

The ATPs act as a local showroom for Amway wares for the "try before you buy" rural consumer. The typical model of a central warehouse shipping out products would never work in India for Amway. It quickly understood that the rural consumer wants a "touch-and-feel approach to the products he/she buys."[16] Further, a mistrusting rural consumer may not know of Amway's pedigree or global success. A physical showroom like an ATP, where Amway products are displayed, goes far in convincing the rural consumer that the company is legitimate.

The showroom mentality has driven the thought, innovation, and insight behind Apple's retail strategy. Apple stores now account for 20 percent of total revenue for the company. And that percentage is growing. In 2007, Apple reported $1.25 billion in fourth-quarter revenue for its stores, out of a total $6.2 billion in revenue—a 42 percent increase over the fourth quarter in 2006. As the *New York Times* reported at the tail end of 2007, Apple's 203 stores around the world "feel like gathering places, [and] the bright lights and equally bright acoustics create a buzz that makes customers feel more like they are at an event rather than a retail store."[17]

Substitute the word *mela* for the word *event,* and it is evident that the key to successful retailing in rural India is being mirrored by one of the most successful retailing operations in US history. More important, as the *Times* piece points out, is the "secret formula" to Apple's success: the personal attention paid to customers by the sales staff. The Genius Bars—computer and peripheral help centers staffed by Mac wiz kids who give personalized attention to every problem without charge—are supported by store roamers armed with handheld credit card swipers, so purchases can be made on the spot and without a wait in line. Apple also staffs its stores with professionals who give free lectures on subjects like filmmaking, music production, publishing, graphic arts, and design. Personal shoppers are also available by appointment.

Switching to a Mac from a PC is no small choice to make. For millions of PC users, it means learning something unknown, unproven, and somewhat foreign. ("What, no right-click? What kind of computer is this!") It is a somewhat difficult mental transition to make as a consumer. The Apple store is where that transition takes place, and it is here that reservations are assuaged through personalized attention. Consumers are given full and unfettered access to try out and play with the entire lineup of Apple products—Macs, iPods, iPhones, and peripherals. The mental transitions—and the first impressions created by something new or cool—are quickly converted to sales with on-the-spot transactions.

Apple stores aren't simply retail operations: they are hubs of a branded consumer experience. The stores create the ideal conditions to convert visitors into consumers by catering to their every need, even after the sale is made. (More than half of Apple Store staff is dedicated to post-sale support.) It is a try-before-you-buy mecca. It is not uncommon to see people checking out their emails, updating their résumés, or finishing up a creative project in the stores. The staff doesn't mind. It's a hands-on kind of operation. This type of branded consumer experience is a key to reaching consumers in India. Because what works for Steve Jobs and the über-hip urbanista will also work for Rakhiba Khatoon in Baniyapara.

In the same vein as Apple stores, India's Titan Industries has increased its share of the national wristwatch market despite the entry of foreign brands such as Timex and Swatch. It understood that Indians, who expect a good price even for old newspapers, do not throw their watches away lightly, so Titan has over 700 after-sales centers that will replace straps and batteries for free.

It's not just a matter of service; it's a matter of personal respect. An exchange at an Apple Genius Bar is predicated on the same humanistic principles as that at a Titan watch shop. It is a relationship as old and fundamental as human history itself: people coming together to communicate, commiserate, and conduct transactions. In the case of Brazil's Casas Bahia, a massive appliance, electronics, and furniture retailer catering to millions of poor Brazilians, the personal interaction between a consumer and store employee is at the heart of the brand's success.

The bonds between the company and its loyal customers are so strong that it is said that only the delivery trucks from Casas Bahia are left unmolested by the thugs and gang members who control the shantytowns of São Paulo, Rio de Janeiro, and Brasília. The company regards its truck drivers as their best brand ambassadors, as they are the ones who have the privilege of delivering a much-awaited product into the homes of poor people.

Do not underestimate the act of delivering a product into a household—usually packed with cohabiting relatives—that has known only poverty. The symbolism of hope and the merit of hard work is embedded in the things that we may take for granted. When a TV is delivered to a poor family that has never owned one in the past, that experience deserves the best that a company or brand can give to its customers. Casas Bahia understands this dynamic very well, and its drivers take their role extremely seriously.*

This is just one aspect of the Casas Bahia experience. Founded by a Holocaust survivor named Samuel Klein in 1952, the company started as a door-to-door operation to sell linens and towels. It is now the largest retail chain in Brazil, with more than 330 stores, 10 million customers, and 20,000 employees. Samuel Klein is a venerable man in Brazil among the poor. Every day, ordinary people who come into one of his stores ask one of the sales clerks to pass along their good wishes to the old man or to his two sons, who now run the day-to-day operations. Casas Bahia literally transforms lives every day in Brazil, giving the poor consumer an aspirational celebration with every purchase.

It doesn't take a lot of observation to conclude that poor consumers are very aspirational. That should be no surprise, as they are all striving for a better life. Well-known brands are therefore not only symbols of product superiority and lifestyle branding but manifestations of success. Yet big brands come with big price

---

* All the managers at Mexican bakery brand Bimbo must also work as company truck drivers for a limited time in order to become better acquainted with the company's customers. The company owns Thomas' English Muffins, among other brands, in the United States.

tags. So the challenge to large firms is to make aspirational products affordable to poor consumers. Casas Bahia does it with credit, and herein lies another aspect to a business that relies closely on a personal relationship with its customers.

Casas Bahia has used a number of innovations to, as it says in the stores, "fulfill the dreams of its customers." Casas Bahia has developed the now famous *carne*, or passbook, that allows its customers to make small installment payments for the things they buy at the store. The stuff can be paid off in one to 15 months. The passbook is payable only at Casas Bahia stores, and every month customers must come into the store to pay their bill personally. This is a key component to growing and maintaining the relationship between Casas Bahia and its customers. The passbook itself, a simple twist on credit, drives the business model for the retailer: the financed sales represent 90 percent of all sales volume while 6 percent are cash purchases and 4 percent are credit card sales.[18]

When the customer is in the store to make a credit payment with the passbook, a Casas Bahia sales representative—preferably the one who made the original sale—engages the customer in friendly banter and in doing so, ascertains how things are going. Most of the customers are day laborers and low-level underemployed workers who are prone to frequent ups and downs in their income. In fact, income volatility is so high for its customer base that Casas Bahia has developed a recurring promotion that offers customers "unemployment insurance." If a customer loses his or her job, Casas Bahia will swallow the first six installment payments.*

Sales reps know that times can be tough, and empathy is a key training focus for Casas Bahia. A simple conversation between a company representative and the customer can put up a red flag

---

* Parenthetically, Casas Bahia likes to delight its customers with altruistically slanted promotions. For instance, in 2002 the company pardoned the debt of customers who had defaulted on their payments five years prior, in 1997. In doing so, they unlocked millions of repeat purchasers.

that a late payment is imminent, or a green flag that the customer is ready to make another purchase.

If a customer is not approved by the mandatory government credit check, the Casas Bahia sales rep will direct the customer to an in-store credit analyst—one of the most well-trained and rigorously tested positions at Casas Bahia—who is asked to evaluate the customer's credit needs. In 10 minutes, based on training and experience, the credit analyst will ask a series of questions about the customer's credit worthiness and teach the customer the basic tenets of credit and payment. Most of the time, based upon the empathy and trust built up during the personal interaction, the analyst will override the system and grant the customer store credit to make the purchase. In doing so, the company creates an immediate relationship with its customer, one that is certain to continue because of the face-to-face interactions within the store and at the point of delivery.

Sales at Casas Bahia are predicated on personal transactions. The face-to-face relationship translates into good business: the company's default rate is about 4.5 percent, whereas its closest competitor's is closer to 16 percent.[19] This relationship transcends into lifelong commitment: 77 percent of customers who open an account at Casas Bahia make repeated purchases.[20] Personal interaction between customer and company is a significant consumer trend in emerging economies, as well as a key differentiator for brands in the United States.

At its most basic, the one-to-one interaction involves two human beings coming together. One-on-one interactions also lead to marketer empathy, a crucial component of customer service. The future of marketing is based on these interactions, resulting in meaningful dialogue between a marketer and consumer. Marketing invariably becomes more relevant, and therefore, more effective.

The Future of Global Marketing

Conservatively, rural India comprises roughly 770 million people. But the rural Indian consumer—potentially the most lucrative consumer on the face of the planet—is unlikely to consider a brand unless there is an experience-based demonstration or a personal outreach to his or her cultural heartstrings. This makes marketing a much harder proposition than simply airing a spot, buying print, or getting on the radio. There needs to be much more depth to the communication. For this rural consumer, the prosumer of India, experiential marketing plays a much bigger and more effective role within the marketing mix.

Especially in a marketplace where cash transactions are more common than credit, a clear value for money needs to be communicated. A team of uniformed teenagers handing out single-use samples isn't one-on-one marketing. There is no value to the rural consumer in that. The value rests in experience.

Traditional media such as radio are using festivals and cultural congregations to activate the brands that no longer want to advertise on their stations. The hottest business in radio is to stage events for brands at massive *melas* and religious festivals and surround those events with radio ad time and programming. A *Business Standard* article in late 2007 estimated that brand activation can account for about 15 percent of a popular radio station's total revenue.[21]

For instance, an FM radio brand called Radio City used a holiday called Raksha Bandhan to activate the Cadbury brand of chocolates. The holiday is a Hindu festival that celebrates the relationship between brothers and sisters. A sister will tie a *rakhi*, or holy thread, onto her brother's wrist, and in return he offers her a gift and vows to look after her. They also feed each other sweets. A *rakhi* can be given to any male—a cousin or a good friend— whom the sister has "adopted" as a brother.

The radio station brand launched an SMS-driven on-air contest for brothers and sisters across six radio stations, in Mumbai, Delhi, Ahmedabad, Vadodara, Jaipur, and Lucknow. Radio City also set up a "Celebration Bandhan Wall of Fame" at major malls in these cities. The walls encouraged brothers and sisters to write messages to each other and win gift baskets of Cadbury sweets.

Other than radio, another truly ancient form of advertising is surging in rural India: wall murals. They are akin to billboards here in the West, although they are often much more intricate, colourful, expressive, and artistic. The days of wall murals—the ones on the sides of factories and hotels in Times Square, Milwaukee, or Evanston that still appear as faded nostalgia in downtown squares—may be back again. In India, they are simply a continuation of a trend started thousands of years ago by the Indus Valley civilization.

It's fitting, therefore, that annual OOH media growth in India has climbed to 17 percent.[22] The tradition of wall murals—coupled with more modern techniques like wall projections, digital billboards, and point-of-purchase displays—has enchanted major marketers into using the medium heavily in rural markets. Consumer packaged goods companies like Hindustan Unilever and telcos like Bharti are using wall paintings to effectively explain the value and benefits of their products by depicting everyday people engaged in everyday activity.

Van tours, such as those employed by Nokia, have become a widely used tactic—for shampoo brands, Bollywood flicks, local politicians—as a rudimentary experience-based method of delivering branded communication. Thousands of vans now traverse the Indian rural landscape, equipped with speakers, AV equipment, and a team of brand ambassadors who rustle up crowds in tiny villages. Many even do sales on the spot. (If the van carries a shipment of the product, the local shop gets a delivery.) More often than not, each van also transports two trained actors who perform a branded theater skit in front of increasingly coin-rich farmers. Often, these skits are performed in town halls or village squares to no more than 200 consumers at a time. The van can also carry three promoters equipped with bicycles, a boom box, and a flip chart to provide a simple backdrop for scaled-down presentations to audiences of only a few people at a time. After each presentation, some branded tchotchkes are handed out. And sales, of course, are made.

This type of van-based marketing can seem uneconomical or primitive to a Madison Avenue exec. And yet it encompasses the fundamentals of experience-based marketing: a personal, highly engaging, and sensorial experience that delivers a brand insight through rich contextual narrative. In other words, this type of marketing is replacing traditional, mass-media marketing across the globe. It may be a historical mainstay in the rural heartland of India, but experience-based marketing is the future in the developed world.

More than half a million villages are scattered throughout India. The distances between them and the infrastructural hurdles to be overcome are enormous for marketers seeking to deliver branded communication and to sell products there. Whereas TV and radio seem to be ideal media to effortlessly traverse the terrains, the realities suggest otherwise.

Because of the myriad languages and 1,600 local dialects found from valley to valley, the reach and frequency of regional programming is limited, and there is very little viewer loyalty. Because there is no visual element to the message, radio engagement is very low in rural India. Low literacy rates make print media a tenuous proposition.

Although TV penetration is growing by leaps and bounds in rural India, more than half of TV viewing in rural India is still a communal affair. In fact, an illuminating and simply brilliant piece of campaigning by the DMK Party in a 2007 election for the state of Tamil Nadu can shed light on the state of TV penetration in rural India. Since farm workers cannot afford to buy a TV set on their measly daily wages, the DMK promised a brand new set for every farmer who voted for the party. Inevitably, the DMK won in a landslide. No one would readily admit that the party was literally buying votes—each set cost about $60—because even competing parties agreed that TV penetration was vital to the development of the rural hinterland.

India marketers and advertisers are devising experiential techniques to memorably reach a relatively unreachable consumer audience. Marketers are quickly realizing that an experience-based approach is an integral part of a pan-Indian advertising strategy, one that uses a rich narrative legacy in its above- and below-the-line activations to mobilize the grassroots.

The Rural Yuppies

The experience-based marketing that comes to Indian *melas* and *haats* in the forms of van marketing or live theater is especially popular with the "rural yuppies" of Indian villages: males 15 to 34 years old who are moving off the farm to work in nearby towns and cities and sending money home to the family. Rural youth are therefore becoming opinion leaders in their villages, a position that was occupied by village elders or the collective vote for hundreds of years. The rural yuppie isn't a TV watcher. Therefore, touch-and-feel campaigns in the rural villages—branded plays and product demonstrations—have been at the heart of successful national launches for hundreds of Indian brands. For this particular rural consumer, access to media has unleashed a deep desire to discover brands.[*] And his rurally honed value consciousness has developed a keen ability to discard or replace them.

Urban centers are a magnet for poor people across the globe. By 2015, there will be more than 225 cities in Africa, 903 in Asia, and 225 in Latin America. More than 368 cities in the developing world will have a population of 1 million or more. Collectively, these cities will account for close to 2 billion people.[23] In India, it seems that national trends are now being born in second-tier cities and smaller towns, not in the urban hotspots of Mumbai or Bangalore.

A study conducted by Euro RSCG Worldwide in 2007 found that in 12 second-tier cities in India, the 15- to 34-year-old consumer is a hyper-aspiring one, exposed to brands in an almost urgent manner.[**] Youngsters in smaller towns like Ludhiana, Chandigarh, Kanpur, Jaipur, Kochi, Mangalore, Coimbatore, and Murai are more aggressive and more confident than their cohorts in the bigger cities. The majority of small-town consumers, according to the study, "believes that greed is good, with many consumers wanting foreign trips, a great career and a beautiful wife almost immediately." It is telling indeed that 80 out of every 100 Mercedes S-class cars sold in India are sold in Ludhiana. When Volvo entered the Indian market, it started with a showroom there first.

The study also suggests that the suppressed aspirations and desires of this emerging consumer class are the same as those of consumers in the rest of the developing world. That seems intuitive. But the suggestion goes further.

Suman Srivastava, Euro RSCG India's CEO, is quoted in the study: "We have observed that 20 to 25 percent of all consum-

---

* Ernst & Young said in 2007 that the hottest-selling item in India's smaller cities is skin-lightening creams for men.

** Industry analysts broadly define metro cities as being in the Tier 1 category, state capitals and bustling towns as Tier 2, and other semi-urban and rural centers as Tier 3.

ers [in Tier 2 cities] become *prosumers*—customers who are more involved with the brand than others. They would typically explore and research about brands, search brand history on the Internet, etc. There's a series of six questions that we ask to a customer and the ones who strongly agree or disagree with four out of six questions are declared prosumers. Therefore, when prosumers recommend a brand or start spreading the word around a brand—that becomes a much bigger trend."[24]

It is no wonder then, that the secret to successfully reaching the Indian marketplace—and, arguably, the billions of poor consumers around the world—rests with a growing class of prosumers who are determining how brands connect with them. These prosumers' first interactions with brands have most likely been experiential. Branded experiences allowed them to engage with brands both contextually—the brands went to their towns and villages—and through compelling insights delivered via local narrative. The experiences got them to try out the brands first-hand. And these prosumers are taking their impressions of and interactions with brands into the bigger cities, where marketers rely more on mass media advertising.

The Merrill Lynch *World Wealth Report* estimates that 1 million people per week will move into urban areas every week in the emerging markets in the next 25 years.[25] India reflects the trend. Its prosumers are its rural yuppies. They are coming up from the rural villages and towns, and the numbers are growing.

For the most part, they are young: 72 percent of India's population is under 35 years of age, and 50 percent is below 25.[26] From experience-based rural marketing to SMS-based Bollywood promotions delivered to the cell phone, this prosumer class is eager to engage with brands.

They are seeking experiences. And the revolution will allow them to access the world—broadband Internet is notoriously lacking in India—will be breathtaking. The consumer engagement model that has been touted for years by the telephony industry is beginning to take shape in the rural hinterlands and secondary cities of India. The third screen—the holy panacea that will cure Madison Avenue's ills by transferring 30-second spots into 5-second bits—is being birthed in India, where it is said that a new customer is signing up for a cell phone every second of the day.

Certainly, a cell phone is not just another screen to receive ads. In fact, it is a tool that connects people. In India, it connects hundreds of millions of people. In our world, it will connect billions. Brands wishing to engage with emerging markets around the globe must consider telephony as their primary mode of branded dialogue, either through compelling services or contextual content.

Indian conglomerate Spice introduced a cell phone priced below $20 "to target surging demand for cheap phones in emerging markets in Asia" in early 2008 at Barcelona's Mobile World Congress, the world's biggest telecoms conference. The company will sell its "People's Phone" line from $10 to $20, and compete with market leaders Bharti Airtel and Vodaphone Essar in India. Spice has also unveiled a pilot scheme for ad-supported free calls, a first for India, and invented the world's first phone able to play films, downloaded from a disc like a DVD or CD. Clearly, for a challenger brand like Spice, the mobile marketplace battle will be waged in the rural hinterlands, where price matters and entertainment is at a premium. Interestingly, Spice's corporate motto is "By the people, for the people, of the people."

Market Differently

Emerging markets like India, and the emergent consumers who stoke them, are blazing new and unique ways to market their goods and services. For instance, two companies in the Philippines are winning consumers over by reinventing the traditions of doing business.

Manila Water, which serves 5.1 million residents, has implemented a system of collective billing to keep the taps running. In addition, the company has so far trained more than 1,000 engineers to service the system and uses micro-lending to support thousands more local entrepreneurs to act as couriers and pipeline contractors. Furthermore, it distributes millions of dollars in aid to schools and hospitals in impoverished areas each year. The Filipino mobile company Globe Telecom also gives millions of dollars in food, education, and training aid to poor but emerging communities throughout the country. By benefiting entire communities, the company can successfully work with local leaders to safeguard cell towers and ensure the safety of their employees working on the lines.[*]

By reaching out to village elders, school principals, mayors, religious leaders, community board members, and residents, Manila Water and Globe Telecom are thriving in low-income areas. And in doing so, they are reinventing their businesses for the better.

For instance, Manila Water shifted the paradigm of how a water company behaves by allowing the communities themselves to decide how they want to engage with the company. Manila Water offers its consumers three options: one meter per household, one meter for three or four households, or a bulk meter for 40 or 50 households. When households coalesce, the connection fee can fall by as much as 60 percent, depending on the number of customers who shoulder the cost of pipes, the meter, and installation. Sub-meters measure water usage in each household, and everyone in

---

[*] Since 2002, lawless elements have damaged more than 30 of Globe Telecom's cell sites over the company's refusal to pay "revolutionary taxes." Moreover, copper cables are routinely cut and sold for scrap.

the group takes responsibility for paying the bill. This, in effect, gives Manila Water and its consumers a form of group insurance coverage on payment. According to a McKinsey report, about 30 percent of the urban poor serviced by Manila Water pool their bills, and the company collects 100 percent of the money it is owed.

Selling prepaid mobile service cards for 300 and 500 pesos was proving too ineffective to reach the massive block of low-income Filipinos looking to get networked. In response, Globe Telecom introduced and perfected the practice of over-the-air (OTA) reloading: instead of paying for calling cards, consumers can pay a licensed distributor for network access. Since the costs of OTA reloading are insignificant, the consumer can reload his or her phone with any amount he or she wants, even a single peso. The consumer takes a mobile phone to a local village stall or roadside *sari-sari* store and gives the clerk the money. The store clerk then uses a mobile phone to transfer the credit to the customer's phone, which is used to make calls until the credit is used up. Through this simple scheme, Globe Telecom has invented an entire small-entrepreneur economy of OTA shops and empowered millions of consumers.

Is it any wonder that the trends emerging from developing countries are becoming increasingly important in influencing corporate strategy in the developed world? But relatively few companies in the West act on the trends coming from "over there," and if they do act on them, then they do so in an overly timid—and therefore ineffectual—way. In a recent study, 8 out of 10 C-level execs consider the growing number of consumers in emerging economies to be an important trend for global business. Six out of 10 respondents think it will have a positive impact on their companies' profits. But only 3 in 10 say that they are doing anything to address the trend.[27]

This is a dire mistake to make, because we are not only losing out on tapping a burgeoning market overseas but also neglecting innovative ways to reach their existing consumers, who are increasingly resistant to traditional marketing methodologies. If we were to take a relativist, global outlook, it would be clear that the marketing that we do in the developed world essentially revolves around selling products and services in a hemispheric marketplace, where it's fairly easy to motivate the typical consumer. There is more than enough wealth to go around for thousands of brands to get snatched up by an enthusiastic consumer who has the deepest pockets in the world. We've got it good here.

But what about the majority of the world, which is composed of much poorer nations? Marketing in the developing world is a tough job. But marketers there are coming up with unique, innovative, and outright exemplary marketing strategies. It's imperative that we know about them, simply because a large stratum of consumers in North America are resistant enough to mainstream brands and stingy enough about major purchases that marketing to them may mean looking for examples from the Third World.

A growing number of consumers who don't (or can't) eagerly translate traditional marketing into purchases—for instance, students and low-income youth who are frequently un(der)employed and media cynical—are many times more affluent than the average Russian or Indian, but their lagging propensity to purchase imposes the need for some creative marketing.

In Brazil, the cost of buying a vehicle is prohibitive. In response, Brazilians have come to rely on pooling money with other buyers to form a *consórcio*. A number of buyers pool small payments, and at the end of each month a lucky winner is chosen by lottery to use the car for the month. If enough people chip in, two cars may be distributed, one by chance and the other going to the person who contributed the most that month.

What a great idea for a North American auto maker when marketing to the student consumer or first-time buyer. A car for this psychographic is a refuge from parents and pressure; it's newfound mobility and freedom, as well as the prime catalyst for entering consumer society and growing up. But insurance and maintenance of a car are also huge financial strains. As bundled services and payment options have become a commodity among car suppliers, a fearless marketer can take these operations to the next level with a *consórcio*-type model, and the first to respond will be the youth demographic—because it's new, simple, peer based, and makes sense.

These types of purchasing incentives are almost ideal for a young consumer in the United States who has no financial or credit history, the mobile and connected young adult who wants to avoid costly cell charges and fixed lines, not to mention parents who are confounded by their monthly statements. Nokia, for instance, is producing phones with multiple address books for as many as seven users per phone. Again, the inspiration behind this was the notion of *consórcio*, or the pooling of resources, a prevalent practice in hyper-markets like Brazil. The *consórcio* model—a form of crowd sourcing that sees crowds of strangers coming together to perform a common task—could also be an ideal way for struggling car manufacturers like GM and Chrysler to reinvigorate their business through innovative pricing mechanisms based on social networks and psychographic tribes.

Furthermore, consumers in the developed world are increasingly becoming brand atheists and purchase resisters. Every day it gets harder to successfully influence them, while new and differentiating ideas and executions from marketers are slow in coming. More often, they are coming from hyper-developing markets. In short, the low-end, emerging marketplace is the ideal source of innovation and insight for businesses going forward in a brand new marketplace.

In a funny bit of coincidence, the pervasive use of mobile technology—the so-called third screen—is being steered by the so-called Third World.* Farmers in Botswana and Uttar Pradesh alike are using their mobile phones to access micro-loans and their bank accounts. In the slums of Dharavi and São Paulo, a single mobile phone acts as a bank branch for thousands of new consumers. In the Philippines, South Africa, and Kenya, money can be sent by text message between two people. They've been doing business through SMS for years now, but this type of service has only just reached the US market.

For centuries, the world's consumer markets have followed the lead of the most advanced nations. Poorer ones emulated and imitated. Yet today, it is the poorer, hyper-developing markets that are dictating the pace of change and the introduction of paradigm-shifting technologies.

For instance, an Indian financial company called Basix sends its field reps into slums and villages to scout for prospects. They help them fill out a rudimentary application, then use a digital camera, scanner, and printer to create a smart card that displays the consumer's image and a biometric fingerprint. To make a deposit or withdrawal, the consumer can visit any of thousands of agents in the community who use a special mobile phone to access account information on the consumer's smart card. If it's a withdrawal, the agent enters the amount on the mobile phone, gives him or her the money, and prints out a receipt. When the consumer wants to send money back home to a remote village, the mobile phone is used to activate an agent near the village, who then personally delivers the money to the family.

In another ingenious invention for the mobile phone industry, Ugandans routinely use the shared village phone as a banking

---

* More than half of all cell phone users now live in developing countries, making the mobile phone the first electronic technology to garner more users in the Third World than the First.

center and micro-finance hub. The practice is called *sente*, an innovative way to use prepaid airtime as a way of transferring money from place to place. Moreover, it doesn't require any banks or financial institutions, which are rather tenuous in African nations. Here's how *sente* works: I want to send $5 to my mother back in the village. I buy a $5 prepaid calling card and then call the village phone operator. I don't use the card to make this call. Instead, I read the village operator the code on the card. The operator loads $5 on to her phone, and gives my mother the money, minus a small commission. These village "phone ladies" are not only revolutionizing the way mobile technology is used in their countries but also driving economic growth. For instance, Grameenphone used its innovative village-phone program to become Bangladesh's largest telecom provider, with annual revenue well over $1 billion.[28]

In early 2007, *The Economist* reported that a Ghana-based company called TradeNet had launched an eBay-type service for agricultural products that connects 12 countries across West Africa to let buyers and sellers transact business through SMS.* A Luxembourg-based company called Millicom International Cellular is taking lessons learned from operating in seven African countries, from Chad to Mauritius. The company has innovated to the point of selling prepaid seconds instead of minutes. That's right. You can buy 23 seconds of talk time, if you want. Millicom has also wholly changed the way that these minutes . . . er, seconds . . . are sold by turning street vendors into its service providers through simple SMS. In a *Wall Street Journal* interview, Millicom's CEO, Marc Beuls, declared, "We're selling minutes like Coca-Cola is selling soft drinks."[29]

---

* Nigerian Jimi Agbaje is the first politician ever to use Bluetooth advertising on the campaign trail. At an upscale fundraiser dinner, he announced to all his politician and celebrity friends that his political platform and personal ringtones were available to anyone who switched on the Bluetooth function of his or her mobile phone. Agbaje's campaign slogan was "New Thinking. New Lagos."

Millicom's e-Pin technology allows a customer to pay cash to a street vendor, who then sends a text message to Millicom with the buyer's phone number and minute request. By selling fewer calling cards, Millicom has significantly reduced reload costs, a savings it has passed on to its customers. More interestingly, anyone who has a cell phone can become a Millicom vendor. The company allows its customers to send a text message requesting that minutes be transferred from one phone to another. It's like a minute donation, the terms of which can be worked out between the parties. Similarly, the company's "share balance" program allows a customer with no more minutes left to send a free text message to a friend asking for more. The receiving customer can send a text message to Millicom to transfer minutes to his or her friend's phone.

Dynamic consumer-based innovation like this is prompting some brave Western companies to take serious heed of the trends being birthed in developing nations. In the Netherlands, a company called Finnish Ferratum has launched a small-loan service based on SMS. The practice of micro-lending—perfected by Grameen Bank and Nobel Peace Prize–winner Muhammad Yunus—has led to the runaway success of sites like Kiva.org, which in less than two years has garnered more than $19.5 million worth of loans from more than 220,000 individuals wishing to finance small businesses and start-ups in countries like Kenya, Bangladesh, and Samoa. Not only are these people helping out the world in a small way but their loans are almost always repaid: the default rate is 0.16 percent. The runaway success of Kiva has made its founders cap loans at $25 because there are more people wanting to contribute than there are people applying to receive the contributions.

Taking the notion of micro-financing a bit further (well, a lot further), EA Games announced in early 2008 that its forthcoming blockbuster game, Battlefield Heroes, will be free to download. The company will instead source revenue from microtransactions such as the sale of in-game items like helmets or beards that enhance and customize the game's characters and, therefore, the game play experience of the consumer. In a similar innovative leap, Rockstar Games released its hotly anticipated Grand Theft Auto IV with more than 200 songs licensed for the game, the largest soundtrack of any video game ever released. But more significant, Grand Theft Auto IV is also the first video game that allows its players to tag songs they hear in the game to be purchased online at a later time. If a player likes what he hears when rolling through Liberty City—a fictional version of New York—he can use his game controller to buy the song from Amazon.

In another bow to trends rising from emerging economies, a number of youth-focused fashion and sports retailers partnered with NBA star Stephon Marbury to create the Starbury Collection of urban-inspired apparel and footwear, which featured its crown jewel—the Starbury II—which Marbury wears on the NBA court. It's a basketball shoe that's positioned squarely up against the $100 Converse and $200 Nike Air Jordan. But it's sold for only $14.98.

And in 2008, a retailer called Steve & Barry's partnered with actor Sarah Jessica Parker to create the Bitten collection of sportswear for women. All of the collection's 500 pieces were to be priced at $19.98 or less. According to the company website, Steve & Barry's is "a company of engineers. We strive to find solutions in every corner of our business, big or small, that allow us to charge incredibly low prices. Our innovations extend from the way we buy paper clips and desk chairs to the way we ship and distribute our products. It's in our culture and our nature to scour for savings wherever we can find them." Because of the financial meltdown in late 2008, however, Steve & Barry's has since filed for bankruptcy.

In the same vein, to produce and bring to market the first-ever $2,500 car, India's Tata Motors had to discover ways of removing superfluous costs in every aspect of the car's design. The result—the Nano—is a feat no other car company in the world has been able to accomplish.

Accordingly, the Ford Motor Company announced in 2008 that it would move its small car development hub to India. According to the *Boston Globe,* global car makers like GM, Suzuki, and Hyundai are moving their design and engineering operations to India—"not because the engineers are cheaper, but because they better understand the needs of developing world consumers."[30]

The emerging countries—those that are still fundamentally composed of poor people—are the new frontiers for brand breakthroughs and business paradigms. For instance, a project called One Laptop per Child seeks to put low-cost computers into the hands of kids in developing countries for as little as $100.* The first countries to sign up to buy the machine—called the XO—included Brazil, Argentina, Uruguay, Nigeria, Libya, Pakistan, and Thailand. Importantly, in order to cater to the needs of the poor, the XO has been developed with an interface different from Linux, Windows, or Apple. It is, in effect, a brand new user interface that could soon replace the folders-and-desktop mode of personal computing.

In mid-2008, Dell unveiled a line of computers designed for business in developing countries. Two notebooks will be available in more than 20 emerging counties, with a price tag of about $475. The desktops in the company's Vostro line will cost less than $440, including the screen. Dell currently gets half of its revenue from outside the United States. In Brazil, Russia, India, and China, Dell's revenue rose by a combined 58 percent in the first quarter of 2008, accounting for 9 percent of $16.1 billion in revenue. It is not inconceivable that two-thirds of Dell's revenue will come from outside the United States five years from now.[31]

---

* In 2006, the average price of a laptop was $1,070, according to *Forbes* magazine.

Nokia is seeing record profits and growing global market share based on its performance in emerging areas like Africa, the Middle East, and Asia. Clearly, with US financial markets reeling and growth in established markets continuing to trend downward, multinational marketers need to look toward the poorer nations to offset their dwindling numbers. They would much rather celebrate a hyper-market deluge than an established market demise. It should go without question that the success of the former is instrumental to that of the latter.

The advertising and marketing industries must recognize this playing-field shift or risk becoming obsolete. They need to recognize the impending shift at home, too. According to the Congressional Budget Office in Washington, 28 million people in the United States used government food stamps to buy essential groceries in 2008. This number is the highest ever for the program, which was introduced in the 1960s.[32] Would it be safe—or sage—to say that marketers in the United States need to understand the poor more than ever?

CONCLUSION

It's an Ad, Ad, Ad, Ad World

In the emergent global marketplace, the fundamental trump card for all marketing endeavors and branding strategies is "the Idea." Big ideas can come from anywhere, but the majority of them will likely come from the hyper-developing world. Indeed, the consumer trends and emerging cultures of hyper-developing nations—particularly the BRIC countries—are now shaping the advertising, marketing, public relations, and digital media industries in the so-called developed markets. We have no choice but to recognize, integrate, adapt, and adopt these marketing strategies and tactics. And we can no longer assume that breakthrough marketing campaigns, paradigm-shifting products, and top-tier global brands will be exclusive to the West.

Consider this: when the head of Latin American operations for the McCann World Group (a massive advertising network owned by the Interpublic Group) polled 15 of his largest global clients, the majority of them identified the world's poor as their next big market, and potentially the most lucrative. So McCann launched a $2-million effort to find fresh proprietary insights in Latin America, drawn from its poorest consumers. The company now sends many of its staffers—junior and senior—to Colombia, Chile, and Mexico, where they spend up to two weeks living with low-income families. The hope is that this type of immersive, experiential exercise will give the agency an unrivaled understanding of how brands are perceived by the poor, as well as a sense of how marketing initiatives might motivate and influence these consumers.

At McCann, and at many other agencies, marketers know that many future successes depend on how well they can engage the poorer masses and what knowledge they can glean from them to invigorate the consumer markets elsewhere. The new marketing imperative to engage the hyper-developing world isn't simply a matter of reading business case studies, attending trade shows and workshops, or even spending a week in a leaky, overcrowded hut with a family that makes less than $100 per month. Sure, all of those activities have the potential to generate significant insights. But the future of marketing—the complex system that innovates, produces, and sells products and services to a global marketplace—rests on the mantra: *Think Differently.*

The concept of "thinking differently" is being promulgated in Brazil, Russia, India, and China. Within the geopolitical, economic, social, and cultural borders of these countries, this philosophy is effortlessly but profoundly ingrained in the business mores and marketing strategies of the leading brands and companies. Many of these innovations are still in the incubation stage, and many more remain undiscovered, misunderstood, misapplied, or ignored by the developed world. But the emergence of a new global brand order is well underway, and to deny the marketing campaigns, media tactics, and pop culture trends that are rocking the hyper-developing world is utter folly.

Every day it is becoming clearer that a break with the past is necessary. In fact, a vision of the future is already on the horizon.

The hyper-market is no longer being forged by the BRIC economies alone. Many economists and executives have started adding other letters to that acronym to form BRICKS, which includes Korea and South Africa in the hyper-market boom. Turkey, Mexico, and Chile will likely join the club soon. And what about Poland, Hungary, Ukraine, and Romania? What of Colombia, Peru, and Argentina? Israel, Egypt, and Morocco? Indonesia, Malaysia, Thailand, Taiwan, Pakistan, and…?

This brand new world is reshaping and redefining what marketing and advertising is in our lifetime, and what it can become in our lifetime as well. The survival of Western brands—and the persuasion economy that serves them—now depends on the hyper-developing world. The calamitous collapse of US and European financial markets in late 2008 ensured that multinational marketers will need to look to hyper-markets like India and China to counter domestic blows. General Motors, for instance, saw 2008 sales grow by at least 10 percent in China and 20 percent in the BRIC countries as a whole. PepsiCo International grew over 20 percent in revenue and over 30 percent in profits that year. IBM grew about 8 percent in the Americas in 2008, but its worldwide income grew 22 percent—with two-thirds of its revenue coming from outside the United States. And DuPont's international sales rose 18 percent last year, compared to 5 percent growth in the domestic market.[1] Between 2001 and October 2008, the equity markets in BRIC countries drastically outperformed the S&P 500 in the United States, racking up returns of 180 percent compared to a 23-percent-loss for the US benchmark.[2]

It is clear that the hyper-market is instrumental to the success of the global economy, but not solely in economic terms. Understanding how to market in these countries will indubitably reshape the way we think about consumerism altogether. The future of the world's economies is today being determined by thinking and practices that are unprecedented in modern times. Quite simply, we are in uncharted territory. It is impossible to predict how the economic winds will blow, as the world's economists and business leaders have certainly failed to predict the global financial tailspin that we are now struggling to correct. But it is wholly possible—if not probable—that traversing the unexplored economic seas will yield discoveries that can change our world forever. I believe that most, if not all, of those discoveries will come from the hyper-markets—particularly the emergent markets in Brazil, Russia, India, and China. And out of these discoveries the brand new world will emerge.

Am I suggesting that we adopt violent and duplicitous ways of doing business, as many oligarchs have done on their way to amassing billions, in this brand new world of ours? Of course not. Instead, I rather extol the oligarchs' keen sense of history and their audacity to seize the moment. I would advise the marketers of the world to imitate the oligarchs' ability to think big and find new ways to reinvent the system. Wouldn't such thinking benefit a global marketplace that is currently undergoing such a radical reinvention?

Will all global ads come from India in the near future? The answer is certainly no. But the ability to tap into a global empathy will be compulsory for any ad agency or global marketer seeking to win business in the brand new world. And it is within India's burgeoning advertising community—and the creative industries that surround it—that this ability is being refined. Moreover, the sheer amount and variety of content creation that is occurring in Mumbai alone is leading to new paradigms in how people outside of the Western hemisphere consume, distribute, and value entertainment. Marketers understand that their brands and campaigns thrive on insight and inspiration from the creative class. And India could very well be the focus of the emergent global empathy, the uncrowned standard-bearer of the brand new world's creative ethos.

Conclusion

The protected piracy that thrives in thousands of China's cities—and is widely exported to receptive markets throughout the developed world—will fundamentally transform that way brands are developed, launched, and appropriated in both developed and developing markets. Marketers and advertisers are no longer in control of their brands. How could they be when those brands are being sold at Silk Street at a fraction of their value? Anything visual can be copied, but the personal experience certainly cannot be duplicated. In a brand new world, we will appraise brands and products based on their ability to create unique experiences rather than on their tendency to create unique logos. Brands will therefore be judged by the total experiences they deliver rather than the identity they present. The Chinese ambivalence to the importance of the brand leads to some profound lessons for the brand new world: the health and success of a brand—global or local—will be increasingly dependent on an experience-based proposition, and so will the marketing that surrounds it.

The marketing in a brand new world will also have to be *better*. Not better in terms of funnier or more contextual, but in terms of actually improving the social condition. The mere possibility of an outdoor advertising ban in a mega-city like São Paulo must be disconcerting to those advertisers not accustomed to the brand new world. In the case of São Paulo—and Moscow, Paris, Shanghai, and countless other mega-cities—we have proof that the citizens, and the politicians who rise to meet their populist sentiment, can fundamentally change the dynamic between marketer and consumer. This isn't a bad thing at all. Marketers must understand that they are now obliged to adhere to a new standard of behavior, one that is based on a trade-off between brand messenger and consuming recipient, a trade-off that is ever more often favoring the latter and making the former irrelevant. In the case of São Paulo, outdoor advertising was outlawed in favor of a "better quality of life." Wouldn't it behoove the advertising industry to start thinking of ways to do just that, making people's lives better?

This question becomes a fundamental strategic springboard when Western marketers begin to think of ways to serve the global poor—billions of people who are still relatively untouched by branding, advertising, or marketing. It is precisely because they have been unmarked and unaffected by the 60-odd years of Western-style marketing that they are so vital to the brand new world: the billions of poor people on this planet, and their varying consuming penchants and proclivities, will fundamentally shape the way products and services are developed, marketed, bought, and sold in the future. In the brand new world, the poor will demand more than aspirational commercials and pithy taglines from the companies that are asking for their hard-earned money. They will expect marketers to do what marketers have avoided for so long—walk the walk instead of talking the talk. And in doing so, they will direct the persuasion industry away from marketing-as-image to marketing-as-service.

Perhaps this notion is best explained by using an example. For years it has been reported that Jim Stengel, Procter & Gamble's head of marketing, had been trying to persuade his company—and the thousands of brands that it controls worldwide—to expand its role in society, to be a provider of benefits rather than a seller of goods (with either good or bad results, depending on whom you ask). No company in the world spends more on advertising than P&G. And no company boasts more leading big brands and veteran subsidiaries worldwide. So it is telling to hear Procter & Gamble's chief marketing officer calling for an end to the clutter of mass media. In the place of this clutter, Stengel wants to refocus P&G's efforts on the experiences of its consumers at the grassroots level.

A breakthrough example of this new approach appeared for the company in 2006. According to a *Financial Times* profile of Stengel that year, the Pampers brand saw double-digit sales increases the moment after P&G fundamentally changed the way it viewed the brand and product. Instead of looking at Pampers—a diaper brand launched in 1961—as a way to keep babies dry, the company repositioned it as an aid in child development. In other words, rather than looking at a brand as a brand, the marketers of Pampers began to look at their brand as a service.

The marketing naturally followed. P&G launched a site not only to sell Pampers but also to help parents care for their children. Pampers.com immediately garnered millions of visitors. (Stengel has gone on record to state that Pampers.com reaches most of the new mothers in the United Sates every month.) The online marketing program focuses on giving expectant and new moms the things they need: companionship, community, empathy, and information. The commercial side of the site features Pampers coupons and a personalized electronic reminder tool, based on children's actual birth dates, that prompts moms to increase diaper sizes as their children grow. The community features of the site allow P&G to query moms on new products and monitor their needs and interests. In fact, one of the company's fastest-growing brands, Kandoo (wet wipes and foam soaps designed to aid in toilet training), was launched in response to customer concerns posted on the Pampers website.

According to Stengel, "Pampers.com is, at the end of the day, a service. I don't know how much we are going to monetize services [but] the important thing for us is the mentality of delighting consumers, being of service to them."[3] This sentiment is not restricted to consumers in North America or Europe; it is applicable to the entire world. But nowhere is it more crucial than in the poorer nations. To succeed there requires looking at marketing as a way to help people achieve their existential dreams and fulfill their commercial potential. In effect, to succeed in the hyper-markets means re-evaluating what marketing means. For the brand new world, marketing is the service—or conversely—service is the marketing.

Hyundai followed in these footsteps. In the midst of an economic recession and an automotive market meltdown, the company bought a Super Bowl television spot. This commercial promised Americans who bought a new car that if they lost their job or income within a year, they could return the car at no cost and with no dent to their credit rating. The new marketing program—called Hyundai Assurance—saw the company's sales rise by 14 percent in one month and its market share nearly double.[4] Rather than resort to even more discounts to sell cars, Hyundai simply offered a service that was extremely compelling for consumers in uncertain times and shaky economic conditions. And in doing this, the car brand's marketing became a force for good, a service that turned buying a car into a beneficial experience, and increased the company's sales at a time when other major car manufacturers were on the brink of bankruptcy.

Hyundai's marketing campaign comes straight out of the Casas Bahia playbook. In the face of economic uncertainty, the car manufacturer understood that tight budgets and slim wallets meant a new and more beneficial approach to its marketing was needed. The results were immediately positive. In the brand new world, forward-thinking marketers will quickly discover that doing good is good marketing. In doing good, they are carving out a competitive advantage for doing business in the hyper-markets for years to come. But there's more to this world and this life than a competitive advantage. In doing good, brands and businesses throughout the world are able to tap into the emerging global empathy to create better products, stories, and experiences.

In order to do good, marketers must ask themselves honestly: what does the next phase of global commerce look like? What kind of action do we want the people of this planet to take? How can we all change the world for the better? We will not be able to thrive in the global economy without asking ourselves these simple, but wholly fundamental, questions. This book has touched on a number of major trends and ontological themes—albeit from a marketing and advertising perspective—that are instrumental to the success of the brand new world.

ENDNOTES

A SNEAK PEEK

1. David Olive, "Globetrotters Circle the World Looking for New Opportunities," *Toronto Star,* 18 February 2008.
2. Navin Chaddha, "India's Economy: Off the Launch Pad," *BusinessWeek,* 8 March 2007.
3. Tom Doctoroff, "Brands in China," *Huffington Post,* 10 December 2007.
4. Normandy Madden and Emma Hall, "With US Economy Reeling, Advertisers Pin Hopes on Emerging Markets," *Advertising Age,* 18 September 2008.
5. Ibid.
6. "China's Vast Television Audience Draws in Olympic Sponsor," *Voice of America News,* 27 March 2008.
7. Harold L. Sirkin, James W. Hemerling, and Arindam K. Bhattacharya, "Global-ity: Competing with Everyone from Everywhere for Everything" (New York: Hachette Book Group, 2008).
8. Ibid.
9. Ibid.
10. Ibid.
11. Jacqueline Thorpe, "Chinese Becoming Avid Shoppers," *Financial Post,* 24 July 2006.
12. "Russia to Become Europe's Largest Consumer Market," *Russia Today,* 5 November 2007.
13. Manu Bhaskaran, "China, India Guarantee Global Economic Growth," *The Nation,* 10 April 2007.
14. "India Biggest Job-Spinner among BRIC Nations," *India Times,* 19 June 2007.
15. Harold Sirkin, "India and China Wise Up to Innovation," *BusinessWeek,* 30 January 2007.
16. "PC Growth Riding the BRIC Wagon," *India Times,* 12 June 2007.

17. Loretta Chao, "Motorola Dials into China's Under 30 Set," *Wall Street Journal,* 20 December 2007.

18. Ibid.

19. Ibid.

20. "We Are the BRIC," *Economic Times,* 26 June 2007.

21. David Barboza, "Internet Boom in China Is Built on Virtual Fun," *The New York Times,* 5 February 2007.

22. Steve King, "Ad Spending in Developing Countries Outpaces Average," *Advertising Age,* 20 June 2007.

23. Andrew Leonard, "One Company: 300 Million Chinese Cellphone Users," *Salon.com,* 23 January 2007.

24. Sean Leow, "QQ Raking in the Dough," *psfk.com,* 26 March 2008.

25. "Fresher Cookers," *The Economist,* 6 December 2008.

26. Sara Corbett, "Can the Cellphone Help End Global Poverty?" *The New York Times,* 13 April 2008.

INTRODUCTION: A Note from an Ad Man

1. William Mellor and Le-Min Lim, "BRIC Shoppers Will Rescue World, Goldman Sachs Says," *Bloomberg.com,* 2 December 2008.

2. Ibid.

CHAPTER ONE: Think Like an Oligarch

1. Jeanne Sahadi, "World's Most Expensive Cities," *CNN Money,* 19 June 2007.

2. Mikhail Khmelev, "Russian Real Estate Is the Best Investment," *RIA Novosti,* 19 March 2007, en.rian.ru.

3. Matthew Chance, "Eye on Russia: Russia's Resurgence," *CNN.com,* 18 June 2007, www.cnn.com.

4. Matthew Taylor, "From Russia, with Love for the More Exclusive Side of London Life," *The Guardian,* 13 April 2007, www.guardian.co.uk.

5. "Moscow: New World Capital for Billionaires," *Brietbart.com,* 5 March 2008, www.brietbart.com.

6. Chance, "Eye on Russia."

7. Ibid.

8. Alex Shifrin, "Celebrity Endorsements: A Failing Experiment," *The eXile* (Moscow), 1 June 2007, www.exile.ru.

9. Nick Paton Walsh, "She Has a TV Show and a Porsche: Now Moscow's Paris Hilton Wants a Party Too," *The Guardian,* 3 June 2006, www.guardian.co.uk.

10. "Russian Forbes Publishes Top 50 Celebrities List," *Russia Today,* 27 July 2007, www.russiatoday.com.

11. Sebastian Smith, "Putin Mania Takes Grip on Home Front," *Evening Standard* (London), 23 April 2007, www.thisislondon.co.uk/standard.

12. Heidi Dawley, "Russian Media: Blossoming, if Bloody," *Media Life*, 12 July 2007, www.medialifemagazine.com.

13. Luybov Pronina, "Ad Spending in Russia Grows with Economy," *International Herald Tribune*, 15 August 2007.

14. Ibid.

15. Ibid.

16. Vladislav Grinkevich, "Vodka: Russia's National Drink May Be Russian No More," *Malaysia Sun*, 23 July 2007.

17. "Roustam Tariko," *BusinessWeek* special report, 7 June 2004, www.businessweek.com.

18. Ibid.

19. Becky Ebenkamp, "Aquafina Adds Beauty SKUs to Enhance Liquid Assets," *Brandweek*, 7 May 2007, www.brandweek.com.

20. Ibid.

21. Rance Crain, "Why Russians Ads Are Attacked," *Advertising Age*, 17 September 2007, www.adage.com.

22. Abhay Singh and Subramaniam Sharma, "India Billionaire Mallya Isn't Showing Shareholders Everything," *Bloomberg.com*, 21 February 2008, www.bloomberg.com.

CHAPTER TWO: Insights Outsourced

1. Sam Dolnick, "Newspapers in India Enjoy Boom," *Columbus Dispatch*, 29 May 2007, www.dispatch.com.

2. William Underhill and Jason Overdorf, "Bottom to Best," *Newsweek*, 10 September 2007.

3. Ibid.

4. Ibid.

5. Ibid.

6. Ashish Sinha and Suvi Dogra, "Ad Industry to Grow 61%," *Business Standard* (New Delhi), 10 December 2007.

7. Ibid.

8. "India Has the Potential to Redefine Advertising," *Hindu Business Line*, 27 December 2007, www.thehindubusinessline.com.

9. "India Whizzes China in Creativity Alley," *Economic Times* (New Delhi), 9 December 2007.

10. "Offshore Dream Factories: Advertising Can Be Outsourced," *Economic Times* (New Delhi), 27 September 2007.

11. "Is Advertising India's Next BPO Opportunity?" *Business Standard* (New Delhi), 11 July 2007.

12. Saurabh Turakhia, "Ad'vantage India," *Hindustan Times*, 25 July 2007, www.hindustantimes.com.

13. Irshad Daftari, "We Will Do a Lot of Global Work out of India: Wright," *Economic Times* (New Delhi), 4 July 2007.

14. BBH, Axe—Billions, www.youtube.com/watch?v=eo2iQHCbV-M.

15. Matthew Creamer, "Gillette Taps 9,000 Creatives Online," *Advertising Age*, 17 September 2007.

16. Eric Pfanner, "On Advertising: A Web Link between Buyers and Sellers of Ideas," *International Herald Tribune*, 11 February 2007.

17. Robyn Meredith, *The Elephant and the Dragon: The Rise of India and China and What It Means for All of Us* (New York: W.W. Norton, 2007), 84.

18. "Marketers Require Better Insight into Rural Demographics," *Hindu Business Line*, 10 January 2007, www.thehindubusinessline.com.

19. Niti Bhan and Brad Nemer, "Brand Magic in India," *BusinessWeek*, 8 May 2006, www.businessweek.com.

20. Gouri Shah, "Today, Ideas Are What Matter," *LiveMint.com*, 31 March 2008, www.livemint.com.

21. Prasoon Joshi, "Why Indian Creatives Bring Great Ideas to Global Brands," *Advertising Age*, 20 August 2007, www.adage.com.

22. Helen Coster, "Biker Bajaj," *Forbes.com*, 2 October 2006, www.forbes.com.

23. Daniel H. Pink, *A Whole New Mind: Why Right-Brainers Will Rule the Future* (New York: Riverhead Books, 2005).

24. Rian Steinberg, "Want to Squelch Ad Skipping?" *Advertising Age*, 9 June 2008.

25. Michael Maiello, "India's Elvis," *Forbes*, 13 August 2007.

26. Ibid.

27. "India Has the Potential to Redefine Advertising," *Hindu Business Line*, 27 December 2007, www.thehindubusinessline.com

28. Jason Overdorf, "Bigger than Bollywood," *Newsweek*, 10 September 2007.

29. Joe Leahy, "Sony Goes to Bollywood and Learns a Lesson," *Financial Times* (London), 19 March 2008.

30. "Indian Entertainment Industry to Top $27b by 2011," *Sify.com*, 25 March 2008, www.sify.com.

31. Richard Siklos, "Time to Short Facebook, Buy Bollywood," *CNNMoney.com*, 5 November 2007, www.cnnmoney.com.

32. Meena Iyer, "Bollywood Owes Biz to 10–24 Age Group," *Times of India*, 13 April 2008, www.timesofindia.indiatimes.com.

33. Siklos, "Time to Short Facebook."

34. Ines Forster, "Marketing across Borders," *PR Domain*, 11 October 2007.

35. Steve Diller, Nathan Shedroff, and Darrel Rhea, *Making Meaning* (Berkeley: New Riders, 2006), 32.

CHAPTER THREE: **Bought at Silk Street**

1. Ted C. Fishman, *China Inc.* (New York: Scribner, 2006), 242.

2. Ibid., 246.

3. *China Daily* (Xinhua), press release, 24 January 2008.

4. Ming Zeng and Peter J. Williamson, *The Hidden Dragons* (Boston: Harvard Business School Press, 2004).

5. Fishman, *China Inc.*

6. "Beijing Is China's Largest Advertising Market," *China Daily* (Xinhua), 22 February 2008.

7. David Lague, "Selling to China? Which One Is It?" *International Herald Tribune*, 16 January 2006.

8. Jing Wang, *Brand New China: Advertising, Media, and Commercial Culture* (Cambridge, MA: Harvard University Press, 2008).

9. Focus Media Holding Limited, press release, 5 March 2008.

10. Frederik Balfour, "Catching the Eye of China's Elite," *BusinessWeek*, 31 January 2008, www.businessweek.com.

11. Matt Chapman, "Nintendo Calls on US to Kill Piracy," *Vnunet.com*, 18 February 2008, www.vnunet.com.

12. "China Sued Over Web Music Piracy," *BBC News*, 4 February 2008, http://news.bbc.co.uk.

13. Stephanie Bodoni, Hugo Miller, and Naween Mangi, "Asian Counterfeiters Shift Focus to Consumer Goods from Luxury Goods," *Bloomberg.com*, 15 June 2007, www.bloomberg.com.

14. "China's Piracy & Counterfeiting Problems," *Wikinvest.com*, 22 May 2007, www.wikinvest.com.

15. Jonathan Landreth, "Spider-Man 3 Will Land in China before N. America," *Hollywood Reporter*, 30 March 2007.

16. "China's Piracy & Counterfeiting Problems."

17. David Radd, "Piracy Is Big Business," *BusinessWeek*, 13 March 2007, www.businessweek.com.

18. David Barboza, "Smugglers Return iPhones to China," *The New York Times*, 18 February 2008.

19. James Surowiecki, "The Piracy Paradox," *The New Yorker*, 24 September 2007.

20. Ibid.

21. Surowiecki, "The Piracy Paradox."

22. Heather Timmons, "Online Scrabble Craze Leaves Game Sellers at Loss for Words," *New York Times*, 2 March 2008.

23. Rachael King, "Building a Brand with Widgets," *BusinessWeek*, 3 March 2008, www.businessweek.com.

24. Ibid.

25. Stuart Whitwell, "Brand Piracy: Faking It Can Be Good," in *Intangible Business Limited Report*, May 2006.

26. Ibid.

27. Adrienne Fawcett, "Conscientious Consumerism Drives Record New Product Launches in 2006," *MediaPost*, 24 January 2007, www.mediapost.com.

28. Wang, *Brand New China*.

29. Ibid., 123.

30. Allison Mooney, "Reebok x Maeda = Emoretion," *PSFK*, 19 March 2008, www.psfk.com.

31. Joseph Pine and James Gilmore, *Authenticity* (Boston: Harvard Business School Press, 2007).

32. Ibid.

33. Dexter Roberts, "Don't Know Li Ning? Ask Shaq," *BusinessWeek*, 8 October 2007, www.businessweek.com.

34. Joseph Chaney, "Watch Out Nike: China's Sports Brands Coming on Fast," *Reuters*, 21 February 2008, www.reuters.com.

35. Pine and Gilmore, *Authenticity*, 13.

36. Ibid., 149.

37. Cited in various sources, also found in Bruce Lee, Bruce Lee: A Warrior's Journey (Warner Home Video, 2000).

38. Angela Natividad, "Modernista! Entrusts Identity to Able Hands of Internet," *Adrants*, 19 March 2008, www.adrants.com.

39. Paul Sweeting, "Media Wonk," *Content Agenda*, 20 March 2008.

40. Dimitry Dokuchayev, "The Cost of Making a Russian Toast Set to Rise," *Moscow News*, 8 August 2007, www.mnweekly.ru.

41. Steven Eke, "People's Vodka Urged for Russia," *BBC News*, 11 November 2006, http://news.bbc.co.uk.

42. Dokuchayev, "Cost of Making a Russian Toast."

CHAPTER FOUR: No Logo Metropolis

1. Vinicius Galvão, interview by Bob Garfield, NPR, On the Media excerpt, *AlterNet*, 21 August 2007, www.alternet.org/story/60084?page=2.

2. Jason Leow, "Beijing Mystery: What's Happening to the Billboards?" *The Wall Street Journal*, 25 June 2007.

3. "Visual Pollution," *The Economist*, 11 October 2007.

4. Patrick Burgoyne, "São Paulo: The City That Said No to Advertising," *Business-Week*, 18 June 2007, www.businessweek.com.

5. Calvin Leung, "Out-of-Home Advertising: Marketing Ubiquity," *Canadian Business*, 18 February 2008.

6. Katy Bachman, "OAAA: Outdoor Advertising up 8%," *MediaWeek*, 14 March 2007, www.mediaweek.com.

7. Claudia Penteado and Andrew Hampp, "A Sign of Things to Come?" *Advertising Age*, 1 October 2007, www.adage.com.

8. "Giant Adverts Set for World's Busiest Runways," *Reuters*, 25 September 2007, www.reuters.com.

9. Penteado and Hampp, "A Sign of Things to Come?"

10. Alycia de Mesa, "A Branding New Year," *BrandChannel.com*, 12 February 2007, www.brandchannel.com.

11. Elizabeth Gettelman and Dave Gilson, "Ad Nauseum," *Mother Jones*, January–February 2007.

12. Ibid.

13. Matthew Creamer, "Caught in the Clutter Crossfire: Your Brand," *Advertising Age*, 1 April 2007, www.adage.com.

14. David Lieberman, "New Media Expected to Get More Ad Dollars," *USA Today*, 25 March 2008.

15. "Brazil Beats a Path Online," *eMarketer*, 19 June 2007, www.emarketer.com.

16. Antonio Regaldo and Kevin J. Delaney, "Google under Fire over a Controversial Site," *Wall Street Journal*, 19 October 2007.

17. Gary Ruskin, "A Death Spiral of Disrespect," *Commercial Alert*, 26 April 2004.

18. Bill McKibben, "What's My Damage—A Call for Mental Environmentalism," *Adbusters* 38 (November–December 2001).

19. Ibid.

20. "Russia Moves toward Full Ban on Tobacco Ads," *Moscow News*, 17 January 2008, www.mnweekly.ru.

21. Angelique Chrisafis, "Sarkozy to Ban Advertising from State Television," *The Guardian*, 10 January 2008, www.guardian.co.uk.

22. Guo Shipeng and Ben Blanchard, "China Asks Web Sites to Eradicate Porn, Violence," *Reuters*, 22 February 2008, www.reuters.com.

23. Steve Hall, "Anti-Advertising Efforts Backfire, Cause More Advertising Overload," *Adrants*, January 2008, www.adrants.com.

24. Best Marketing Ideas in the World," *Brandweek*, 10 December 2007, www.brandweek.com.

25. Kimberly Anderson Kelleher, "Good Matters to Consumers," *Advertising Age*, 10 December 2007, www.adage.com.

26. Ibid.

27. Ibid.

28. Piers Fawkes, "Interview with Benjamin Palmer of Barbarian Group," *PSFK*, 6 November 2006, www.psfk.com.

29. Piers Fawkes, "Interview with Johnny Vulcan of Anomaly," 8 November 2006.

30. JCDecaux, Development Services, "Cyclocity," www.jcdecaux.co.uk.

31. "Vive la Velorution," *The Economist*, 20 September 2007.

32. John Ward Anderson, "Paris Embraces Plan to Become City of Bikes," *Washington Post*, 24 March 2007.

33. John Dalla Costa, "What Really Matters Now," *Marketing*, 7 January 2002.

34. Stuart Elliot, "An Honor for Creativity Fuels Ode to Tap Water," *The New York Times*, 17 November 2006.

35. "About," *Tap Project*, www.tapproject.org.

36. "When Fashion Met Famine: Benetton's Third World Crusade," *The Independent* (London), 9 March 2008.

37. Brooke Capps, "Study: Kids Connect with Social-Conscious Marketers," *Advertising Age*, 3 November 2006, www.adage.com.

38. Ibid.

39. "Analysis: Ethical Marketing," *UTalk Marketing*, 23 March 2007, www.utalkmarketing.com.

40. Capps, "Study."

41. Sara Corbett, "Can the Cellphone Help End Global Poverty?" *The New York Times*, 13 April 2008.

CHAPTER FIVE: The World Is Poor

1. Nadeem Bhat, "Poverty in India," *Newstrack India*, 29 May 2007, www.newstrackindia.com.

2. "A Flourishing Slum," *The Economist*, 19 December 2007.

3. Ibid.

4. C.K. Prahalad, *The Fortune at the Bottom of the Pyramid* (Upper Saddle River, NJ: Wharton School Publishing, 2005), 12.

5. "India Marketing Summit Superconsumers," *Financial Express* (Bangladesh), 29 August 2007.

6. Anjana Pasricha, "India's Mobile Phone Market Fastest Growing in World," *Voice of America News*, 28 October 2007.

7. Heather Timmons, "For the Rural Poor, Cell Phones Come Calling," *International Herald Tribune*, 6 May 2007.

8. "Mobile Operators to Invest $20b in 2 Yrs," *Times of India*, 1 April 2007, http://timesofindia.indiatimes.com.

9. "India Adds 8.17 mln Mobile Users in Dec—Regulator," *Yahoo! India News*, 23 January 2008, http://in.news.yahoo.com.

10. Nandini Lakshman, "Online Extra: India's Cell Phone Ride Out of Poverty," *BusinessWeek*, 24 September 2007, www.businessweek.com.

11. Ibid.

12. Sravanthi Challapalli, "The Great Rural Goldrush," *Hindu Business Line*, 8 April 2004, www.thehindubusinessline.com.

13. Kenneth Hein, "Study: Purchase Intent Grows with Each Event," *Brandweek*, 28 January 2008, www.brandweek.com.

14. PQ Media, "Branded Entertainment Momentum Healthy: Report," *Promo*, 12 February 2008, http://promomagazine.com.

15. Ibid.

16. "Amway Going Rural with India-specific Biz Model," *Hindu Business Line*, 24 January 2007, www.thehindubusinessline.com.

17. Katie Hafner, "Inside Apple Stores, a Certain Aura Enchants the Faithful," *The New York Times*, 27 December 2007.

18. Prahalad, *The Fortune at the Bottom of the Pyramid*, 126.

19. Ibid., 127.

20. Ibid., 129.

21. Seema Sindhu, "Taking Promotions to the Outside World," *Hindu Business Standard* (New Delhi), 6 November 2007.

22. Ibid.

23. Prahalad, *The Fortune at the Bottom of the Pyramid*, 12.

24. Pritha Mitra Dasgupta, "Euro RSCG Gets Set for a Big China–India Leap," *Sify.com*, 4 October 2007, www.sify.com.

25. Suzy Mac, "Building BRICs," *Financial Standard*, 11 October 2007, www.financialstandard.com.au.

26. Anita Sharan, "Youth, the Most Sought-After Customers in India," *Hindustan Times*, 2 October 2007, www.hindustantimes.com.

27. "How Companies Act on Global Trends," *McKinsey Quarterly* (April 2008).

28. Sara Corbett, "Can the Cellphone Help End Global Poverty?" *The New York Times*, 13 April 2008.

29. Sarah Childress, "Connecting with the Developing World," *The Wall Street Journal*, 28 August 2007.

30. Rob Walker, "Extra Helping," *The New York Times*, 27 January 2008.

31. Jeremy Kahn, "Third World First," *Boston Globe*, 20 January 2008.

32. Craig Simons, "Dell Unveils Computers for Developing Markets," *Austin American-Statesman*, 28 August 2008.

CONCLUSION: It's An Ad, Ad, Ad, Ad World

1. Donald DePalma, "Keep Plugging Away with Your International Marketing Campaigns," *Chief Marketer*, September 2, 2008.

2. William Mellor and Le-Min Lim, "BRIC Shoppers Will Rescue World, Goldman Sachs Says," *Bloomberg.com*, December 2, 2008.

3. Gary Silverman, "How Can I Help You?" *Financial Times Magazine*, February 4/5, 2006.

4. Nick Bunkley, "Hyundai, Using Safety Net, Wins Market Share," *The New York Times*, February 4, 2009.

INDEX

Index

Index

Clean City Act, 149. *See also* São Paulo, advertising banned in
Clean Start program, 172–73
Clear Channel Communication, 155, 164, 170
clothing, 6, 18, 21, 100, 167. *See also* fashion industry; shoes
Cluetrain Manifesto, The (Levine et al.), 88
co-branding, 35–43, 128
Coca-Cola, 122
Collin, Will, 151
communism. *See under* China; Russia
competition, economic, 39
computers, 58, 123, 207–8, 227
consórcio model, 222
consumer attention, getting and keeping, 92
consumer mindsets, changing, 179–85
consumer packaged goods (CPG), 61
consumerism, 104–5, 162, 163
consumer(s)
    establishing a conversation between brand and, 88 (*see also* empathy)
    proactive (*see* prosumers)
counterfeiting, 94–96, 100, 102n, 103, 108, 110, 120, 138. *See also* authenticity
  imperative; piracy; Silk Street
creating differently, 86–93
creation and customization, 133
creative centers of the world, 57
Creative Commons, 118
Creative Technology, 103
creative work applicable throughout the world, 64. *See also* marketing world as flat
Cyclocity, 169–71

D:2.5, 83
Dalla Costa, John, 174
Darkness at Dawn (Satter), 46
delivering products to households, 208–9. *See also* Casas Bahia
Dell, 227
democracy, managed/sovereign, 20
Deripaska, Oleg, 5
Dharavi, 66, 187–89, 223
Diageo, 123
digital approach to Bollywood, 83–84
digital billboards, 164

Index

Index

Index

Index

Oshiuri, 65

out-of-home (OOH) media, 163–64. *See also* advertising, banned
    importance, 150–57

outsourcing, 54–61

"outsourcing creative," 57

over-the-air (OTA) reloading, 220

Palmer, Benjamin, 167–68

Pampers, 235

Panerai watch, fake, 94, 95, 98–99, 115

Pawar, Bobby, 65–66, 68–69, 199–200

pay-offs. *See* bribery/pay-offs

Pepsi-Co, 36, 39, 58

Philippines, The, 56

Philips, 175

Photoshop, 102

Pine, Joe, 130, 132

Pink, Daniel, 75

piracy, 99, 103, 107, 233. *See also* authenticity imperative; counterfeiting;
  limited-edition products; Silk Street
        software, 101–2

piracy paradigm, 108–19

piracy paradox, 114

pirate mentality, 39, 49

pirated brands, future of, 120–26

plagiarism, 52–54

Plastinina, Kira, 20–21

platform, 91

poor people, 186–90, 209, 229–30. *See also* emerging markets, marketing differently;
  low-income consumers; prosumers

Popcorn, Faith, 154

power elite, 17–18. *See also* Russian oligarchs

Prahalad, C.K., 190n

Proctor & Gamble (P&G), 172, 180–81, 234–35

product demonstrations, 215

prosumers, 133, 179, 190, 192, 217
        definitions of, 191–92

protectionist policies, 55

Pushkin Square, 1

Putin, Vladimir, 2, 3, 5, 12, 18, 20–22, 46

Putinka, 22

Index

Index

Index